D0113846

The Governments of
GERMANY

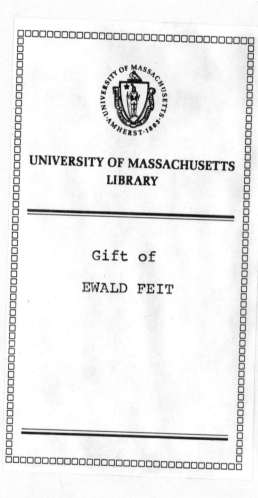

The Governments of GERMANY Second Edition

Arnold J. Heidenheimer UNIVERSITY OF FLORIDA

THOMAS Y. CROWELL COMPANY
New York   Established 1834

CROWELL COMPARATIVE GOVERNMENT SERIES

TO THE MEMORY OF
OTTO KIRCHHEIMER, 1905–1965

EDITOR'S FOREWORD

In our time the study of comparative government constitutes one of many fields or specialities in political science. But it is worth recalling that the most distinguished political scientists of the ancient world would have had difficulty recognizing the present-day distinction between the study of comparative government and study in other subject areas of the discipline. Think of Plato, for example, whose works abound in references to the political systems of his own and earlier days. Or consider Aristotle, whose *Politics* and related writings were based on an examination of more than one hundred constitutions. Twenty centuries after Aristotle the comparative emphasis continued strong in the work of Montesquieu and Rousseau, among others. In the nineteenth century the comparative tradition entered upon a period of decline, but there are signs that the merits of comparative political analysis are once more gaining recognition. At many colleges and universities, the introductory course in political science is no longer focused exclusively on American government. The comparative approach—in politics, in law, in administration—is becoming increasingly important in the political science curriculum.

This book, one of a series, is designed to reflect that approach without, however, marking a sharp departure from the substance and method of most comparative government courses. Thus most of the books in the series deal with one national government. Several volumes, however, deal with more than one government, and the approach of the entire series is distinctly comparative in at least two senses. In the first place, almost all of the books include material descriptive of other political systems, especially that of the United States. In addition, the books follow a common outline, so far as possible, that is designed to promote comparative treatment. Of course, there is nothing to keep the instructor or student from treating a particular governmental system in isolation, if he chooses to do so. On the other hand, his lectures on political institutions and functions can be as comparative as he wishes.

A further advantage of this series is that each volume has been written by a distinguished scholar and authority in the field; each author is personally and professionally familiar with the political system he treats. Finally, the separate books make it possible for the instructor to design his course in accordance with his own interest or the interests of his students. One book may be substituted for another or any book put aside for one semester without affecting the others. The books, in short, unlike most one-volume texts, give the instructor maximum freedom in organizing his course. This freedom will be virtually unlimited as the forthcoming titles in this series complete a survey of representative governments of the world.

But to return to Aristotle once again, it remains true that the best judges of the feast are not the cooks but the guests. I have tried to indicate why, in my view, the recipe for the series is a good one. Let all those who teach comparative government, and all those who take courses in that field, proceed to judge the books for themselves.

ARNOLD A. ROGOW

PREFACE

I am grateful that the good reception accorded *The Governments of Germany* by both colleagues and students since it first appeared in 1961 seems to have justified the preparation of a second edition five years later. In writing the appropriate revisions, I have sought not merely to up-date but also to keep in mind the differences the passage of five years has made—in the outlook of successive generations of students, in the life of a nation and its political system, in the discipline of political science, and in regard to the impact of particularly important individuals.

Thus, the generation of students who will read through the pages of this edition will differ from their predecessors in that their lives will not have coincided at all with that of Adolf Hitler. They and the political system of postwar Germany are, in fact, contemporaries, both having been conceived and born in the late 1940's. Perhaps this generation will be sympathetic to pleas that the societies which have been shaped in Germany since 1945 ought, now that twenty-one years have passed since the end of World War II, to be evaluated for what they are rather than for what they once were.

Having achieved solid marks during an adolescent testing period, having proved capable of eclipsing the faulty patterns of earlier generations—so the argument goes—the West German political system should now be treated as a fully mature and democratic one. Thus, President Luebke has argued that the German "postwar period" be officially considered as having been concluded. This book should help the reader decide whether German institutions ought now to be accepted as much on face value as those of other democratic Western systems.

As regards progress toward German unification, however, very little has occurred during the five-year period. Considered as both societies and political systems, West and East Germany are still very much the hostile twins they were in 1961, when the Berlin wall was built. In spite of the many threats to change the status quo during this period, none of them resulted in significant alterations. At another level, the political integration of Western Europe has also not advanced very rapidly, although no forward-looking observer of German politics can overlook the continuing impact of West European economic integration.

Since publication of the first edition, two national elections were held in the Federal Republic, as well as many state and local ones; their results are analyzed in the text. No one was reported killed or wounded during the campaigns, voting turnout remained high, and the outcomes were universally accepted. The winning party has always been the same since 1949, making the Federal Republic the country with the least governmental turnover of any major country with a multiparty system. In the process, the CDU/CSU has far outstripped the NSDAP with respect to the length of time it has controlled a national German government, a paradox we try to explain.

The most difficult maturational problem West Germany has had to face during the past five years is that of finding entry into the "post-Adenauer period." Defying biological laws, Adenauer long remained omnipresent: at age 85 he promised to quit as Chancellor, but at age 90 he was still trying to purge his successor, Ludwig Erhard. How West Germans react to the radical change in style of leadership will continue to bear close scrutiny.

In the previous edition I expressed my gratification at being able to "present to students a synthesis based on the efforts of as capable a group of men as those who have devoted themselves to the study of German politics in the postwar period, particularly in the United States." Many of them have since continued to be helpful, directly and indirectly, as the additions to the bibliography in part indicate. But I acknowledged an especial debt to the inspiration and friendship of Otto Kirchheimer. That acknowledgement must, alas, be translated into the past tense for this edition, for "OK," the friendly and sensitive skeptic, the generous friend, the wanderer between cultures, died in November, 1965. His discriminating mind contributed much, often in the face of adversity, to our knowledge of German politics and our understanding of constitutional systems. Many of his keen analyses will be consulted for a long time to come. It is to his memory that this volume is dedicated.

A. J. H.

March, 1966

BIBLIOGRAPHICAL NOTATIONS

At the end of each chapter, except the last, is a short bibliography of items particularly relevant to the subjects covered. There, as well as in the footnotes, frequently cited political science journals have been abbreviated as follows: *APSR–American Political Science Review; FA–Foreign Affairs; JP–Journal of Politics; PSQ–Political Science Quarterly; PVS–Politische Vierteljahresschrift; WP–World Politics; WPQ–Western Political Quarterly.*

In recent years, a convenient tool for following current German affairs has become available in the form of *The German Tribune* (Hamburg, 1962–), a weekly English translation of articles from the German press. Its use is recommended. For culling data from this and numerous other sources, I am indebted to my graduate assistant at the University of Florida, Peter W. Nixdorff.

CONTENTS

The Governments of
GERMANY

PART ONE
GERMANY: ITS HISTORY, PEOPLE, AND SOCIETIES

ı: The Molding of Modern Germany

THE LONG ROAD TO UNIFICATION

An understanding of the tumultous character of much twentieth century German political experience requires some appreciation of the complex political history of the country and its people. The existence of a German state, characterized by a central government and a uniform splotch of color within definite boundaries on a map, has been, historically speaking, a very short-term phenomenon. When Hitler came to power in 1933 with dreams of subjecting all Europe to German rule, Germany itself had existed in this form for only two generations. For centuries before that, from the Middle Ages right into the nineteenth century, Germany consisted merely of those areas of central Europe whose inhabitants spoke one or another of the German dialects. They had no common flag, no common rulers, and not much in the way of shared history. This situation was in marked contrast to that of most other countries of northern and western Europe, particularly England and France, where a feeling of national identity had been fostered by many centuries of rule by powerful kings who had imposed uniform systems of law and administration.

The common political traditions that Germans could look back upon were remote in time, such as the heritage presumed to have been left by the old Germanic tribes which Tacitus had described. In these early German communities there was little in the way of organized government, the settlement of breaches of the law being left to the person injured and his near relatives. There was an emphasis on liberty, but in the peculiar autarchic sense that any man had a right to freedom if he was strong enough to defend his rights by himself. This old Germanic tradition was established in pre-Christian times and continued to be powerful into the Middle Ages when it was superceded by legal and other institutions based on Roman influences.

A second German political tradition looked back to the unity Germans had enjoyed within the latter-day Roman Empire, particularly under Charlemagne. This tradition emphasized the bonds that—through institutions like Christianity, the inheritance of Roman law and a common European culture—tied Germany to the Western and the Latin world. Indeed, German princes inherited the nominal leadership of the remnants of the old Roman Empire (First Reich), within which the German areas remained very loosely held together until the time of Napoleon. The emperorship rotated among various German princes and electors until the fifteenth century, when it was finally bequeathed as an empty relic to the Hapsburgs, rulers of Austria.

The decay of the imperial power led to the decentralization of political power and to the complex sets of loyalty typical of the feudal structure, with prelates, free cities, princes, and even minor nobility carving out their own realms. By the thirteenth century there were ninety-three ecclesiastical and fourteen lay princes. A century later there were forty-four lay princes, and their number continued to multiply as partitions took place between heirs. Many parts of the country were converted into tiny fragments of territory incapable of fulfilling the tasks of a state. During this time the free German cities, ruled by a wealthy merchant class, reached the pinnacle of their political and economic power. But changing trade routes, misdirected investments, and war led to their decline in the sixteenth century, thus preventing the further development of a strong German middle class. The weakness of the kings and lay political power allowed the church not only to claim for its clergy exemption from the criminal jurisdiction of the state, but the right to try laymen in its ecclesiastical courts. In England such courts were gradually integrated into the king's courts, where application of the Common Law discouraged localism. In Germany royal courts did not endure, and lay justice was administered by territorial judges applying laws of a strictly local character. When, later in the Middle Ages, lawyers trained in the Roman law entered on the scene, they did so as allies of the princes, rather than as servants of the Emperor.

Administration, too, evolved strictly on the local, or at most regional, level. In the smaller territories the prince often exercised a personal kind of rule, and the evolution of a professional officialdom was slow. Representative institutions contributed little in the way of a centralizing force. Originally the Imperial Reichstag consisted only of those great princes who elected the Emperor.

In the fifteenth century the admission of lesser princes and free towns gave this institution a somewhat greater representative character. But the great lords, the lesser princes, and the representatives of the towns met in separate colleges, with the effect that the Reichstag was both less representative and more divided than the English parliament. In this way did German particularism manifest itself in a multiplicity of political institutions which for centuries defied effective integration. At the same time the narrow outlook and lack of awareness of a common bond were not only obstacles to unification, but actually contributed to the formation of deep historical prejudices among the peoples of the different German states and regions.

The great social and economic changes which marked the gradual transition from a predominantly agricultural and feudal to a predominantly capitalist and urban society might yet have generated enough centralizing forces to bring some measure of unity to the German lands. But two factors prevented such a culmination: Germany became the storm center of a European ideological struggle of unprecedented dimensions; and her geographical position, which had allowed her cities to achieve such great prosperity, became more than ever before a great political handicap as her territories became a battleground for rival foreign armies. The Reformation constituted a revolution rending the Christian web which had maintained a European cultural unity, despite feudal particularism. It superimposed on regional and dynastic division schisms based on divergent faiths. The paradox that Luther united Germans as no other before him had—both religiously, in the wake of his movement, and culturally, by establishing a uniform style of written German—while also leaving a heritage of denominational strife which virtually split Germans in two, is characteristic of the contradictory German historical development.

For the cause of German unity and the development of German liberalism, the Reformation, however, had disastrous consequences. Its effect on the rulers was less significant than on the ruled. Much to Luther's annoyance, his followers did not content themselves with breaking theological ties to Rome, but in many regions sought to convert the movement into a large-scale social revolution. A peasant rising of unprecedented proportions was initially successful in large sections of southwest Germany, and many princes were forced to accept reforms such as the abolition of serfdom, the lowering of taxes, and the right of the people to elect their own parsons. But, although vastly superior in numbers to the princes, who lacked standing armies, the peasants suffered from a severe lack of discipline. Their cause was already on the decline when they were bitterly attacked by Luther himself, who called them "murderers and robbers who must be stabbed, smashed or strangled, and should be killed as mad dogs." Increasingly, the emphasis of Lutheranism on the freedom of the spirit gave way to new dogmas and rites and a new, bigoted priesthood. Moreover, Luther's interpretation of the Sermon on the Mount, to the effect that every ruling power, whether tyrannical or not, was ordained by God and hence to be obeyed, placed a heavy political mortgage on German Protestantism. It led to the development of separate state churches, each recognizing the suzerainty of the local prince, and becoming so identified with the prevailing social and political order that they opposed manifestations of liberalism with misplaced fervour and remained insulated from the misery which plagued the lower classes as a result of war and economic change.

The struggles carried on between princes and Emperor in the aftermath of the Reformation brought Germany to a new low ebb of impoverishment and humiliation, and her once proud cities declined. In the early seventeenth century the Hapsburgs made themselves temporary masters over most of an exhausted Germany. But the wars continued as the more powerful rulers of Sweden and France intervened, and for decades foreign armies ravaged the German lands. When the Thirty Years' War came to a close in 1648 Germany was as divided as ever, with power distributed between weak princes and an impotent Emperor.

However, while foreigners lorded over Germans, at least one German ruling house, the electors of the eastern province of Brandenburg, were expanding their realm at the expense of their Slavic neighbors, whom they ruled with unrestrained absolutism. Building in part on the crusading tradition of the Teutonic orders, these rulers gradually shaped the kingdom of Prussia, in which military priorities reigned supreme. In this impoverished and culturally backward area, a succession of brilliant rulers developed politics of a style new to Germany, with an efficient state machinery and an excellent army ruled by kings who knew how to harness their nobles to the task. Frederick the Great turned the Junkers (the East Prussian landed aristocracy) into administrators, spent the bulk of his resources on the army, and while demanding great sacrifices from his subjects engaged in a series of limited wars which moved Prussia into the ranks of the great powers, a rival to the Hapsburg Emperors for the political leadership of Germany. For a century and a half it was difficult to predict who would become the instrument of unification—the Hapsburgs, who were Catholic, cosmopolitan members of the traditional European "establishment," or the Prussians, who were upstart, disciplined, rough, and, together with their Junker adjutants, oriented much more towards the East than the West.

After the Napoleonic period developments were greatly influenced by the rise of liberalism and nationalism, the two great political movements of nineteenth century Germany. The Napoleonic storm swept away most of the decrepit little dynasties, united them into new states and, most importantly gave Germans the first taste of those political rights which the middle classes in the western countries had established. Feudal privileges of church and nobility were abolished; civil liberties and other Enlightenment ideas found entry into Germany and were warmly welcomed by the hitherto politically apathetic middle classes. But what had been won through revolution in France was imposed on Germany by a foreign administration. Later, when Prussia and Austria joined the grand alliance which sealed Napoleon's doom, most of the middle classes were ready to hail the Battle of Leipzig as signalling the birth of a new Germany.

However, when the Congress of Vienna returned most of the old rulers to their thrones, they still refused to ally themselves with a national movement which they identified with bourgeois radicalism. Some of them granted constitutions, but in Prussia and Austria reaction remained dominant. The German Federation (under Austrian chairmanship) which succeeded the Empire was a sham, and the various Customs Unions had little impact. Nationalist agitation was left to the urban middle class, particularly to the professional class, who still formed a very small segment of a country whose total town population was not much greater than that of contemporary Paris. Their chance came, again as a consequence of outside initiative, when the Paris Revolution of 1848 touched off popular disturbances in Vienna, Berlin, and elsewhere, which the weak and vacillating regimes could not master. The rulers in most of the states were all but overthrown, and agreed to subordinate themselves to the authority of a national government.

The hour of German liberalism had struck, and several hundred delegates of the educated upper-middle classes met in Frankfurt to draw up a national constitution. But their opportunity slipped away as the delegates lost themselves in rhetoric, argued whether to offer the position of constitutional monarch to Austria or Prussia, waxed indignant when Czechs, Poles, and Danes sought to claim national rights for themselves as well, and lost contact with the German masses. This allowed the princes to re-establish themselves, so that when the Frankfurt Parliament finally offered the German Emperorship to King Frederick William of Prussia, he turned it down as a "jester's cap lined in red." The few radical members of Parliament who continued to claim power in Frankfurt were chased out by Prussian and Austrian troops. Reactionaries breathed a sigh of relief. In Frankfurt, the great German philosopher, Schopenhauer, enthusiastically sent his opera-glasses to the officer directing the mop-up from a nearby roof and deeded money to the families of Prussian troops who had participated in restoring order.

Twenty years later a Prussian king did deign to accept the Imperial crown. Speaking in 1871 at the field headquarters for his successful campaign against France, King William agreed to respond to "the unanimous call of the princes and free cities to create the German Reich . . . and to reestablish the Imperial crown." Significantly, he accepted the commission from the princes and not from his subjects. The political happenings of the two previous decades were crucial for this culmination. These included the expansion of Prussian political power in North Germany, the gradual rapprochement between the nationally-oriented middle classes and the ruling forces of militarist-aristocratic Prussia, the deathblow to Austrian ambitions delivered in the brief Austro-Prussian War of 1866, and the subsequent creation of a North German Confederation. The Franco-German War merely served to arouse the patriotic sentiment which swept the reluctant South German states (except Austria) into the Imperial fold. In doing so they acted true to the blueprint of Otto von Bismarck, who had risen from a provincial East Prussian background to become chief minister of Prussia and, through immensely skillful use of the forces of diplomacy, military power, and political blackmail, the real creator of the Second German Reich.

Bismarck's influence continued to be dominant for another two decades, during which he firmly established the constitutional traditions of the Empire and indirectly influenced those of subsequent regimes. His genius synthesized the contradictory elements in the German political tradition. How did it prove possible to reconcile German regional diversity and the continued existence of most of the smaller kingdoms and principalities with Prussia's desire to give strong unified leadership? Bismarck devised a federal structure within which the various states had equal standing but assured Prussian dominance by providing that Prussia's chief minister would automatically become Imperial Chancellor. How to reconcile the middle and lower classes' demands for political equality with the upper classes' insistence on the retention of their special privileges? Bismarck responded with a clever dual policy under which elections to the national legislature, the Reichstag, were held on the basis of universal suffrage, while the Prussian state legislature, which shaped the lion's share of domestic legislation affecting most Germans, retained an archaic electoral system which allowed the reactionaries to remain in control. In like manner, the Chancellor met the problem of reconciling demands for constitutionalism with the autocratic traditions of Prussia by allowing the Constitution to give the illusion of popular influence on the government, while in fact the real decision-making powers remained lodged in the hands of those tried servants of hierarchical authority, the civil service and the army.

The Reich Constitution of 1871 combined elements of political institutions of the "old" Empire with those of the Constitution of the North German Federation of 1866, parts of which were taken over intact. The Emperor's powers had a dual basis: as Emperor he controlled foreign and military affairs and appointed the Imperial Chancellor; as King of Prussia he ruled over the domestic affairs of his state, as did the other German princes. The integrating function within the federal system was played by the *Bundesrat*, which was composed of delegates from the various states. This body, under dominant Prussian influence, met in secret and had extensive powers both in the legislative and executive areas. (In effect, it combined most of the functions that in the United States are divided among the Cabinet, the Senate, and the Governors' Conference.) Its president, the Imperial Chancellor, who held his job by virtue of Imperial confidence, while being at the same time the only minister responsible to the popularly elected Reichstag, was the pivot about which the German constitutional system revolved.

This extremely complex structure functioned with reasonable efficiency as long as the pivotal position was occupied by its architect. But in its relations with Parliament the Imperial government was involved in strenuous constitutional conflict from the very start. For in pursuit of his policy of killing parliamentarianism through Parliament, the Iron Chancellor sought both to limit the Reichstag's powers to nonessentials, and to harass and discomfit the legislative parties so that they would fearfully respond to his wishes. He largely succeeded in depriving the Reichstag of ministers whom it could hold responsible for policy, and he almost succeeded in depriving it of its most basic power, that of approving the budget. Even so, he frequently bullied the legislature into voting military appropriations for as long as seven years at a time. In this way the legislature was placed in a position where it could neither affect the tenure of the Chancellor and his ministers, nor effectively hamper passage of the most important pieces of legislation. Furthermore, the Constitution prohibited simultaneous membership in the government and the legislature, thus setting a legal barrier to the introduction of parliamentary government. In contrast to the British system, where ministers sit amongst their parliamentary colleagues on the front bench of the government party, the members of the government in Germany sat on a raised rostrum, looking down on the semicircle of deputies.

Because of his clever and unscrupulous manipulations, Bismarck was never matched against the whole of the Reichstag in his greatest political struggles, but always managed to isolate the parties in an attempt to crush them one at a time. He was ready to cooperate with almost any party in order to achieve his ends, but he usually destroyed them when they gained enough confidence to make strong demands. In turn, he collided with the Zentrum, representing the Catholics of West Germany, the Conservatives, representing the Prussian old guard, the National Liberals, representing the democratic middle class, and the Social Democrats, representing the Marxist-influenced working class. His successive campaigns against the Catholics and the Socialists involved an all-out use of police power, the suppression of meetings and newspapers, and the imprisonment of priests and party leaders. These attempts at suppression backfired. The two parties whom the Chancellor accused of "opposing national development by international methods and fighting against the nation state" were able to resist, not because of aid from the Vatican or the Socialist International, but because of the stubborn cohesion of their adherents, who greatly increased their party voting turnout in the face of official repression. But on the whole Bismarck did succeed in intimidating the parties. By limiting them to ineffective debate, he prevented them from forming effective competition to the administrative elite. By blocking their leaders' roads to public office, he prevented them from recruiting the best political talents of their time.

To understand German politics under the Empire it is necessary also to understand the prevailing political goals, and their degree of acceptance. It might have been expected that nationalist fervor would ebb after the achievement of unification. But Germany's rulers would not have it so. They could not resist the temptation of averting criticism of their policies by keeping the attention of both the educated elite and ordinary folk fixed on the promises implicit in a policy of national expansion. Talk of German colonies, German preparedness, and the superiority of German culture were the order of the day. New generations were inculcated with memories of the Franco-German War, and under Emperor William II a vigorous start was made on the creation of a navy which would eventually rival Britain's. The virtue of war was the subject of sustained glorification. Whereas earlier philosophers like Kant had written of the hope of achieving a state of perpetual peace, now generals like Moltke attested that, "Perpetual peace is a dream and an unlovely one at that, while war is a link in the divine order of the world. In it are developed man's purest virtues, courage, faithfulness to duty and the willingness to make sacrifices. Without war the world would sink in the swamp of materialism." Such sentiments were expressed outside of Germany as well, but nowhere else were they so well received as in a country permeated with militaristic influences, through institutions like the reserve officer corps and the martial figure of the Emperor himself.

Consensus on national goals was, however, far from complete. Sentiment in South and West Germany remained skeptical of the military ambitions of the Prussian rulers. Catholics found it difficult to identify with a dynasty which had allowed their persecution. Radicals poked fun at the self-conscious posturing of members of the official establishment. Historians like Mommsen bemoaned a "miscarriage of national feeling." Marxists resisted demands for the strengthening of national power by calling for international solidarity of the workers. Each of these groups, as well as the various factions supporting the government, developed complex philosophical systems to buttress their political positions. These ideologies or *Weltanschauungen* did much to shape political movements and at the same time to lend intellectual reinforcement to the divisions that continued to exist among the German people despite the cloak of unity their rulers imposed. The ideologies of the more extreme left and right promoted militancy, but at the center the middle-class liberals reacted in the main by retreating from active participation in politics. Writing at the turn of the century, Friedrich Naumann noted that forty years earlier a bond had still tied the educated classes to liberalism. "But this tradition was lost as Bismarck's greatness crushed liberalism. The majority of the educated . . . believed in the greatness and power of the single great man. . . . The disdain with which Bismarck treated the parliamentarians was taken over as though it was a permanently valid value judgment. And as Bismarck was forced aside and then died . . . a great vacuum remained in the intellectual consciousness of the educated German. He fell back into the apolitical attitudes of the eighteenth century."

Thus, by the time that socio-economic developments came increasingly to favor the German middle classes in terms of wealth and numbers, their political ideas were adulterated and they had lost their self-confidence. In England, where the difficult stages of industrial "takeoff" had been completed in the early nineteenth century, the self-confident middle classes could press gradually toward a political victory over the aristocracy. In Germany, on the other hand, the middle classes looked back on a string of political defeats and became increasingly worried about a working class which was only then being exposed to the hardships and strains through which the British workers had passed earlier. By playing the middle classes off against the Marxist-led workers, Bismarck's regime managed to retain absolute political control.

Though it arrived belatedly, German industrialization assumed tremendous momentum in the decades after unification. Backed by a dynamic banking system, built on the fruit of intense scientific and technical research, and developed within tight cartel structures, German industry grew phenomenally on all fronts. In the four decades after 1870 German iron production increased ten-fold, surpassing Britain's output along the way. In the course of this period Germany was transformed from a land where two out of three people lived in villages and hamlets to one where three out of five lived in urban, predominantly industrialized centers. The Ruhr developed into a mighty arsenal of cartelized heavy industry, ready to forge the Emperor's weapons. The new industries demanded and got high tariff protection, while the small tradesmen were pushed increasingly to the side. These changes did place the hierarchical order under great strain, but buttressed by a phalanx of bureaucratic, academic, and military supporters, it held fast without having to make too many concessions, except to the new captains of industry, who were granted places within the ruling class. Kaiser Wilhelm II, who assumed personal control after Bismarck was eased out of office in 1890, was still basically ruling a great industrial nation much as his forefathers had imposed discipline on the ignorant peasants of a frontier province.

Outwardly, German society presented a picture of sobriety and orderliness. Its members knew their place according to their titles and ranks, whether as reserve officers, commercial counsellors, or assistant deputy street cleaners. But in the twilight zones new forces were generating strength. The Socialist-led working class, embittered by its exclusion from decision-making, sought to beat the state at its own game by developing a supremely disciplined political organization, drawing on those same qualities of sacrifice and courage which the militarists had idealized. Growing stronger with every election, until they received almost one-third of the vote in 1912, the Socialists represented a vast unintegrated political element, which was divided between its commitment to revolution and its eagerness to display its political responsibility, if only given the chance. Among the artisans and shopkeepers a movement based on political anti-Semitism found considerable response. Despite the Emperor's friendship with leading Jewish capitalists, many of his subjects and even his court chaplain participated in the movement, though it was not nearly as strong as in Austria and some other countries. Elsewhere, too, dissatisfaction was rife. In East Prussia the great landowners were alarmed at their worsening economic position, and sought to compensate by retaining political power on the basis of the reactionary Prussian election law. There was strong pressure to extend the vast welfare program, including health insurance and social security which Bismarck had introduced. But efforts to introduce reforms from above, even through an incorruptible civil service, lost much of their value, because the masses were not allowed to feel that they had won victories for themselves.

The acid test of the political system which Emperor William II developed on Bismarck's foundations came in World War I, unleashed in good part by hazardous German diplomacy. At first the system and the German population lived up to the Emperor's highest expectations. Regional jealousies disappeared as the nation dedicated itself to the national cause. The Reichstag voted huge military credits with barely a murmur. Even most of the Socialists gave wholehearted support to the war effort, rationalizing their disavowal of previous commitments to international workers' solidarity with the assertion that they were aiding the cause of progress by helping a conservative regime to defeat an even more reactionary one, that of the Russian Czar. But as the German victory failed to eventuate, the tensions which the Bismarckian system had sought to submerge came to the surface. Liberal and Catholic politicians asked themselves why they were supporting an autocratic regime against countries whose governments had granted their citizens the privileges of parliamentary government and ministerial responsibility. The workers, tired of providing cannon fodder and bearing the brunt of economic sacrifices, were encouraged by their leaders to ask why they were dying for an Emperor who did not deem them worthy of an equal vote in the Prussian legislature. Awkwardly the Emperor made promises of reform, but they came too late. Under the impact of unceasing Allied pressure, morale on the home-front sagged noticeably. Then, in November, 1918, inevitable defeat was hastened by the political unrest in German cities which quickly developed into demonstrations demanding bread, an end to hostilities and the overthrow of the regime. As the revolutionary spirit spread to units of the army and navy, German leaders saw the ground slip beneath their feet. The army high command, which had indirectly ruled Germany since the outbreak of war, advised the Emperor that further resistance was useless and suggested that he seek refuge in neutral Holland. Thus did the German Empire crumble.

THE WEIMAR REPUBLIC, 1918–33

After the downfall of the Emperor's regime, Germans were suddenly presented with the opportunity to follow the dominant political tradition of the West by establishing democratic political institutions. Surprisingly, the opportunity caught most German political parties unprepared. Even the progressive groups had prepared only piecemeal reform plans looking at most toward a constitutional monarchy. There were virtually no republicans. Earlier liberal democratic sentiment had atrophied or been stunted. Of all the German parties only one carried the word "democratic" in its name, and this by its program was pledged to achieve a socialist revolution. To most Germans domestic democrats seemed like political animals out of the dim pre-Bismarckian past. They thought of great-grandfathers who in the early nineteenth century had cursed into their beer at the arrogance of the local prince, or had climbed grandiloquently onto makeshift barricades in the picture-book revolutions of 1848.

In the interval, the vast bulk of educated German opinion had drawn broad philosophical conclusions from limited historical experience, so that they saw in the decay of liberal movements proof that democratic forms were not suited to German politics. The experiences of the Western countries were dismissed as inapplicable. The German upper-middle class tended to share the snobbish ethos of the old ruling classes, who looked askance at Britain as a country of traders where even the nobility had accepted mercantile values. Parliamentary institutions were conceived as suitable for the compromise or sordid economic interests, but not adequate for a nation of poets and philosophers. As Thomas Mann wrote in 1918: "Away with the foreign and repulsive slogan 'democratic.' The mechanical democratic political institutions of the West will never take root here."

The dominant influence of the tradition of philosophical idealism deriving from Hegel, which depreciated the significance of objective phenomena, had an important influence in causing Germans to reject Western political values. Western concepts of liberty, which stressed the absence of inhibitions on such external acts as freedom of speech and assembly, were dismissed as vulgar and superficial. *German* freedom was conceived as the freedom of the inner man to engage in poetic flights of the imagination and daring metaphysical speculation. Its exercise depended little on the will of the official legislator, except that the passions aroused under a popular form of government were likely to disturb the tranquility required by the creative mind. Moreover, the sharp class cleavages in German society had led to the perpetuation of exaggerated notions of the intellectual and moral weakness of the average voter, whose voice would be decisive under a democratic system. Although Germany had achieved a higher degree of literacy than any country, much educated opinion—the crucial elite who controlled German administration, culture, and education—expected that "the masses" would give free rein to their low instincts and install a political system which would smash the proud achievements of German culture. Conservative German constitutional lawyers argued that if a people sought to exercise sovereign rights through a legislature, power would inevitably fall into the hands of parties and factions which would corrupt the national will by tearing it into little pieces.

It was a tradition molded by such concepts which had to be overcome by the politicians entrusted with the task of drafting Germany's first republican constitution. Their meeting place, Weimar, the city of Goethe and Schiller, was symbolic of the democrats' attempt to link up with an earlier, pre-Bismarckian tradition which, if not democratic, was at least humanistic. Significantly, they did not meet in Hamburg, Berlin, or one of the other large cities where revolutionary skirmishes had actually taken place and where radical sections of the working class movement were strongly in favor of emulating the Bolshevik precedent set in Russia. Actually the Socialist government which took over responsibility for maintaining order did set up workers' soviets, but, though Marxist in programmatic commitment, the majority of the Socialist leaders had come to accept gradualist aims. They opposed the radicals' suggestion that they establish a proletarian dictatorship and initiate a sweeping revision of the social and economic systems, which could only have been achieved through the use of force. When the radicals sought to enact their plans anyhow, they were suppressed by their fellow Socialists with the aid of regular troops and reactionary volunteers. This led to a division within the German working-class movement, and the beginning of that tradition of hostility between German Socialists and Communists which was to contribute to the downfall of the Weimar Republic.

Having split with their own left wing, the majority of the Socialists cooperated in drafting the constitution with the two other parties which by 1919 had accepted the republic, namely, the progressive German Democratic party (DDP) and the Catholic Center party (Zentrum). That the constitution was to bear a primary liberal democratic, rather than Socialist, character was borne out by the fact that the drafting work was entrusted to a Democratic party constitutional law professor. There was wide agreement that the constitution should establish a parliamentary system, but little in the way of German traditions to build on. Looking abroad, the drafters found appeal in the relative stability of British governments, but mistakenly attributed this to a constitutional balance of power between the King and Parliament. Thus they concentrated on creating a constitutional figure, the president, who would take the place of the British monarch as the authoritative balancing force which could help shape order out of the diversity of opinions represented in the powerful and popularly elected legislature.

The changes between the Weimar Constitution and its predecessor are well brought out by the different sequence of sections in the two documents. In the 1871 document the section dealing with the princes' organ, the *Bundesrat*, was followed by those dealing with the executive and the popularly elected Reichstag.

In the Weimar Constitution, the section dealing with the popularly elected legislature took first place. The Reichstag was given the predominant share of legislative power and, in contrast to earlier practice, the power of approving and dismissing the Chancellor and his ministers. Second place, but potentially equal power, was given to the president as head of state, elected directly by the people so that his mandate would be as strong as that of the Reichstag. He was also given the power to nominate the Chancellor, dissolve the Reichstag, and rule through emergency decree. Closely linked to the sections dealing with the presidency came those dealing with the political executive, the Chancellor and the cabinet. The cabinet was viewed as a link between president and Parliament, and thus made dependent on both institutions. Finally, in last place, were the sections dealing with the considerably weakened federal element within the Constitution. As befitted a constitution with a strong centralist bias, the second chamber, the *Reichsrat*, which included representatives of the *Land* (state) governments, was endowed with extremely limited powers, mainly of an administrative nature.

Structurally, the experiment with the creation of a dual authority, Reichstag and president, neither of which carried executive responsibility, was a dubious one. The two Weimar presidents were distrusted by large segments of the population; Friedrich Ebert (1919–1925), because he was a Socialist ex-saddler, Otto von Hindenburg (1925–1934), because he was a conservative ex-general. Most precarious of all was the constitutional position of that organ which was most important in shaping the political prestige of the regime. For the cabinet was given little power to maintain itself against a demanding legislature, and successive ministries found themselves at the mercy of either the president's pleasure, or shifting legislative majorities, or both. The weakness of the cabinet, moreover, was directly related to the functioning of the party system, which the Constitution's drafters did not adequately take into account. In order to stay in power, cabinets had to retain the confidence of a legislative majority, which meant the confidence of parties. Parties were thus the supremely important institutions, but the Constitution neither recognized nor regulated their position. The stability of the larger democratic parties was threatened by the ease with which splinter groups could sap their strength because of the prevailing system of proportional representation, which allowed even minute parties to gain parliamentary representation. Finally, the ease with which anticonstitutional parties could contribute to the overthrow of

successive governments made the position of the parties supporting the regime increasingly difficult.

In many respects the Weimar Constitution was a very progressive document. But its drafters lacked sufficient understanding
of practical political relationships, and in too many ways they
tried to face in two directions at once. A good example lies in
their treatment of civil rights. Compared to the Constitution of
the Second Reich, which had left civil rights entirely to the
Land constitutions, the Weimar charter pledged the national
government to protect the citizen against the many threats to
his liberties. Then, having enumerated civil rights admirably,
they added another article (Article 48), which gave the president
power to cancel the same guarantees if the public security were
threatened. The same sweeping article also provided the president with power to suspend large parts of the Constitution, by
allowing him during crises to direct the Chancellor to enact legislation even without the support of the Reichstag.

The Weimar Constitution might nevertheless have served as
the basis for a stable democratic state if subsequent political
conditions had been more favorable. As it was, the antidemocratic groups were given an initial advantage by the fact that
the democratic parties, who acted as midwives to the Constitution, also had to take responsibility for accepting what practically
all Germans regarded as a humiliating and ruthless peace treaty.
"Versailles" became a club for the extreme nationalist groups
which soon organized amidst the chaos caused by civil strife and
economic hardship, followed by ruinous inflation. By arguing
that "traitors" on the home-front had caused defeat by stabbing
the army in the back, the extremists won the cooperation of
many reactionary officers, who had lost economic position and
social status as a result of the virtual disbanding of the German
army. (The peace treaty provided for a Reichswehr of only
100,000.) The nationalist fanatics showed their determination
by assassinating some of the most prominent of the new republic's statesmen, including the ministers Erzberger and Rathenau,
who belonged respectively to the Center and Democratic parties.
Further difficulties for the regime were caused by the French
occupation of the Rhineland and the need to pay large reparations
to the victor nations, in addition to having to renounce claims
to all German colonies.

By the mid-twenties, however, the regime was beginning to
gain stability amid world-wide prosperity. The working class
reaffirmed its support of the moderate constitutional policies of

the Social Democrats, who remained the most solid backbone of the regime. The SPD (Sozialdemokratische Partei Deutschlands) discarded much of its semirevolutionary ideology and, together with the dominant trade union movement to which it was affiliated, supplied the bulk of the mass electorate, local officials, and grass roots support which sustained the regime among the people. From its ranks also came most of the volunteers who joined the prorepublican organizations which kept the Nazi and Communist street gangs in check. The other of the two original "Weimar" or prorepublican parties proved less stable. Most of the German Democratic party's middle-class voters deserted it in the course of the twenties, mainly in favor of two more conservative parties, the moderate right-wing German Peoples' party (DVP) and the nationalist-Protestant German National Peoples' party (DNVP), whose attitude toward the republic was much more critical. Gradually these two parties shared in assuming governmental responsibility, and the DVP even produced the single outstanding parliamentary figure of the Weimar Republic, Gustav Stresemann, who as Foreign Minister went furthest in seeking to strengthen German ties to the Western world, particularly to France. Cabinets including representatives of these parties alternated throughout the twenties. Even the victory in the 1925 elections for the presidency of the right-wing parties' candidate, Hindenburg, caused no grave concern, for the venerable ex-general pledged himself to support the republican Constitution.

But the regime proved unable to radiate the political magnetism necessary to convert either its grudging supporters or its open enemies, or to solve through political means the social and economic problems which served to keep Germans deeply divided among themselves. Some of its most serious weaknesses lay within the governmental structure. Large proportions of the civil servants and judges carried over from the preceding regime served the republic with questionable loyalty. Relying on the sacrosanct German tradition of civil service tenure and on the lack of qualified candidates for high office from outside the old ruling classes, these officials felt free to flaunt their reactionary commitments. Right-wing agitators, libellers of republican politicians, and virulent anti-Semites could pursue their aims with relative impunity, for the republic's courts were rarely severe with their kind. Even those clearly guilty of assisting Adolf Hitler in his attempt to initiate an overthrow of the government in Munich in 1923 were sentenced to only a few years' imprisonment. In the Reichswehr, which became an increasingly important political

factor during the last years of the republic, officers with democratic sentiments were a distinct rarity. Outside these official
circles, a considerable portion of the intellectuals allied themselves with a movement which called for a "conservative revolution" to end the party quarreling of Weimar and which sought
to replace the parliamentary system with some form of authoritarianism based on national solidarity.

But while considerable portions of the educated elite served
as the republic's grave-diggers, the most direct threats were to
come from political movements which attracted large segments
of the masses. Leading the groups which sought to destroy
democracy through the use of democratic elections were the
National Socialists and the Communists. Both recruited strong
cores of members dedicated to the establishment, respectively,
of Fascist or proletarian dictatorships. But, though well organized
and able to agitate with relative impunity, these movements
proved no serious threat during the period of prosperity. In 1928
the total anticonstitutional vote of these and similar movements
was less than 15 per cent. (The Nazis polled only 2.6 per cent.)
But the repercussions of the world depression aggravated the
underlying economic and social tensions. The failure of the
market mechanism seemed to lend support to those prophets of
doom who had long predicted that both liberal democracy and
capitalism were on their last legs. Large social groups became
disaffected because of very severe grievances. Small businessmen
felt themselves driven to ruin by the bankers and the cartels.
Farmers rallied to use force to prevent foreclosures. Skilled
artisans rebelled against the pressure to join the industrial pro-
letariat or even the long line of the unemployed. Workers of all
kinds lent a ready ear to radical exhortation, as the cutbacks in
production cost them their jobs and the government's attempt
to maintain balanced budgets cut into their meagre unemployment benefits. University-trained intellectuals and technicians,
unable to find responsible jobs, joined the antidemocratic forces
in droves, and the universities became hotbeds of radicalism,
mainly of the rightist kind. Finally, the disgruntled among the
insecure lower-middle classes rallied in large numbers to the siren
songs of the splinter groups and the totalitarian movements.

Under the resulting pressures, the party alliances which had
supported the regime began to crumble. Interest groups within
the larger parties made irreconcilable demands and frequently
split off into special interest parties. On election day the voter
was wooed by as many as twenty parties. The air was full of

party strife as policies based on economic interest calculations were superimposed on older programs based on ideological traditions. If there was little agreement on substantive questions there was even less on procedural ones. Extremist groups espoused a variety of radical solutions. Among the larger parties, the DNVP and the DVP began to edge away from their earlier, partial commitment to the Constitution and called for the creation of a presidential regime and other strong-man solutions. The workers shifted their strength from the Socialists to the Communists. But the biggest gains were made by the Nazis.

The real political crisis of the republic began with the 1930 elections, brought about by the inability of the democratic parties to agree on basic economic policies. They showed a sharp increase of public support for both the right-wing and Nazi parties (the latter jumped from 12 to 107 seats) which began to coalesce into a powerful anticonstitutional force. Viewed with suspicion by the moderate left and denied the cooperation of the right, the Center party Chancellor, Heinrich Bruening, sustained his government even without the support of a parliamentary majority, as a result of President Hindenburg's delegation of powers to rule by emergency decree. From that point on, government on the basis of democratic legitimation ceased, and administration based on a negative impasse began. The decrees issued by the Bruening government remained in force, not because they were accepted by the legislature, but because the Social Democrats dared not vote to annul them for fear that the Chancellor's resignation would lead to new elections in which the antidemocratic parties would make still greater gains. But the Nazis were gaining strength steadily—in membership, in the size of their paramilitary formations, and in local and Land elections. In July, 1932, after they had succeeded in forcing new Reichstag elections which resulted in their capture of 230 Reichstag seats, they became by far the largest party. At this point the pro-democratic parties ceased to be influential forces altogether. Widespread rioting, unceasing economic crisis, and virulent agitation by nationalist, Nazi and Communist forces made the state's continued existence dependent on the limited power of the Reichswehr and the fading will power of the aging president. From then on, the only alternatives open to Hindenburg were to entrust the government to military-conservative groups who would seek to ignore the deeply divided Parliament and public opinion, or to appoint as Chancellor the leader of a party openly dedicated to using its control of government to suppress all political opposition. Hindenburg was loath to turn power over to the "Austrian corporal," but he was equally tired of bearing lonely responsibility for controlling a political system whose forces he did not understand. In the final negotiations, Hitler proved extremely adept at playing up to the image which both the right-wing parties and the president wanted to form of him, that of a leader who would forget his more excessive commitments once entrusted with the mantle of authority. The DNVP supported his claim to the Chancellorship and so did many of the president's military and civilian advisers. On January 30, 1933, Hitler was duly invested as the last Chancellor of the Weimar regime which he had sworn to replace with a one-party dictatorship.

With the wisdom of hindsight, we can easily deduce that the German democratic system of the interwar period was not adequately prepared to sustain itself against the threat of totalitarian movements seeking to capture it from within. But can we pinpoint the faults? Was the constitutional system badly designed, or was distortion caused by the political forces which operated it? Were the electoral machinery and party leaders at fault, or were the Germans so hopelessly divided that neither leadership nor constitutional devices could save them? Was the republic doomed because of the Germans' want of experience with self-government and lack of commitment to democratic values, or because powerful minority groups unscrupulously encouraged a demagogic leader's mad ambitions? Experts are still very much divided on these questions, but a number of statements can be made about the lessons of Weimar, especially as perceived by those Germans who sought to reinstate democracy after the Nazi regime had collapsed:

(1) The Germans' first national experiment with self-government occurred both under extraordinarily unfavorable circumstances and at a time when too many Germans were still too divided on too many basic political ends, as well as on how to achieve them. A basic prerequisite of parliamentary democracy is a wide consensus on national goals, or at least on acceptable alternatives. This did not exist in Germany for most of the period of the republic.

(2) German political and interest group organizations, and especially the leaders who guided them, were not well adapted to functioning within a democratic system. Too much influenced by outdated ideological systems and/or narrow concern for special interests, they were unable to grow beyond their earlier subordinate positions and to produce leaders who could define,

shape, and confront the larger issues. Even parties which were intellectually committed to democracy proved unable to redirect their energies from the effective criticism of an authoritarian state to the effective strengthening of a democratic state.

(3) The Weimar Constitution was not well adapted to regulate the political system and in part contained the seeds of its own destruction. The ease with which methods contrary to the spirit of the Constitution were legally invoked through use of emergency powers weakened appreciation of the importance of rules and procedures. The creation of a strong presidency encouraged the legislature to act irresponsibly, while the cabinet's lack of political power led to executive instability and administrative irresponsibility. The legislature failed to evolve basic rules which would lead to meaningful decision-making within the parliamentary system. The liberal spirit of the Constitution also led its defenders to display misguided tolerance toward the regime's open enemies.

(4) While the Nazi movement built its large popular support on the basis of the chauvinism, gullibility, and short-sightedness of the German middle classes especially, it also found fertile ground among the frustrated and embittered German masses at large. It could not have developed momentum without the tolerance of large sections of the intellectual elite and the active support of influential power-holders, particularly among the industrial leaders. Unable to distinguish their distaste for democracy from the fear of communism, many who held the highest positions in Germany's economic and social life gave the Nazis both the financial means and the cover of respectability which they needed to make possible their swift rise from the gutter to the Chancellery.

NAZI TOTALITARIANISM

With Hitler's assumption of the Chancellorship Germany was rapidly coordinated into a totalitarian state and society, and eventually into an armed camp for the subordination of other peoples. To emphasize the theme of national revival, the regime was called the Third Reich. In guiding its course, Hitler, as Fuehrer and dictator, aroused intensities of blind loyalty and immeasurable hatred matched by no other modern politician. He amazed the world and delighted most Germans by rapidly turning an economically listless, politically divided, and dispirited country into a prosperous, self-confident, and aggressive world power. Vast construction projects were undertaken, welfare programs were greatly strengthened, and the wholesale annihilation of millions of human beings was commenced. In little over a decade his regime produced so staggering an exhibit of deliberate violations of basic human, individual rights that it cast the dismal records of other totalitarian regimes into the shade. Indeed, his ability to appeal to the hidden, irrational motivations of an educated nation has had a lasting, dampening effect on the optimistic political assumptions of Western liberal democrats.

Nazi Germany produced many variants of the characteristics usually associated with totalitarian dictatorships. Ideologically, the Nazi movement created initial appeal by exciting popular resentments and jealousies. It promised to protect a "downtrodden" Germany from the evil machinations of "international" Jewry, the "decadent" rapaciousness of Western democracies, and "subhuman" Marxists. The center of its crude philosophical basis was a melodramatically developed concept of race, according to which the Aryans (i.e., Germans) were the master race and all other peoples were destined to either subservience or extermination. An attempt was made to explain all aspects of man's existence in terms of the Nazi racial theories, much as extreme Marxists seek to explain all phenomena in terms of materialistic causation. Finally, the Nazi ideology also promised the future paradise typical of totalitarian appeals. Under the "new order," carefully bred blond Aryans were to create a new culture on the ruins of a decadent Western civilization. These were the aims of the Nazi party which, as in other totalitarian one-party states, was organized on a hierarchical principle and completely intertwined with the state machinery. It recognized neither constitution nor law, only the will of the leader. Leader and party in turn felt free to employ a system of police terror to achieve those ends which enticement and threats could not attain. Under the Fuehrer, the Nazi party and its allied organizations finally assumed complete control not only over the machinery of the state, but also over communications and most social organizations, and indirect control over the armed forces and all branches of the economy.

Adolf Hitler was born into a minor Austrian official's family, had a difficult childhood, some scrappy art training, and while still in his youth began to imbibe the virulent racialism that sprouted in the occult intellectual underworld of prewar Vienna. After volunteer service in the wartime German army, he was demobilized in Munich as a corporal and found temporary employment as an observer of radical political groups for an army intelligence unit. Finding one of these groups to his liking, he took out membership (he had card No. 7) and began to display extraordinary speaking abilities in public meetings. Attacking the West and the Jews, he soon drew beerhall crowds in thousands and achieved a prominence which brought him into contact with other extreme nationalists, including reactionary generals. He played a leading role in drawing together the diverse elements which feared or hated Communists, democrats, and labor unions, synthesizing them into a new movement. Officially, the German National Socialist party was born in 1920 in Salzburg as a result of the merger of various small groups which had support on both sides of the border. (Most Germans at this time wanted to bring Austria into the Reich.) Its party symbols brought out the hotchpotch of influences which it sought to reflect: the swastika was taken over from the reactionary Free Corps who were fighting the Marxists, the red color from revolutionary socialism, the "Heil" from older German usage, the raised-hand salute from the Italian Fascists. The following year Hitler became the movement's official head, and began to receive support from "respectable" people in society and big business who hoped that he would cut the ground from under the leftist movements. The Nazis promised the masses radical action in the name of "national" rather than "Marxist" socialism. In November, 1923, working hand-in-glove with reactionary confederates in the army and government, Hitler gambled all to lead a coup d'état which sought to overthrow the Bavarian government in Munich as a prelude to a march on Berlin. The attempt was squashed, but because of friends in high places (the Bavarian Justice Minister entered Hitler's cabinet a decade later), Hitler was given a prison sentence just long enough to permit him to write *Mein Kampf*, which was to become the movement's bible. During the middle twenties the movement was reorganized and established roots all over Germany, building up an organization of several hundred thousand devoted members and activists in its tough fighting formations, the brown-shirted SA and the black-shirted SS, the latter sworn to personal loyalty to the Fuehrer.

The defeat of the Munich putsch persuaded the Nazi leaders to abandon attempts at violent overthrow of the state and to concentrate instead on winning strength in electoral contests. As early as 1928 Joseph Goebbels, whose name later became a byword for propaganda lies, openly stated the party's intent: "We are going into the Reichstag in order to seize our supply of weapons in the very arsenal of democracy. We are becoming deputies only in order to use its own institutions to undermine the values of the system. If the democrats are so stupid as to reward us for this . . . with legislators' pay and free railroad tickets, that is their affair."

CONSOLIDATION: When he assumed the Chancellorship many conservative Germans believed that under pressure from Hindenburg and other parties Hitler would forget his extreme statements and settle down to rule together with the Nazi and conservative ministers who made up his cabinet. They failed to understand how fanatically he was committed to his program and underestimated his ruthless acumen. Confident that he could force the divided opposition to yield him complete power legally if he played his cards right, Hitler exploited Nazi control of the pressure and communications channels of the Reich and Prussian governments in an attempt to win an outright majority in the elections scheduled for March, 1933. Events played into his hands. In late February, a heroically demented Dutch anarchist, whom the Nazis used as an unwitting tool, set fire to the Reichstag building. The Nazis blamed this sensational act on the Communists, and demanded and received an emergency decree from the dazed President Hindenburg which allowed the Chancellor to suspend civil liberties and to take over police control in *Laender* (states) where "threats to public security were not being adequately met." This allowed the Nazis to imprison political opponents with the appearance of legality, seize police power where it was held by non-Nazi Land ministers, and use it for purposes of getting out an immense Nazi vote. For the record, the election results demonstrated the stubbornness of non-Nazis, for despite terrorism and propaganda, the Nazis did not quite succeed in winning the desired majority. But the seventeen million votes cast for their ticket constituted 44 per cent of the total vote; together with his German National allies, Hitler had a majority.

After outlawing the Communist party and arresting most of its deputies, Hitler resorted to the idea of getting the Reichstag to pass an Enabling Act under which the legislature would yield its powers to the Chancellor, in effect liquidating itself without formal constitutional amendment. By means of threats, promises, and pledges of good behavior, the Nazis succeeded in inducing the Center party and the remaining Liberal and Conservative deputies to vote for the ignominious act which marked the formal end of the Weimar system. Only the remaining Socialists stood firm to vote against Hitler. A few months later all non-Nazi parties were declared illegal and dissolved.

In the following year the Nazis laid the basis of their dictatorship, even though the senile Hindenburg remained president. Large numbers of Socialists, intellectuals, and other potential opponents were arrested, and the concentration camps were organized. Jews began to be weeded out of the civil service and the professions. Editors unfriendly to the regime were forced to resign and were replaced by Nazis. Free trade unions were taken over and converted into a state-controlled Labor Front. Nazi-oriented clergy were encouraged to take over the Protestant churches, and Catholic opposition was cleverly diminished by Hitler's promise to respect church rights in a Concordat with the Vatican. Leaders of all mass organizations were put under pressure to give evidence of their loyalty to the new regime, and the ranks of the party expanded greatly as they and many others sought to climb onto the bandwagon. The use of terror became widespread as the dread secret political police (Gestapo) expanded its network. Although the scales fell from the eyes of many Germans who had previously evaded the dark side of nazism, there was little active resistance. Just as the democratic mass organizations, such as the trade unions, had surrendered without struggle, so most of the moderate officials, officers, and professors lacked the civil courage to make a show of protest. Some even took heart from the fact that in April, 1934, Hitler purged that part of the Nazi leadership which had advocated radical anticapitalist action. But the blood-bath which annihilated some of his oldest party comrades also claimed many conservative opponents and should have served notice of things to come. Opposition, however, occurred only underground, mainly among Socialist and Communist groups in contact with their exiled colleagues abroad. In August, 1934, the death of Hindenburg finally allowed Hitler to do away with the last shred of constitutionalism. He declared himself both head of state and Chancellor, and as Fuehrer demanded and received a personal oath of loyalty from all servants of the state.

Like the masters of all totalitarian systems, the Nazis were not content with seizing control of the state and merely expanding its functions, but aimed at controlling all phases of economic, social, and even personal life. Gradually, satellite organizations were developed to carry the Nazi ideology and the Fuehrer principle into the most remote sectors of the social structure. But complete control could not be brought about at once by the party alone, even in highly organized Germany and with a rapidly swelling party apparatus. Instead, the party infiltrated and took over the most crucial organizations, taking some into partnership, and making concessions to others (such as the Catholic church) to buy a benevolent neutrality until the regime was stronger.

For the first five years, something of a division of authority was arrived at between the Nazi hierarchy on the one side and its allies in the army and business on the other. The latter groups were generally left alone as long as they followed over-all government policy. They were allowed to continue as a kind of second force, not politically, but in the sense of commanding executive positions parallel to those of the government and party. Thus the expanding army organization, based on its corps of professional officers, as well as the business-controlled sector of the economy, were allowed for a time to resist open nazification. This also held in part for the state bureaucracy, another institution with a tightly organized group life which the Nazis did not want to disturb since they depended on it to carry out their orders.

But all other economic, professional, and labor organizations were taken over directly by the placement of tried Nazis at their helm. The Labor Front became an important subsidiary organization of the state, as the Nazis tried to lure the workers over to their cause. Welfare benefits were expanded, the unemployed were guided to new jobs created by the armaments industry and the vastly expanded public works program, and recreation and vacation programs were set up in which amusement and propaganda were cleverly mixed. Less complex were the problems of enlisting the support of peasant and artisan groups. These had been strongly pro-Nazi even before the take-over, their loyalty won by the way the party glorified romantic pre-industrial ideals. Their antidemocratic sentiments were now redirected so as to bring about identification with the party's political and economic programs. Some trouble occurred when the artisans found that the Nazis were not going to carry out their earlier promises of carving up or taking over their hated big business rivals. But the Nazis succeeded in persuading these lower-middle class groups to see their enemy only in Jewish-controlled big business, and to regard the German capitalists as fellow workers in the Fuehrer's vineyard.

"National solidarity" was the slogan successfully employed to bring the uncommitted into line, especially as the Fuehrer's policies led to such successes as the return of the Saar by a referendum of its population, Western acceptance of the illegal German militarization of the Rhineland, prestigious German intervention in the Spanish Civil War, and the "bringing home" of Austria in 1938. But as the Nazis' domestic strength grew and plans for military aggression were developed, it was found advisable to extend party control over sectors previously left a certain independence. Thus the army was "nazified," at least at the top, by the retirement of its traditional leaders and their replacement by generals loyal to the regime. Civil servants were no longer allowed to remain aloof but were expected to join the party. Business also was drawn more completely under state influence, though it remained in private ownership until the end.

The Nazi state was based squarely on the cult of one individual. Submission to the will of the leader who somehow embodied the national will was the beginning and the end of Nazi political theory. The party saw itself only as an instrument for rendering the state completely submissive to the Fuehrer's will. Hitler was fond of telling young party fanatics that the only basic rules were "blind discipline and the absolute recognition of authority." Even a top-ranking leader like Hermann Goering proclaimed, "I have no personal conscience; Adolf Hitler is my only conscience." This dependence on the personal whim of one person was difficult to reconcile with the efficient running of even an autocratic administration, which would normally be based on some coherent set of rules. But Hitler wanted to be bound by nothing. Neither the Weimar Constitution nor most pre-Nazi laws were ever really replaced because Hitler refused to be bound by any kind of legal norms. He placed supreme confidence in his ability to make correct decisions based on intuition.

But since Hitler could not make every decision necessary for the running of a state, it was inevitable that a division of powers should develop within the Nazi state, lack of legal basis notwithstanding. Basically, the authority of the various Nazi organizations and ministries depended on the degree of confidence that Hitler had in their leaders at any one time. In the resulting competition among the Nazi paladins, Heinrich Himmler, the head of the SS, gained a dominant position soon after the take-over, which he solidified by gaining effective control over the entire German police system. Vital areas of administration were taken away from regular government agencies and placed under his indirect control. The SS quickly eclipsed in authority the party bureaucracy itself, which was preoccupied with integrating its vast membership and exercising indirect control on the local level. The party organization in fact was relegated to the status of a control organ over the masses, making sure that non-Nazi groups and individuals were deprived of any opportunity to make effective decisions.

Throughout the Hitler period power ebbed and flowed among the Nazi leaders in the party organization, the SS, the army, the bureaucracy, and their subdivisions. After 1941, when Martin Bormann was named party secretary, the party organization began to reclaim much power from the SS apparatus. But in the meantime, the SS had built up a virtual state within a state. It had suborganizations that competed in foreign policy with the Foreign Ministry, agencies that developed occupation policies which conflicted with those of commanding generals, and it also ran its own system of prison and extermination camps. It even developed its own army, the Waffen-SS, which, recruited all over Europe, grew to almost a million and was beyond the jurisdiction of the army high command. After the war it expected to carve out its own model state, which was to be made up of sections of France and Belgium with the capital at either Ghent or Dijon. The official language was to be German, but at the beginning the people were to be allowed to continue to speak French.

While the Nazi leaders fought each other for power and control over the vast conquered areas of Europe, the rest of the German administrative and military elite worked with customary efficiency to keep the vastly swollen state machinery functioning relatively smoothly. It was this elite that worked out the difficulties arising from the erratic policies and battle commands which emerged from the Fuehrer's headquarters in an endless stream, and prevented the contradictory pressures from the various Nazi cliques from causing fatal internal conflicts. Though largely excluded from the inner councils, members of the elite maintained an extraordinarily high discipline which allowed Hitler to make even greater demands. Though many secretly rejected the Nazi regime or even belonged to the "inner immigration," they followed the dictates of obedience and duty to the Fatherland which generations of forebears had shaped. The idea of measuring orders and official policies by the moral yardstick of personal values was alien to the German bureaucratic outlook. It took even the bravest among them years of soul-searching before they could bring themselves to attempt what reason and basic concern for the national destiny commended as the only possible solution, to end the Nazi regime by overthrowing Hitler. The attempt on Hitler's life in his East Prussian command headquarters on July 20, 1944, was the culmination of years of planning in a number of highly secret resistance groups which consisted mainly of the most courageous members of conservative German social groups. But the handful of aristocrats, generals, high civil servants and labor leaders failed in their endeavor to end the regime which was leading Germany to the abyss. Their attempt did achieve symbolic value for postwar Germans seeking to restore some measure of national self-respect.

The horrors inflicted on European populations during World War II finally convinced the world of Hitler's earnest determination to carry out the program first outlined in *Mein Kampf*, and subsequently elaborated in his tirades before the Nazi party meetings and in the private conversations since published in his *Secret Conversations*. Developments bore out his declaration of November, 1933, that he had not become Chancellor in order to do otherwise than he had preached for the past fourteen years. His phenomenal success in carrying out seemingly fantastic plans, first of internal, then of world revolution, can be attributed in large part to his extraordinary readiness to gamble all previous achievements for yet higher stakes. Because of his unchallengeable position he was able first to use the party as an instrument to capture Germany, and then Germany as an instrument to capture control of Europe. When by 1942 German armies had overrun almost the entire continent of Europe and also penetrated into North Africa, his promise of turning the Germans into a master race seemed well on the way toward realization. Hitler took personal command of operations on the warfront, and the success of operations based on his intuition impressed not only the generals, but his people and the world.

However Hitler was not content with fulfilling the positive promises of greater "Lebensraum." Confident of eventual victory almost to the end, he ordered an energetic start to the "reforms" which formed part and parcel of the establishment of the new order. High priority was given to the elimination of "the Jewish problem." First in Germany and then in the occupied countries Jews were deprived of all civil rights, herded together into ghettos, and eventually transported to areas in Poland and Czechoslovakia. Ostensibly they were to be resettled in isolated "pales," but in reality this was the road to the awful "final solution" that led to the mass murder of millions of human beings in the gas chambers and ovens of the extermination camps. Carried through with terrifying efficiency by special SS and other units under the direction of genocide engineers like Adolf Eichmann, this operation was duplicated on a smaller scale by many other programs designed to eliminate groups considered undesirable under Nazi racial theories. Thus gypsies and the mentally retarded were methodically dispatched, as were hundreds of thousands of political opponents, resistance fighters, and civilian hostages. Seldom had absolute power corrupted so absolutely what had initially been accepted by many as an idealistic program for national regeneration.

The extermination programs were kept relatively secret, and after the war most Germans declared that they had known nothing of these and other abominations. Indeed, only a small minority of selected party fanatics had been shaped so completely by the totalitarian mold that they were able to suppress their consciences altogether. But large numbers of "average" Germans who held positions in the party and its affiliated organizations had come to adapt themselves to the regime's excesses, rationalizing acceptance with the argument that they were inevitable or that they were more than balanced off by the regime's positive achievements. Even the very large number who conformed only outwardly could not help but be carried along by an unceasing propaganda campaign. The exposure to years of uninterrupted nationalist frenzy, exhortations to discipline, acceptance of party orders, and self-submersion in racialist mystique made such a deep impression on Germans of all backgrounds that those few thinking of recreating a democratic order after the inevitable defeat frequently had to ask themselves whether Hitler's handiwork might not require several generations to undo.

THE AFTERMATH: With the collapse of the Nazi regime and Hitler's suicide in Berlin in April, 1945, as the Soviet and Western armies swept their way deep into German territory, German political development had turned full cycle. What had begun a century earlier as an attempt to unify diverse states culminated, after sporadic attempts at domestic integration and external expansion, in the complete disintegration of the German Reich and the assumption of German sovereignty by the victorious occupying powers. As a result of inter-Allied agreements reached at Yalta and Potsdam, the central European map was completely recast. Territories which Germany had annexed from Poland and Czechoslovakia in 1939 were returned, and Austria was recreated. In addition, very large sections of Germany east of the Oder and Neisse rivers, which were German even before 1933, were turned over to Poland and the Soviet Union "for administration." Although their final status was to be determined in the peace treaty, they were in fact annexed, and their indigenous

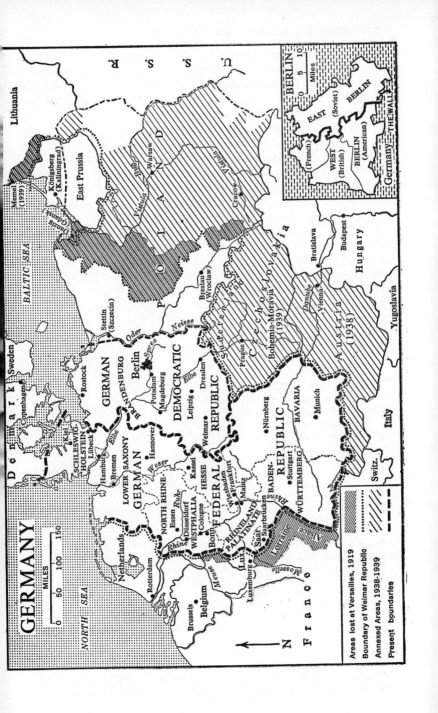

GERMANY

MILES
0 50 100 150

N →

NORTH SEA

BALTIC SEA

D e n m a r k
Sweden
Copenhagen
Kiel
SCHLESWIG-HOLSTEIN
Lübeck
Rostock

Netherlands
Rotterdam
Brussels
Belgium

Hamburg
Bremen
LOWER SAXONY
Hannover
NORTH RHINE
WESTPHALIA
Essen Ruhr
Düsseldorf
Cologne
Bonn
RHINELAND-PALATINATE
Meuse
Luxembourg
Lux.
Saarbrücken
Saar

Elbe
Weser
Rhine
Mosselle

GERMAN
BRANDENBURG
Berlin
Potsdam
Magdeburg
Leipzig
Weimar
HESSE
Kassel
Frankfurt
Wiesbaden
Mainz

Spree
Oder
Neisse

Stettin
(Szczecin)

GERMAN
DEMOCRATIC
REPUBLIC
Dresden

FEDERAL
REPUBLIC
Nürnberg
BADEN-WÜRTTEMBERG
Stuttgart
BAVARIA
Munich

Lorraine
ALSACE
Rhine
France
Switz.

P O L A N D
Lithuania
Memel (1939)
Königsberg (Kaliningrad)
Danzig (Gdansk)
East Prussia

Vistula
Bug
Warsaw
Vistula
Cracow

Breslau (Wroclaw)
S u d e t e n l a n d
C z e c h o s l o v a k i a
Bohemia-Moravia (1939)
Prague
Danube
A u s t r i a (1938)
Vienna
Bratislava
Budapest
H u n g a r y
Yugoslavia
Italy

U. S. S. R.

BERLIN
0 5 10
Miles
EAST (Soviet) BERLIN
WEST BERLIN (American)
WEST (British)
(French)
Germany — THE WALL

Areas lost at Versailles, 1919
Boundary of Weimar Republic
Annexed Areas, 1938-1939
Present boundaries

German population of about ten million was driven out. Finally, the rump of German territory was divided into zones of occupation, administered respectively by American, British, Soviet, and French military governments, while Berlin was divided into sectors occupied by the same powers.

The Allied agreements had left open the question of what final political status Germany was to be granted. East-West tensions soon began to hamper the operation of the Inter-Allied Control Council, which never succeeded in coming to grips with the problem of reconciling contradictory policies among the occupying powers, and ceased to function in 1947. For a time Germany was divided into what were in effect four zonal states. The three Western powers gradually moved first toward the economic, and then toward the political, merger of their zones. This process culminated in 1949 in the creation of the Federal Republic (West Germany), to which the Soviets responded by quickly establishing a rival German Democratic Republic (East Germany) in their zone.

BIBLIOGRAPHY

Germany to 1918

ALEXANDER, EDGAR, "Church and Society in Germany," in J. Moody, ed., *Church and Society* (New York, 1953).

CLAPHAM, J. H., *Economic Development of France and Germany, 1815–1914* (Cambridge, 1936).

CRAIG, GORDON A., *The Politics of the Prussian Army, 1640–1945* (Oxford, 1955).

EYCK, ERICH, *Bismarck and the German Empire* (London, 1950).

HALLOWELL, JOHN H., *The Decline of Liberalism as an Ideology with Particular Reference to German Political-Legal Thought* (Los Angeles, 1943).

HAMEROW, THEODORE S., *Restoration, Revolution, Reaction: Economics and Politics in Germany, 1815–1871* (Princeton, 1958).

HERTZ, FRIEDRICH, *The German Public Mind* (London, 1957).

HOLBORN, HAJO, *History of Modern Germany* (New York, 1959).

KOHN, HANS, ed., *German History: Some New German Views* (Boston, 1954).

KRIEGER, LEONARD, *The German Idea of Freedom* (Boston, 1957).

MEINECKE, FREIDRICH, *Weltbuergertum und Nationalstaat*, 4th ed. (Munich, 1917).

NAUMANN, FRIEDRICH, *Die Politische Parteien* (Berlin, 1913).

PROSS, HARRY, *Die Zerstoerung der Deutschen Politik: Dokumente 1871–1933* (Frankfurt, 1959).

SELL, FRIEDRICH, *Die Tragödie des deutschen Liberalismus* (Stuttgart, 1953).

TAYLOR, A. J. P., *The Course of German History* (London, 1948).

VALENTIN, VEIT, *The German People* (New York, 1953).

VERMEIL, EDMUND, *Germany in the 20th Century* (New York, 1956).

THE MOLDING OF MODERN GERMANY—33

The Weimar Republic

BLACHLEY, F. F., AND OATMAN, M. R., *The Government and Administration of Germany* (Baltimore, 1928).

BRACHER, K. D., *Die Aufloesung der Weimarer Republik*, 2d ed. (Stuttgart, 1957).

BRECHT, ARNOLD, *Prelude to Silence* (New York, 1944).

ESCHENBURG, THEODOR, *Die Improvisierte Demokratie der Weimarer Republik* (Laupheim, 1954).

EYCK, ERICH, *Geschichte der Weimarer Republik*, 2 vols. (Munich, 1956–57).

FLECHTHEIM, OSSIP K., *Die Kommunistische Partei Deutschlands in der Weimarer Republik* (Offenbach, 1948).

HALPERN, S. WILLIAM, *Germany Tried Political Democracy* (New York, 1946).

HEBERLE, RUDOLF, *From Democracy to Nazism* (Baton Rouge, 1945).

KLEMPERER, KLEMENS VON, *Germany's New Conservatism* (Princeton, 1957).

ROSENBERG, ARTHUR, *A History of the German Republic* (London, 1936).

SCHULZ, GERHARD, *Zwischen Demokratie und Diktatur* (Berlin, 1963).

SONTHEIMER, KURT, *Antidemokratisches Denken in der Weimarer Republik* (Munich, 1962).

WATKINS, FREDERICK M., *The Failure of Constitutional Emergency Powers Under the German Republic* (Cambridge, Mass., 1939).

WHEELER-BENNETT, JOHN W., *The Nemesis of Power* (New York, 1954).

The Nazi Period

ALLEN, WILLIAM S., *The Nazi Seizure of Power: The Experiences of a Single German Town, 1930–1935* (Chicago, 1965).

BAUMONT, MAURICE, et. al., eds., *The Third Reich* (Praeger, 1955).

BRACHER, KARL DIETRICH, SAUER, WOLFGANG, AND SCHULZ, GERHARD, *Die Nationalsozialistische Machtergreifung* (Cologne, 1960). Yale University Press will publish an English version of this classic study.

BULLOCK, ALAN L. C., *Hitler: A Study in Tyranny* (New York, 1952).

FRIEDRICH, CARL, AND BRZEZINSKI, ZBIGNIEW, *Totalitarian Dictatorship and Autocracy* (Cambridge, Mass., 1956).

HALE, ORON J., *The Captive Press in The Third Reich* (Princeton, 1964).

HEIDEN, KONRAD, *Der Fuehrer* (Boston, 1944).

HITLER, ADOLF, *Mein Kampf* (Boston, 1943).

JARMAN, T. J., *The Rise and Fall of Nazi Germany* (New York, 1956).

KOGON, EUGENE, *The Theory and Practice of Hell* (New York, 1950).

LEWY, GUENTHER, *The Catholic Church and Nazi Germany* (New York, 1964).

MEINECKE, FRIEDRICH, *The German Catastrophe* (Cambridge, Mass., 1950).

NEUMANN, FRANZ, *Behemoth* (New York, 1942).

NEUMANN, SIGMUND, *Permanent Revolution* (New York, 1942).

PRITTIE, TERENCE, *Germans against Hitler* (London, 1964).

REITLINGER, GERALD, *The Final Solution: The Attempt to Exterminate the Jews of Europe, 1938–1945* (New York, 1953).

SEABURY, PAUL, *The Wilhelmstrasse: A Study of German Diplomats under the Nazi Regime* (Berkeley, 1954).

SHIRER, WILLIAM L., *The Third Reich* (New York, 1960).

TAYLOR, TELFORD, *Sword and Swastika* (New York, 1952).

TREVOR-ROPER, H. R., ed., *Hitler's Secret Conversations, 1941–44* (New York, 1953).

VOGELSAND, THILO, *Reichswehr, Staat und NSDAP* (Stuttgart, 1962).

2: Society and Economy in West and East Germany

POPULATION STRUCTURE

It is important to remember that the Germans constitute the largest national group in all of Europe west of the Soviet Union. It was this fact which led the French to build the Maginot Line and which today makes unification so much more difficult. There are many on both sides of the Iron Curtain who do not relish the idea of a powerful state made up of some seventy-five million Germans. As things stand, war and its aftermath brought considerable dislocation of large population groups, particularly expulsion of the bulk of the German population from East Prussia, Silesia, and the other "Oder-Neisse" territories, as well as from the Sudetenland in Czechoslovakia and German populated areas in the Balkans. The following figures suggest the magnitude of these changes:

GERMAN POPULATION CHANGES, 1939–64 (in millions)

	1939	1964	Gain or loss
West Germany (Fed'l Republic)	40.2	56.1	+15.9
East Germany (Dem. Republic)	15.1	16.1	+ 1.0
West Berlin	2.7	2.2	− 0.5
East Berlin	1.6	1.1	− 0.5
"Oder-Neisse" territories	9.6	1.1	− 8.5
TOTAL	69.2	76.6	+ 7.4

It is noticeable that the over-all effect of the redistribution has been to increase greatly the population of West Germany. This is because the bulk of the expellees did not care to remain in the Soviet zone but headed for the western parts of the country. In addition, the "Democratic Republic" suffered an exodus of some two to three million, mostly younger, productive inhabitants who crossed into West Berlin and the Federal Republic between 1949 and 1961. In those years its population remained almost static, since the number of those leaving about balanced the natural population increase. By contrast, the population of the Federal Republic increased by some eight million between 1947 and 1958. The over-all increase in the German population is explained by the fact that the influx of ethnic Germans who had previously lived outside the Reich (i.e., in Poland, Yugoslavia, Rumania) plus the natural population increase has more than made up for the six to seven million military and civilian casualties of World War II.

The German population in both East and West is predominantly urban. In West Germany (including West Berlin) about a fifth of the population lives in eleven large cities with more than 500,000 inhabitants each, about 45 per cent in small and medium-sized towns and cities with populations of over 5,000, while slightly over one-third lives in smaller, rural communities. In the Democratic Republic there is a somewhat greater population concentration in rural communities and medium-sized towns, but there too population tends to be concentrated in heavily industrialized areas. Thus the heavily industrialized Land Northrhine-Westphalia and the Dresden-Leipzig-Karl-Marx-Stadt district each contain a third of the population of the two states.

In the East the administrative districts have relatively equal populations, but in the West the Laender, embodying in part traditional boundaries, vary greatly in population, almost as much as American states. Some Laender embody strong regional traditions, especially those like the Hanseatic city-states of Hamburg and Bremen or heavily agricultural Bavaria. The dialects of simple people from these areas vary quite as much as do the accents of a New Yorker and a South Carolinian. Another distinct group are the Rhinelanders, proud that after a century of rule from Berlin the West German capital was established in one of their towns by one of their own political leaders. But Land boundaries do not necessarily correspond to traditional loyalties. The occupying powers caused the Rhinelanders to be divided between two Laender, while the citizens of Wuerttemberg and Baden subsequently found themselves united into one Land. Natives did not always welcome the influx of expellees, who were at first heavily concentrated in the poorer agricultural areas of Schleswig-Holstein, Lower Saxony, and Bavaria. However, as cities and factories were rebuilt, they spread out more evenly.

Considerable political significance attaches to the religious structure of the population, and not only to the proportions between Protestants and Catholics, but also to their regional distribution. Since the formation of the Second Reich, Catholics, though predominant in certain sections, have been outnumbered about two to one in the country as a whole. They were always influential in predominantly Catholic areas like Bavaria, the Rhineland, and Silesia, but they lacked power nationally. The division of Germany has changed this situation radically. Within the Federal Republic they now claim almost half (45 per cent) of the population, a fact which has been of much greater advantage to the West German Christian Democrats than to the Social Democrats. The religious affiliation of East Germans is by contrast predominantly Protestant; only 11 per cent are Catholics. Traditionally, the Catholic church has been both better organized and more successful in maintaining touch with its following than have the Protestant churches. This is due to the fact that the Protestant churches were organized predominantly on a Land and regional level, and only loosely unified within several national church organizations. In addition, the Protestant churches almost completely lost contact with the working-class population, while the Catholics were much more successful in sponsoring a whole network of working-class organizations which helped maintain this important link.

THE WEST GERMAN ECONOMIC SYSTEM

The differences in economic policy between West and East Germany were not as stark initially as they were to become later. This was because under the crisis conditions of the immediate postwar years it was found necessary in both West and East to continue the system of rationing and tight economic control introduced under the Nazis. The critical parting of the ways occurred in June, 1948, when the futility of attempts to achieve unified Allied policy had become evident and the United States and Britain introduced a new currency in their zones and allowed the German economic administration to initiate a policy of radical decontrol of the economy. This policy was carried through under the direction of the future Federal German Minister of Economics, Ludwig Erhard, who, with the support of the non-Socialist parties, gambled that the incentives of a free market economy would serve to liberate long dormant productive capacities. His policy proved phenomenally successful as Germans eagerly sought to earn more of the new hard currency in order to buy goods which shopkeepers had previously withheld, while manufacturers rapidly expanded production facilities in order to keep up with the swelling demand for goods which were now made available on a nonrationed basis for the first time in almost a decade.[1]

[1] Henry C. Wallich, *Mainsprings of German Revival* (New Haven, 1955), Chap. 4.

WEST GERMANY'S POSTWAR ECONOMIC RECOVERY

	1948	1950	1953	1957	1960
Crude steel production (million tons)	5.6	12.1	15.4	24.5	34.1
Employment (millions)	13.5	14.3	16.0	19.0	20.4
Unemployment (millions)	.8	1.3	.9	.4	.1
Standard of living (private per capita consumption compared to prewar standard; 1936 = 100)	—	92	114	151	171

SOURCES: UN Statistical Yearbooks; Wolfgang Stolper, *Germany between East and West* (Washington, 1960); unofficial estimates for 1960.

The subsequent increases in production were impressive. In many industries production doubled within six months. Total industrial production, which had stood at barely half the prewar (1936) figure in mid-1948, surpassed this mark by the end of 1949. With characteristic vigor Germans of all classes—managers, workers, and foremen—worked longer hours than anybody else in Europe in order to expand productive capacities, modernize communication facilities, and rebuild housing. Differences between labor and management were subordinated to the common task. Trade union leaders showed great restraint in making wage demands in order not to impede the German drive to recapture overseas markets, thus setting the stage for a low wage, high profit growth. German technical ingenuity met the challenge of the time to improve production methods and product design in order to catch up with competitors in the United States and elsewhere. Primarily, however, industry sought to fill the demands of the domestic market, shaped by the great acquisitive fervor that gripped the German population once it saw the opportunities for satisfying material wants.

Production continued to increase without any significant recession or real levelling off. Steel production climbed from five million tons in 1945, and by the time it reached thirty million tons in 1960 West Germany had far surpassed Britain to become the world's third largest producer (but it was overtaken by Japan in 1964). Total industrial production doubled once again between 1950 and 1957 as the West Germans marked up annual growth rates averaging 10 per cent, roughly four times the American figure. The Federal Republic's gross national product had already surpassed the 1936 level in 1950, and this figure was doubled by 1957. Records like these were made possible through extremely high investment figures, which continued at a rate of from 20 to 25 per cent of the national income. Though especially encouraged by tax legislation, this indicated that Germans were working not merely to satisfy current demand, but because they possessed real confidence in the future potential of their economy.

Immediately after 1945, considerable amounts of industrial equipment concentrated in the Ruhr area had been dismantled and shipped to countries which German armies had despoiled. The French particularly called for the internationalization of this region, the most powerful industrial complex in Europe. This extreme solution was avoided through a series of events which eventually led to the inclusion of German heavy industry in the European Steel and Coal Community. With the gradual lifting of Allied production limitations, German industry undertook an energetic drive to regain prewar markets and to capture new ones. Conditions were favorable, for in the period following the Korean crisis German industry could supply at low prices goods which had become scarce as a result of the shift to military production in other countries. Success in this endeavor led to a strong interlacing among the economies of West Germany and other Western countries.[2] The great increase in trade between Germany and the Western countries not only made up for lost markets in traditional areas like the Balkans, but also provided a substitute for the intra-German trade which used to be carried on with East Germany and which declined to one-tenth of its prewar significance. Thus whereas in 1936 West Germany had spent 8.6 per cent of its gross national product on imports from East Germany, in 1958 it spent less than 1 per cent, while imports from other countries (mainly in the West) increased from 5.6 per cent to about 13 per cent of gross national product during the same period.[3]

American Marshall Plan aid played a considerable part in supplying the crucial initial capital required for expansion, but further investment was made possible by the very considerable profits which manufacturers and businessmen were able to plough back into their firms. The attempt to restore private business as a dynamic economic factor in the reconstruction of Germany was supported by extremely generous tax policies which favored the creation of new wealth and brought economically

[2] Ludwig Erhard, *Germany's Comeback in the World Market* (New York, 1954), Chap. 1.

[3] Wolfgang Stolper, *Germany between East and West* (Washington, 1960), pp. 10–11.

powerful groups to identify their fortunes with those of the state whose economic basis they were helping to shape. The question of ownership and control of industry was settled in their favor. Originally there had been much sentiment, especially among Socialists and the trade unions, for nationalizing heavy industry, but this impulse was unable to prevail over the newly found enthusiasm for private enterprise. Instead, the Co-determination Law of 1951 gave the trade unions the opportunity to help influence company policies by sending representatives to the board of directors of the large steel and coal companies.[4]

The power of the owners and managers of the very large industrial and commercial firms, who are organized in tightly knit industrial and trade associations, was demonstrated in their ability to undo many of the deconcentration measures introduced under the Occupation. Firms like Krupp, which had been ordered to divest themselves of parts of their industrial empires, were able to avoid the implementation of these orders and even to acquire other large firms which increased their dominance. A similar development occurred in banking. The Allies had broken up the "Big Three" banks which had dominated German banking into thirty independent units. By 1952 these had been reconcentrated into nine banks and by 1957 the "Big Three" were reestablished.

Thus postwar West German economic development has been marked not only by large production increases but also by a return to earlier patterns under which control over large sectors of the economy rests in the hands of a relatively small number of managers and bankers. In view of continued prosperity and full employment this fact has not caused any serious conflicts affecting large parts of the population, but it worries many critics of German big business as well as adherents of the free market economy. Obviously, if concentration of ownership and interlocking directorates continue unabated, the doctrine of free competition will become less and less meaningful. Official policy has sought to deal with these problems, but it has been handicapped by the fact that the government's political backers in industry have opposed the necessary stringent regulations. However, while not making much progress in the area of concentration of ownership, in 1957 the government did pass Germany's first anti-cartel law,[5] and such formerly typical German business practices

[4] Wallich, *op. cit.*, pp. 307 ff.

[5] E. Guenther, "Das Gesetz gegen Wettbewerbsbeschraenkungen im Rahmen der deutschen Wirtschaftspolitik," *Wirtschaft und Wettbewerb*, X (November, 1960), 747 ff.

as price-fixing and market-sharing have been somewhat curtailed. But the organizations representing industry and big business remain the most powerful of economic groups. Where they have led, other economic groups have followed. Labor, farmers, white collar workers, artisans, and civil servants are all highly organized and seek to achieve their ends through the political process as well as through economic bargaining. As in other advanced industrial countries, the government has become the embattled regulatory mechanism of a complex economic system.

FROM RAGS TO RICHES

A politically significant aspect of the German recovery program is that it allowed the West German economy to integrate the millions of exiles from former German areas in Eastern Europe, who had for years been forced to remain in makeshift refugee camps or had been quartered with resentful local families. As new production and service facilities were created, more jobs opened up. This was not immediately the case, for the currency reform caused shortages of credit and capital which led to considerable unemployment. At one time it surpassed the two million mark, and there was some unrest as it continued to hover over the million mark well into the 1950's.[6] But by 1954 the demand for labor began to increase much more rapidly than did the supply, even though the work force continued to be augmented not only by youths reaching working age, but by refugees from East Germany and those returning late from Russian prison camps. Employment increased most markedly in industry and commerce, but significantly also in the restaurant and tavern trades, where it doubled between 1950 and 1956, a phenomenon by no means accounted for by foreign tourists alone. By 1959, unemployment was almost nil (1.3 per cent). Employment had increased by more than 50 per cent in the course of a decade, prosperous housewives were leaving the labor market, and German businessmen were forced to import workers from Italy and even Spain. In 1965, over one million foreign workers were employed in West Germany, and personnel chiefs were sending agents all over Europe to recruit factory hands willing to work for the German mark.

While the economic miracle doubled the number of West German millionaires in four years (1936: 1,957; 1953: 1,566; 1957: 3,502), benefits deriving from economic expansion were fairly

[6] Wallich, *op. cit.*, pp. 79 ff.

widespread. Industrial wages rose gradually. In 1950 the average industrial worker was paid the equivalent of about thirty cents an hour, much to the annoyance of British and other competitors whose labor was more expensive and who felt that German union leaders were not militant enough. By 1965, however, German unions had succeeded in raising the average hourly rate to more than one dollar an hour[7] without delaying economic expansion by more than a minimum of work stoppages. Throughout the 1950's the average German worked close to fifty hours a week, but by the end of the decade the unions were pressing for a reduction, with posters showing a little girl saying, "I want my daddy at home on weekends." Tax returns also showed the general increase in prosperity. In 1950, 54 per cent of all wage and salary earners made less than 900 dollars; in 1957 only 16 per cent were in this category while 53 per cent were earning from 900 to 1,800 dollars a year.[8] During the same interval the number of workers and employees earning more than 2,400 dollars increased from 800,000 to 5.3 million, while the currency maintained its purchasing power better than almost any other, price increases being held to an annual average of less than 2 per cent. Real personal per capita consumption increased by about 6 per cent annually in the first eight years of the existence of the Federal Republic. And between 1954 and 1960 the number of privately owned cars increased four-fold (to four million), those owned by workers twenty-fold (to one million).

By 1964, the total number of private cars on German roads doubled again to more than eight million. Road accidents increased commensurably with 1964 traffic fatalities (16,491) more than twice as high as in Britain (6,922).[9]

What have been the social consequences of this economic revival? For some years observers of German society detected a so-called "restorationist" trend which led Germans to seek to regain social position by competing for material and status symbols. This appears to have been an essentially short-term effect associated with the unexpected rapid ascent from rags to riches of many social groups. A more fundamental trend may

[7] Figures in Deutschmark (DM) are here given at the official exchange rate prevailing since 1960 ($1 = DM 4), after the 5 per cent upward revaluation carried out that year. However, it should be noted, particularly in regard to personal income figures, that specific amounts of money have a much higher purchasing value in Germany than in the United States.

[8] Gerhard Zeitel, "Einkommenstatistik," *Handwoerterbuch der Sozialwissenschaften*, Section 28, p. 65.

[9] *Statistisches Jahrbuch der Bundesrepublic Deutschland, 1965.*

be a development toward the kind of society based on personal achievement typical of the United States. Traditional external signs of status are becoming outdated. Rank in the governmental hierarchy has lost significance as the civil service bureaucracy has become only one among many. Cosmopolitan experience no longer suffices, as millions of workers stream across the Alps to vacation by the shores of the Adriatic. Domestic servants are becoming museum pieces as country girls find that they can earn twice as much in the factory as in the nursery. Family background has declined in importance as vast numbers now leave their native towns in search of new homes or job possibilities. There are many signs to indicate that Germany's social stratification is becoming strikingly similar to that of other industrial countries where feudal traditions were eclipsed earlier or were nonexistent. If the over-all picture still shows somewhat less social mobility than, for instance, the United States, this is partly because of the greater numerical significance of stable groups like professionals (2.9 per cent versus 1.4 per cent in the United States), small entrepreneurs (10.7 per cent versus 6 per cent), and farmers (10.6 per cent versus 5.9 per cent), who tend to pass on positions and status to their children, and the lesser significance of mobile groups like technical and other employees (18.8 per cent versus 30.8 per cent).[10] But basic socio-economic trends tend to bring West Germany closer to the American pattern.

One institution which does not contribute as much to increasing social mobility as it might, or as its equivalents do in countries as different as the United States and the Democratic Republic, is the educational system. The quality of the general German educational system is rightfully held in world-wide esteem both for its successes in bringing literacy to the masses and for its traditional ability to produce outstanding scholars and scientists. But as in most continental countries there tends to be a strong class bias as to who gets advanced education, which is for many the only route to higher social status. Four-fifths of the pupils leave school at the age of fourteen, and those who do go on proceed to the *Gymnasien*, the academic high schools which prepare for university entrance. *Gymnasien* students, however, have always been drawn disproportionately from middle-class families which supply both the incentive and the financial

[10] Morris Janowitz, "Social Stratification and Mobility in West Germany," *American Journal of Sociology*, LXIV (1958), 8.

means. In Britain a concerted effort has been made to remove at least the financial barriers for working-class children by providing aid to families which keep their children in secondary school; there is also a generous public scholarship program for university students. West Germany has not seen fit to follow this example, and one result is that only 5 to 10 per cent of university students come from working-class families, even though all universities in Germany are public, their tuition rates are quite low, and the state does provide other marginal subsidies and a limited scholarship program.

However, most socially-conscious Germans have come to feel fairly satisfied with the social system. As one wrote in 1960:

Tonight, as I dine on oysters flown in by Air France . . . I don't have a bad social conscience. The taxi driver out there could, if he wanted to, occasionally afford oysters and wine. . . . The expellees have been resettled and the manner in which they are looked after is an extraordinary accomplishment of our society. The drug store down the street glitters in chrome, its neon signs promise to bring back lost slenderness. The goodlooking druggist gracefully dims the golden ray of lights as if she were a stage goddess, and gets ready to meet her boy-friend outside an entrance designed by a student of Picasso. They drive off in a white sports car. . . . while the radio plays a soft American tune all about the beauty of Virginia. The girls don't look the way they used to in the days of the Hitler youth movement. They are dressed like their equivalents in New York or Paris, and they wear their hair and cosmetics just as they do in London or Rome. . . . I live in the Federal Republic. Do I live in paradise?[11]

Others emphasize how much changes in German values have eclipsed the traditional stereotypes which foreigners held of the German mentality:

These new Germans don't just live to work, rather they know quite well how to combine self-improvement with all possible comforts. . . . Where once ideals motivated, indifference now reigns. The somber impulses of the "Faustian man" have given way to the clearest sort of calculation. Once-popular concepts of "destiny" are received with knowledgeable smiles and expressions of a "sense of mission" are dismissed with shrugs of the shoulder. Is it possible that a people who before could never do without a rich assortment of *Weltanschauungen* and *ideologies* now yawns at the mention of the thinkers who shaped its traditions?[12]

[11] Wolfgang Koeppen, *Die Welt*, June 11, 1960.
[12] Herman Proebst, *Magnum*, April, 1960, p. 14.

EAST GERMAN DEVELOPMENT

About the same time that the West moved to decentralize economic control through adoption of the "social market policy," the East began to move energetically in the other direction. In 1945 only the larger industrial and business enterprises had been socialized, and even these remained under the control of communal and Land authorities. The change-over to centralized control and planning began in 1948 and found expression in the Two-Year Plan adopted for 1949 and 1950. Subsequently a state planning commission was created on the Soviet model, and it was this agency which developed two additional Five-Year Plans which initially sought to concentrate all energies on the creation of a previously almost nonexistent heavy industrial base. Despite lack of adequate coal and iron resources, steel production was increased tenfold in the period from 1948 to 1958, though at this point West Germany was still outproducing the East by a ratio of twenty-six to three million tons annually.

More recently, within the framework of a new Seven-Year Plan (1958 to 1965) which parallels that of the Soviet Union, the East German economy has been closely integrated with the economies of the entire East European bloc. Thus, East Germany has come to concentrate on expanding its chemical, heavy

INDICES OF THE COMPARATIVE DEVELOPMENT OF THE WEST AND EAST GERMAN ECONOMIES

	1936	1950	1957
Aggregate Gross National Product			
West Germany	100	116	200
East Germany	100	77	122
Per capita Gross National Product			
West Germany	100	92	151
East Germany	100	69	112
Industrial, mining, & electricity output			
West Germany	100	117	233
East Germany	100	75	144
Per capita consumption			
West Germany	100	92	151
East Germany	100	37	95

SOURCE: Wolfgang Stolper, *Germany between East and West* (Washington, 1960), p. 14.

mechanical, and electro-technical industries so as to serve as a specialized supplier to the other "peoples' democracies" as well as to the Soviet Union, for whom it has become the most important foreign source of investment goods. In little more than a decade East Germany has set up not only a planned economy in sharp contrast to the West German system, but has gradually extended the framework within which the planning takes place from the local, to the national, to the supranational level.

The experimentation with planning formulas caused considerable waste and privation, but this did not deter the East German regime from gradually eliminating the remaining private sectors of the economy in line with its ideological goals. Small private factory owners found it increasingly difficult to secure the materials necessary for achieving assigned production targets. Frequently the authorities would find minor infringements of planning or tax regulations and, while the owners were thus under pressure, offer to provide public capital to help modernize the plant.[13] In this way the state became the dominant partner even of enterprises which it did not directly run, and the private sector, which had still made up almost a quarter of East German industry in 1950, was gradually reduced to the vanishing point (1959: 5 per cent). A similar development occurred in areas like the construction industry and wholesale trade, where the "socialist" sector became predominant in the course of the 1950's. Private farmers, artisans, and retail store owners continued to be tolerated as long as they were useful to the state, which was anxious not to overload its economic agencies to the point of organizational breakdown. Ingenious types of "socialist" organization, such as producers' collectives and state-controlled trading cooperatives, were set up with the aim of encouraging the smaller owners to place themselves voluntarily in dependent positions, thus allowing the state to carry out complete socialization at a later date with a minimum of struggle or interruption of economic activity.

The process which by 1960 led to the virtual elimination of private property in agriculture serves to illustrate the manner in which East German collectivization was carried through and its similarity to the earlier Soviet model. The first stage actually created an increased number of private farmers, since the 1945 land reform program distributed the best part of some 7,000 large estates among approximately 300,000 expellees, land-poor farmers,

[13] John Herz, "East Germany: Progress and Prospects," *Social Research* (1960), 147.

and farm laborers, most of whom received less than ten acres. After a period of consolidation comparable to the "New Economic Policy" period in the Soviet Union, pressure began to be brought against middle-sized farmers who owned between twenty and one hundred acres. By means of political propaganda and economic pressure much of their land was incorporated into agricultural collectives. But by 1952 still only about one-quarter of the total land area was in the "socialist" sector, half of this in collectives and half under direct state operation.[14]

When pressure caused the large-scale flight of peasants to the West, the regime substituted a propaganda campaign urging small-scale farmers to deed their land voluntarily to collectives in order to benefit from the preferred position in terms of better machine tractor service and lower production quotas. The pressure was maintained with varying degrees of intensity; it was relaxed during crisis periods like those following the June 17, 1953, uprising and the Polish and Hungarian revolts of 1956, and intensified when conditions stabilized. Between 1953 and 1958 the proportion of land in collective ownership increased from 13.8 per cent to 29.4 per cent, climbing to 45 per cent by 1959. Then in the spring of 1960, the regime decided to stage an intensive drive to complete collectivization. Thousands of Communist activists descended on the villages to undertake a personalized pressure campaign on the peasants still holding out, who were made to see that jail or flight were the only real alternatives to "voluntary entry" into at least a "class-one" collective, in which the peasants gave up their land but kept title to their animals and implements. As newspapers reported district after district achieving 100 per cent collectivization the peasants realized their hopeless position and surrendered title to their land.

The elimination of entire social groups, such as the independent peasants and industrial and commercial entrepreneurs, has been part of the huge social revolution engineered in East Germany. Social mobility has been tremendous as elements of the old middle and lower-middle classes have been forced down the social scale while large masses of workers have been carried upwards. Although the denazification and expropriation processes were most important in eliminating the middle classes' position of influence, other techniques were employed for groups like professionals. Independent practice has been made all but im-

[14] Frieda Wunderlich, *Farmer and Farm Labor in the Soviet Zone of Germany* (New York, 1958).

possible for lawyers and doctors. Like managers, they have been forced to accept positions as employees of the state or one of its subsidiary organizations. Members of the intelligentsia, especially teachers and professors, have had to conform to the twisting party line in their instruction and writings.

In an attempt to replace these groups, the East German regime has from the beginning sponsored a far-reaching program of training workers and peasants for entry into positions in the intelligentsia, the bureaucracy, and managerial positions. Typical perhaps is the engineer, Rosemarie Gutermuth. Originally a humble construction worker, she distinguished herself by winning commendation as an "activist," was promoted to forewoman of her brigade and was then sent to study engineering on a government scholarship. She ended up as a responsible bureaucrat working in the Ministry of Reconstruction and was widely quoted as saying: "What I am and the way I live I owe entirely to our Workers' and Peasants' state."[15] The relatively high salaried elite groups of engineers, managers, and intellectuals who have been funnelled into the new positions created within the apparatus of the planned society after proper ideological indoctrination form one of the key social bases for the regime.

The economic achievements of the German Democratic Republic were for many years far less impressive than those of the Federal Republic. It took the East Germans far longer to reach prewar levels of production and even longer to supply the average citizen with something like his prewar standard of living. This was due not only to successive changes in policy relating to the basic restructuring of the economy and to the losses incurred in the process of the socialization of industry, trade, and agriculture, but also to the fact that East Germany lacked a heavy industry base. Another initial handicap was the fact that the Russians carried through the dismantling program much more thoroughly than the Western Allies, with the result that the East was deprived of a far larger share of its productive capacity. Though possessing only a third of total German resources, the Soviet zone was forced to supply over three quarters of all German reparations, to the value of perhaps ten billion dollars. These factors, together with the problem of a continued labor shortage due in good part to the flight to the West of skilled workers and technicians, handicapped East German reconstruc-

[15] Otto Stammer, "Sozialstruktur und System der Werthaltungen der Sowjetischen Besatzungszone Deutschlands," *Schmoller's Jahrbuch*, LXXVI (1956), 103.

tion. It was only in 1954 that the regime achieved the equivalent of prewar production levels.

Well into the 1950's, however, the emphasis on increasing production goods led to continuing shortages of consumer goods, which caused the regime to maintain rationing until 1958. Until this time currency in East Germany really had two values. Rationed goods were sold at quite low prices, while many goods purchased in the state-run "HO" stores required no ration coupons but were priced much higher. In this way the regime was able to ensure minimum standards of living and at the same time to limit excessive consumer expenditure. Dissatisfaction with the standard of living was one of the causes of the 1953 uprising, since it had been little improved for the past several years and was then some 50 per cent below West German stand-

1963 PER CAPITA CONSUMPTION OF SOME FOODS IN WEST AND EAST GERMANY (in kilograms[a])

Type of Food	East Germany	West Germany
Meat	56	64
Fish	14	7
Butter	12	9
Flour	96	72
Potatoes	159	126
Vegetables	63	45
Fruit	49	88
Coffee	1.6	3.4
Eggs	189	221

[a] 1 kilogram = 2.2 pounds

SOURCE: Leipzig Institute for Market Research as reported in *Duesseldorf Handelsblatt*, August 5, 1965.

ards. In the following years greater emphasis was placed on consumer goods in East Germany, just as in Soviet Russia, and by 1957 the gap between the average East and West German workers' standard of living was reduced to about 30 to 40 per cent.[16] East Germans were gradually able to afford luxury items like radios and vacuum cleaners, while the quality of clothing and similar products improved considerably. Although East Germany did not come close to its propaganda goal of overtaking

[16] Heinz Markmann, "Lohn und Kaufkraft in der Sowjetzone," *Wirtschaft-wissenschaftliche Mitteilungen*, 1959, No. 3, p. 13.

West Germany by 1961 in consumption of the most important consumer goods and foodstuffs, by 1963 the East German food consumption pattern was not too different from that in West Germany. As the table indicates, East and West Germans ate about the same quantities of meat and fish, although the East German diet relied more heavily on fish, as well as on starchy foods like flour and potatoes. Somewhat surprisingly, East Germans consumed more butter than West Germans, but were supplied with less fruit, particularly citrus fruit, and coffee. Although these figures do not take quality factors into consideration, they suggest a closer approach to parity in this sector of living standards than was widely supposed.

The relatively great economic potential of East Germany is not readily apparent to the casual visitor. Such visitors, as a West German author wrote in 1964 ,"will literally stumble over bad roads, or will be thrown about poor road-beds carrying not much better trains. One sees few cars, and while the people are not poorly nourished, they are dressed roughly and in poor

SOME WEST AND EAST GERMAN SOCIO-ECONOMIC INDICATORS, WITH BRITISH AND SOVIET COMPARISONS

Indicator	West Germany	East Germany	United Kingdom	Soviet Union
Per cent of labor force in agriculture	14	19	5	48
Industrial employment as per cent of working-age population	32	30	35	24
Military as per cent of population aged 15–64	.90	.95	1.86	3.02
Private consumption as percent of Gross National Product	58.7	60	66.7	55.8
Inhabitants per hospital bed	100	90	110	140
Radios per 1,000 population	319	348	289	205
Television sets per 1,000 population	109	91	220	28

NOTE: The base periods for most of the statistics cited lie in years 1959–61. Only the East German figure for industrial employment dates from a period considerably earlier than those used for the other countries.

SOURCE: Bruce M. Russett, et al., World Handbook of Political and Social Indicators (New Haven, 1964).

style. The displays in the shopwindows, if one doesn't happen to be in Rostock or Leipzig or East Berlin on the occasion of a fair or festival, are pathetic . . . Nevertheless this DDR is about the tenth most powerful industrial power in the world, and the second strongest in the Eastern block . . . ahead of Czechoslovakia and Poland."[17] It is because they are both, in relation to population and resources, among the world's most advanced industrial societies that the two Germanys remain in many ways more similar than their radically different routes of postwar recovery would suggest. In some ways, as suggested by the indicators in the attached table, the societies and economies of West and East Germany remain more similar to each other than to countries within their respective ideological blocs. Thus the relative significance of agricultural and industrial employment differentiates both states about equally from Britain on the one hand, and the Soviet Union on the other. In holding down private consumption so as to increase investment, both societies have shown a large measure of restraint which, while it does not quite approach that imposed on the Soviet population, exceeds that prevalent in a country like Britain. Data on facilities such as hospitals indicate that both states have maintained a tradition of extensive public services in this area. And even in as politically relevant an area as mass communication systems, as measured in terms of the diffusion of radio and television receivers, East and West Germany remain remarkably similar.

BIBLIOGRAPHY

Economic Structure

ARNOLD, FELIX, *Die Sozialistische Planwirtschaft und der Demokratische Zentralismus in der Volkswirtschaft der DDR* (Berlin, 1959).

ERHARD, LUDWIG, *Germany's Comeback in the World Market* (New York, 1954).

KOENIG, H., ed., *Wandlungen der Wirtschaftsstruktur der Bundesrepublik* (Berlin, 1962).

ORTLIEB, H. D., "Unsere Konsumgesellschaft," *Hamburger Jahrbuch fuer Wirtschafts und Gesellschaftspolitik*, IV (1959), 225-45.

ROSKAMP, KARL W., *Capital Formation in West Germany* (Detroit, 1965).

STOLPER, WOLFGANG, *Germany between East and West* (Washington, 1960).

——, and ROSKAMP, KARL, *The Structure of the East German Economy* (Cambridge, Mass., 1960).

WALLICH, HENRY C., *Mainsprings of German Revival* (New Haven, 1955).

WUNDERLICH, FRIEDA, *Farmer and Farm Labor in the Soviet Zone of Germany* (New York, 1958).

[17] Ernst Richert, *Das Zweite Deutschland* (Guetersloh, 1964), p. 121.

Social Systems

ABENDROTH, W., "Die Soziale Struktur der Bundesrepublik und ihre politischen Entwicklungstendenzen," *PVS*, IV (1963), 150–67.

DAHRENDORF, ROLF, "The New Germanies," *Encounter*, XXII (1964), 50–59. The entire issue of this number is devoted to evaluation of German cultural, political, and social developments.

HERZ, JOHN, "East Germany: Progress and Prospects," *Social Research*, XXVII (1960), 139–56.

HORNSTEIN, ERIKA VON, *Die Deutsche Not* (Cologne, 1960).

JANOWITZ, MORRIS, "Social Stratification and Mobility in West Germany," *American Jl. of Sociology*, LXIV (1958), 6–24.

LOWIE, ROBERT H., *Toward Understanding Germany* (Chicago, 1954).

MERKL, PETER H., *Germany: Yesterday and Tomorrow* (New York, 1965).

PROSS, HELGE, "Die Soziale Schichtung in der Bundesrepublik," *Deutsche Rundschau*, LXXXIV (October, 1958), 916–26.

REIGROTSKY, ERICH, *Soziale Verflechtungen in der Bundesrepublik* (Tuebingen, 1956).

RICHERT, ERNST, *Das Zweite Deutschland* (Guetersloh, 1964).

STERN, CAROLA, *et al.*, "Ulbricht's Germany: Studies in Intellectual Gleichschaltung," *Soviet Survey* No. 34, (1960), 30–73.

WAGNER, HELMUT R., "The Cultural Sovietization of East Germany," *Social Research*, XXIV (1957), 395–426.

PART TWO
THE FEDERAL REPUBLIC

3: Rules, Parties, and Publics

From the perspective of the late 1960's the dominance of patterns of continuity and stability in the Federal Republic presents a sharp contrast not only to previous German regimes, but also to those of most other countries in the contemporary world. Thus the first Chancellor, Konrad Adenauer, held office continuously for a longer period of time than did all his twelve predecessors of the Weimar period taken together. Unlike other rump states in divided nations, such as South Korea, the maintenance of constitutional government has not been threatened by military putsches or the like. True, the governments of the other two major defeated powers of World War II, Japan and Italy, have also been dominated for some two decades by the same conservative parties, but these countries have experienced protests by hostile mass movements, parliamentary crises, political realignments and frequent changes in the premiership, all of which have been notably absent in the Federal Republic. Indeed, it can be said of no other major democratic country in the world that the top governmental office will have been occupied during the two decades from 1949 to 1969 by only two leaders of the same party, as it will have been in the Federal Republic during the terms of office of Chancellors Adenauer and Erhard.

Certainly there have been distinguishable problems and decision-making styles during different phases of the institution-alization process. The changes in physical appearance between the West Germany of 1950, which still bore many marks of wartime destruction, and the highly prosperous Germany of 1965 were paralleled to an extent by changes in political goals and styles. Where the earlier period was dominated by questions of how to equitably share the burdens and dislocations bequeathed by the Nazi regime, in the latter period questions of socio-economic policy revolved increasingly about how to distribute benefits and subsidies from the well-filled coffers of the federal treasury. Whereas earlier West German politicians were still seeking to achieve full sovereignty, later they pondered how to use greatly increased political power to restore the balance of power among their former occupiers. But at no time were there any sharp system-wide breaks. Discontinuities between successive phases were bridged by continuities of either institutions or personal leadership, and often both. Thus the transition from Occupation rule to parliamentary government was softened by the fact that, as Minister of Economics in the first Adenauer government, Ludwig Erhard merely continued the policies he had initiated previously in the Economic Council. When Adenauer in 1963 finally yielded the Chancellorship to Erhard, continuity was maintained by the fact that Adenauer remained as chairman of the Christian Democratic party, while Erhard inherited Adenauer's cabinet.

OCCUPATION THERAPY

The most immediate impact of defeat on the largest number of Germans occurred as the result of Allied policies to uproot nazism, and to punish those who had assisted the Hitler regime. The highest ranking survivors of the Nazi hierarchy and its military and civilian appendices were of course held to account in the Nuremberg War Trials (in which the Soviet Union also participated). But, in addition, millions of Germans were subjected to denazification proceedings in which the attempt was made to investigate the degree of assistance they had given the Nazi regime and to punish them accordingly. Sentences ranged from prolonged imprisonment, through dismissal from office (418,000 in the United States zone) and the payment of heavy fines, to the obligation to spend stipulated periods of time working as ordinary laborers helping to clear up the rubble or repair desecrated Jewish gravestones. But the difficulty was that obvious criteria, such as membership in the Nazi party and its numerous affiliates, were a dubious key to the identity of the worst offenders. In the British and French zones there was relatively little emphasis on punishing the small-time party member, and it was possible to channel considerable energy into a program designed to punish the more active agents of the regime. The Americans, however, decided to have denazification boards review the cases of no less than 3.6 million out of 16 million adults in the United States zone, thus creating a staggering task for the relatively few Americans and proven anti-Nazis who had to carry it out. The result was that denazification proceedings deteriorated; the boards became less thorough and more lenient just at the time when they began to deal with the more serious cases.[1] The Germans, among whom the collective guilt doctrine had created a kind of negative solidarity, were quick to develop theories of self-justification which minimized their role in Nazi excesses and maximized the weaknesses of the denazification process. Gradually the program was replaced by purely German proceedings against individuals guilty of criminal acts under German law.

The Allies were sufficiently wise to recognize that they could not uproot one elite without replacing it with another, and so their policy manuals prescribed that denazification steps were to be matched by democratization actions, not only through the appointment of demonstrated anti-Nazis to public positions, but also through the creation of new institutions which would help Germans with impressive democratic credentials assume positions of influence. In this manner, the leaders of the pre-Hitler trade unions were reinstalled in office long before similar invitations were extended to business and professional groups whose over-all record was far more ambiguous. Similarly, the Occupation authorities began to divest themselves of their initial monopoly in the communications field by issuing licenses allowing certain anti-Nazis to publish newspapers and by replacing the personnel of the state-run radio works. But the most important political instruments of democratization were the political parties, which were licensed only after their programs and membership lists had been screened.

Initially the Western allies pursued rather disparate aims. Thus the French sought to bring about the dismemberment of Germany, while the British and Americans espoused, respectively, a centralized political system based on the nationalization of industry, and a federal system based on the maintenance of maximal private property rights. A change in the situation was brought about, however, by a combination of economic necessity and Soviet intransigence. The Americans and the British were the first to plan the merger of the economic administrations of their economically complementary zones. When the Russians and French refused invitations to join, they began the gradual build-up of interzonal agencies which culminated in the creation of the bizonal Economic Council. The French, recognizing the futility of attempts to hold out for a loose confederation of German states, gradually fell into line, thus turning the bizone into the

[1] John D. Montgomery, *Forced to Be Free: The Artificial Revolution in Germany and Japan* (Chicago, 1957), pp. 10 ff.

trizone. This expansion of German government allowed the German party politicians to look beyond the horizons of their Laender and to think concretely of vying for national power. The two strongest parties, the Social Democrats (SPD) and the Christian Democrats (CDU), staked out their positions in the Economic Council, where the CDU together with the smaller parties upheld Erhard's free market policy. The Socialists, still loyal to the idea of a planned economy, were confident that Erhard would fail and that the support of the impoverished masses would then make them the dominant party.

Meanwhile, the widening rift between the Western powers and Soviet Russia in effect reduced the number of potential alternatives. West Germans could either continue to hope that despite the failure of successive foreign ministers' conferences the Allies would come to an agreement paving the way to an all-German government; or else they could support the much more immediate efforts to create a German rump state based only on the territory of the three Western zones. By the summer of 1948 the mass of West German political opinion was moving toward acceptance of the "Western" solution. All the major party groups were now organizationally cut off from their counterparts in the Soviet zone, while Soviet rejection of the Marshall Plan, followed soon thereafter by the launching of the Berlin Blockade, tended to undercut the arguments of the minority that Germans should support no constitutional arrangements unless based on the unification of all four zones. With varying shades of reluctance, the West German politicians thus accepted the Western Allies' proposal that a constituent assembly be called to draw up a constitution for a West German state, to which the Occupation powers would be prepared to yield the bulk of German political authority. They gave legalistic expression to their reservations by refusing to talk of either a "constituent assembly" or a "constitution," but the "Parliamentary Council" which started meeting in September, 1948, to work on the drafting of the "Basic Law," was to construct more than merely the transitional instrument described in its preamble.

THE BASIC LAW

The members of the Parliamentary Council could not ignore evidence that the traditional operating concepts of the European nation-state were archaic, that the most beautifully drafted constitutions could easily be converted into useless scraps of paper, and that they had little cause to base grandiose plans on an optimistic evaluation of man's political potential. The party complexion of the Council—composed of equally large groups of CDU and SPD delegates, with minor parties holding a balance of power—also discouraged attempts to incorporate basic economic and social policy goals within its framework. But, the name notwithstanding, the delegates did produce a complete constitution, which sought to draw realistic consequences from specific historical experiences.[2]

Contributing causes of the Weimar failure, as the delegates recognized, related to the inability of the legislature to surmount internal party strife, the consequent weaknesses of cabinets and the political executive and, finally, the disappointing function of the president as a guardian of the Constitution. There was some talk of foregoing the parliamentary system altogether, in favor of a presidential system based on the separation of powers. But the lack of European experience with this type of constitution, the unwillingness of all groups, in view of recent experiences, to concentrate as much power in a one-person executive as the American model entails, and a decided distrust of the voters' reliability, led them to discard this idea. Instead, the delegates sought to create a "rationalized" variant of the parliamentary system which would meet the traditional problems of German politics.

As a result, the two institutions which had held greatest power under the Weimar Constitution, the popular branch of the legislature and the presidency, were both retained but their power was greatly reduced. The lower house, whose name was changed from Reichstag to *Bundestag*, was greatly weakened in its ability to overthrow cabinets. The presidency was shorn of most independent political power and almost reduced to the figurehead position of the British monarch. But the people were also deprived, through the abolition of the initiative and referendum, of those direct political powers which the optimistic drafters of Weimar had given them. By contrast, two traditional institutions gained in influence. One was the federal upper house called the *Bundesrat*, which, with Allied encouragement, was made much stronger than its pre-Hitler predecessor. Most importantly, it was the executive, especially the Chancellor's posi-

[2] John F. Golay, *The Founding of the Federal Republic of Germany* (Chicago, 1958), and U.S. Military Government, *Documents on the Creation of the German Federal Constitution* (Washington, 1949).

tion, which was markedly strengthened. The constitutional basis on which Adenauer was later able to develop what many people have called a "Chancellor democracy" was in good part due to the drafters' conviction that the Weimar democracy might have been saved if some of its Chancellors had had greater power to

BASIC RULES OF THE "BASIC LAW"

Article 20

(1) The Federal Republic of Germany is a democratic and social Federal state.

(2) All state authority emanates from the people. It shall be exercised by the people by means of elections and voting and by separate legislative, executive and judicial organs.

(3) Legislation shall be limited by the constitution, the executive and the administration of justice by legislation and the law.

Article 79

(1) The Basic Law may be amended only by a law which expressly alters or adds to the text of the Basic Law. [*Note: Special conditions are applicable for the implementation of certain kinds of treaties.*]

(2) Such a law shall require the affirmative vote of two-thirds of the members of the Bundestag and two-thirds of the votes of the Bundesrat.

(3) An amendment to this Basic Law affecting the division of the Federation into *Laender*, the participation in principle of the *Laender* in legislation, or the basic principles laid down in Articles 1 and 20 is inadmissible.

Article 73

The Federation shall have exclusive legislation on:

1. foreign affairs as well as defense, including both military service for males over 18 years and the protection of the civilian population.

2. citizenship of the Federation . . .

11. statistics for Federal purposes.

Article 74

Concurrent legislative powers extend to the following matters:

1. civil law, criminal law and execution of sentences, the system of judicature, the procedure of the courts, the legal profession, notaries and legal advice;

2. registration of births, deaths and marriages. . . .

23. railroads, other than Federal railroads, except mountain railroads.

impose their policies both on a divided legislature and on fellow cabinet members. The specific constitutional provisions will be examined in greater detail within the context of succeeding chapters, but it is important to become aware at this point of the redistribution of powers through which the Basic Law helped make the politics of Bonn so different from those of Weimar.

The dominant characteristic of the Basic Law consists of the grafting of multiple check and balance mechanisms onto a parliamentary structure. German parliamentarianism had always been heavily adulterated and it became more so. The delegates particularly liked the idea of the American Supreme Court, and they set about creating a Constitutional Court of their own which would assume the role of an arbiter of the Constitution. It was empowered to decide not only the constitutionality of legislation and administrative acts, but also basic questions of constitutional interpretation which were expected to develop both among the various parts of the federal government and between it and the Laender. By thus endowing a novel Constitutional Court with powers to discourage unconstitutional action and to adapt the constitution to changing circumstances, the drafters were confident that they had gone far to eliminate the internal contradictions which had plagued the Weimar system. They allowed very little room for "emergency powers" through which the Constitution could be hollowed out.

The challenge posed by the need to come to terms with the problems associated with the rise of nazism and the abolition of democratic rights was met by the Parliamentary Council in a piecemeal, but by no means ineffectual, manner. The prominence given civil rights is indicated by the conspicuous place accorded the Bill of Rights at the very beginning of the Basic Law, and also by the fact that its provisions are declared to be directly binding on all courts and authorities. Thus the rights of free speech, press, and assembly are strongly anchored, censorship is prohibited, and equality before the law and the equivalent of habeas corpus are guaranteed. German citizens have the right of carrying a constitutional plaint directly to the Constitutional Court. Guarantees of civil rights are reinforced with significant provisions for the general maintenance of the democratic order, particularly through provisions which permit the suppression of antidemocratic movements. Thus, "parties, which, according to their aims and the behavior of their members, seek to impair or abolish the free and democratic basic order" may be declared unconstitutional by the Constitutional Court.

LAENDER AND FEDERALISM

The national political institutions created for West Germany were, as in the case of American institutions of 1789, imposed upon a pre-existent structure of state governments. The traditional German states or Laender had been abolished by the Nazis but resuscitated and reorganized by the Allies, who, in so doing, abolished the previously dominant state of Prussia. In setting up the Laender two kinds of problem were encountered. In south and southwest Germany, loyalty to the Laender was still very much alive, but Occupation geometry had caused zonal boundaries to cut across traditional Land boundaries. In northwest Germany, on the other hand, a century-long Prussian hegemony had largely destroyed regional loyalties, so that after the abolition of Prussia the British had to set up Laender without much regard to local traditions. Apart from the two city-states of Hamburg and Bremen, the only revived Land possessing both live historical traditions and prewar boundaries was Bavaria, a fact which has helped the Bavarians maintain a long-term gain of influence in national politics. With the hope of preventing the re-creation of a strong central government, the French, and to some extent also the Americans, encouraged the small Laender in their zones to set up elaborate governmental machinery and encouraged a largely artificial Land patriotism. The British on the other hand exercised centralized control through zonal authorities, and though they too set up such new Laender as Lower Saxony, Northrhine-Westphalia, and Schleswig-Holstein, they did not attempt to revive archaic boundaries or to encourage Land governments to exaggerate their political significance[3]

The problem of the role of the Laender and of what kind of federal principles the Basic Law should express caused great controversy, both among the Germans and the Allies. As regards the division of legislative powers between the Laender and the federal government, German traditions and preferences for a maximum degree of uniformity favored giving the federal government the lion's share of authority. Among the exclusive legislative powers which the federal government exercises are those which relate to the areas of foreign affairs, citizenship, etc.; the list of federal powers is very similar to that in Article 1, Section 8, of the United States Constitution. A more significant index of the greater legislative predominance of the German federal

[3] Roger H. Wells, "State Government," in E. H. Litchfield, ed., *Governing Postwar Germany* (Ithaca, 1953), pp. 84–117.

government is given by the provisions regarding concurrent powers. Here both constitutional provisions and German practice also leave to the federal legislature the lion's share of power in relation to such subjects as civil and criminal law, legislation relating to economic affairs, agriculture, forests and fisheries, housing, and many other areas which in other countries would usually be left to state or provincial legislation. The Laender's reserved powers were thus kept rather limited, but the Laender do retain the power to legislate in important areas like education, the police, radio and television, and on other subjects which are not listed as either exclusive or concurrent powers of the federal government.[4]

The "federalist" forces influencing the drafting of the Basic Law realized that the bulk of legislative power would remain with the central government, but were concerned nonetheless to reverse the long-term trend under which the Land governments had gradually become subsidiary and dependent units. To strengthen the position of the Laender in the area of administration, they successfully sought a return to the earlier German practice under which the federal bureaucracy was largely confined to policy-making, with the execution of federal legislation on the lower echelons left to the administration of the Laender. In this as in their endeavor to assure the Laender independent tax sources, they were largely successful. But they also wanted to assure the Laender an effective voice in the federal legislative process; here the question was what type of second chamber to create. The "centralists" were in favor of a Senate-type chamber, whose members would be directly elected by the populations of the various Laender, and who would presumably come to represent their parties more than their states. The "federalists," on the other hand, succeeded in winning support for a second chamber which was to be composed exclusively of the Land ministers themselves, and this Bundesrat solution was finally adopted.

THE POLITICAL PARTY SYSTEM

The political party system has contributed much to the achievement of political stability in the Federal Republic. Contrary to pessimistic expectations, the original parties licensed by the Allies managed to both build and maintain independent followings. Moreover, their number did not expand to the point of inhibiting

[4] Carl J. Friedrich and H. J. Spiro, "The Constitution of the German Federal Republic," in *ibid.*, pp. 117–51.

the functioning of parliamentary government, but shrank in the course of the 1950's, with the result that Germany moved closer toward a two-party system than any other continental country. Unlike their predecessors in Weimar Germany or many of their contemporaries in other European countries, the major German parties have avoided significant splits and have maintained a remarkably stable following. For the first time in German history the Federal Republic produced a party which could win the votes of an absolute majority, while between them the democratic parties have attracted the support of all but a tiny minority of the German electorate. In sharp contrast to the Weimar period, extremist parties have hardly counted, and small, special interest parties have had little success in drawing support away from the stable large parties.

THE CHRISTIAN DEMOCRATIC UNION (CDU): The key to an understanding of the changed structure of the German party system lies largely in an understanding of the character and growth of the Christian Democratic Union. This party was newly established in 1945 by Catholics who wanted to overcome the limitations of the all-Catholic Center party of the pre-1933 era and by Protestants, conservatives, and liberals who had previously belonged to half a dozen right-of-center or middle-of-the-road parties. They now rallied to unite, partly because of a recognition of common values, but mainly from fear that they would be overwhelmed by the anticipated strength of the left-wing parties. They never attempted to work out fundamentals or details of their political program, and the party continued to retain quite different complexions in different parts of the country. Many, including the Socialist leaders, expected that this

POLITICAL PARTIES

Article 21

(1) The political parties shall participate in forming the political will of the people. They can be freely formed. Their internal organization must conform to democratic principles. They must publicly account for the sources of their funds.

(2) Parties which, by reason of their aims or the behavior of their adherents, seek to impair or abolish the free and democratic basic order or to endanger the existence of the Federal Republic of Germany, are unconstitutional. The Federal Constitutional Court shall decide on the question of unconstitutionality.

(3) Details will be regulated by Federal legislation.

alliance would soon fall apart, but they were proved wrong. What held the party together was neither its loose organization nor its largely negative anti-Socialist ideology, but strong personal leadership which turned the party's weaknesses into virtues. Konrad Adenauer, a pre-1933 mayor of Cologne who had never played a significant role in national politics, quickly emerged as the leader of the Christian Democrats, first in the British, and finally in all three Western zones. He proved himself an extremely skilled tactician who utilized the party's lack of attachment to organization, program, or ideology to seize the opportunities which the rapidly shifting political situation opened up. In contrast to his great rival Kurt Schumacher, Adenauer never "fought City Hall" but accepted the consequences of the East-West split as inevitable and goaded his party to accept the facts, to get behind successful programs like Erhard's Social Market Policy, and to assume the responsibility of government.[5]

So adeptly did Adenauer play his cards that he found himself installed as Chancellor before the CDU had even formally elected a leader or set up a national organization. He succeeded in identifying himself with Germany's reacceptance into the Western family of nations and with achievements in the area of German reconstruction. By appealing to the German's tendency to support established authority, he succeeded in developing a powerful popular following, both for himself as Chancellor and for the CDU as the party favoring constructive policies. This appeal allowed the CDU, together with its Bavarian branch, the Christian Social Union (CSU), to win the smashing electoral victories of 1953 and 1957, which resulted in successively larger majorities in the Bundestag, thus allowing Adenauer to diminish his reliance on minor party support.

In the early 1960's, when Chancellor Adenauer's power was on the decline and especially after he yielded the office to Erhard in 1963, the CDU began once again to display acute factional tendencies. The lack of any other popular Chancellor candidate forced Erhard's early critics to by-pass the popular leader and to concentrate their attacks on selected cabinet members and their policies. Under Erhard's relaxed leadership the Bavarian CSU accentuated its independence, and for many purposes regarded itself as an independent party. Its long-time boss, Franz Josef Strauss, who had developed a strong power base in the Defense Ministry before his fall from power in 1962, strove for a

[5] Arnold J. Heidenheimer, *Adenauer and the CDU: The Rise of the Leader and the Integration of the Party* (The Hague, 1960), pp. 92–178.

return to power. Adenauer's personal followers and others continued small guerilla campaigns against the foreign policy decisions of Erhard and Foreign Minister Schroeder. With the development of sharp differences between France and the United States the unity which had been forged in the party around foreign policy aims began to disintegrate. Indeed, observers began to discern "Gaullist" and "Atlantic" groupings within the party, and many party followers were appalled by the lack of unified leadership at the top. There were many signs that the long years of government responsibility had at last begun to sap the party's vitality, but these were not paid much heed by the voters in the 1965 elections.

Erhard seemed for some time reluctant to succeed to the CDU party chairmanship, which Adenauer held on to until March, 1966. While uncertainty prevailed, Adenauer and some of his followers in the Rhineland CDU persuaded the young and ambitious parliamentary group leader Rainer Barzel to announce his candidacy for the chairmanship without checking with the Chancellor. Angered, Erhard announced that he would run for the position himself, and thus dared his intraparty critics to precipitate a major upheaval by defeating him. They and Barzel backed down, but grudgingly, and although Erhard was unopposed for the chairmanship, he received only 413 of 548 possible votes, with 80 delegates voting "No." As part of a compromise package, Barzel was elected to the position of first deputy chairman. Also elected as deputy CDU party chairmen were Kai Uwe von Hassell, a Protestant, and Paul Luecke, a Catholic.

THE SOCIAL DEMOCRATIC PARTY (SPD): When Konrad Adenauer, as a septuagenarian, helped found the CDU in Cologne in 1945 he was seeking to check a party which was already well established when he himself was a youth in the Bismarckian era. Founded in the 1860's, the SPD was avowedly a working-class party pledged to the eradication of private ownership of the means of production and the abolition of capitalist society. Though relegated under the Empire to the minor role of an "opposition of principle" which found no common ground between itself and the regime, it rallied increasing majorities of the working class to its banner until it became in the decade before 1914 by far the largest party in the Reichstag. Though the war experience and the subsequent split-off of its left wing into the Communist party halted a further increase in its voting support, the SPD remained throughout the Weimar period a strongly disciplined organization committed to evolutionary social change and the defense of democratic parliamentary institutions. During the Nazi period its leaders went into exile and concentration camps on behalf of their democratic convictions.

After 1945 the Socialists were supremely confident that as the party with the strongest anti-Nazi record, a long history of support of democracy and a strong party organization, they would become the party to lead Germany's reconstruction. Their expectations were frustrated. The shot-gun marriage between Communists and Socialists in the Soviet zone which resulted in the formation of the Socialist Unity party (SED), and the subsequent division of Germany separated the Socialist leadership under the forceful Kurt Schumacher from those areas where they had traditionally enjoyed their strongest support. Next, the success of the CDU created a formidable rival for middle-class and even working-class support. But worst of all, the Socialists found the very strength of their organization and program an embarrassment. The loyalty of the workers maintained their image as a class party, and none of the roles in which Schumacher cast himself—as the champion of German national interests against Allied policies, as an opponent of economic liberalism and German rearmament, and finally even as an opponent of German participation in organizations like the Council of Europe and the European Coal and Steel Community—won the party any significant new share of middle-class votes. Thus, while the CDU succeeded in breaking out of the prewar Center party's traditional "Catholic ghetto," up to 1961 the SPD never succeeded in growing far beyond the industrial working-class districts.

The SPD's failure to win significant new followers among the voters or potential allies among other parties can be attributed to the dysfunctional tactics pursued by Schumacher. As Lewis Edinger's biography forcefully shows,[6] the phychological forces driving this domineering personality in turn caused him to foreclose to the party all chances of achieving power on the national level. After his death it took almost a decade for the party to establish a viable new position.

The groundwork for the SPD's new self-image and role orientation was laid in a new Basic Program adopted in 1959. Named the Bad Godesberg program after the city where that year's special party congress met, it replaced the previous party basic program adopted at the Heidelberg congress in 1925. In doing so it jettisoned most of the Marxist theoretical constructs which had been its heritage for generations. Largely dropping its

[6] Lewis J. Edinger, *Kurt Schumacher* (Stanford, 1965).

earlier commitment to economic policies based on a planned economy and socialization, the SPD embraced the free market economy and accepted private ownership of the means of production as having "a claim to protection and support insofar as it does not hinder the building of a just social order." Philosophically the party also dropped much of its commitment to concepts based on class categories and economic determinism, and showed a desire to embrace new supra-class symbols and more effective styles of communication. The party also sought to end the tradition of hostility toward established religion, and in so doing narrowed its role definition. "A party is no longer regarded as a church or a counter-church. It is not a school of philosophers. It does not feel obliged to explain the history of mankind. This has to be left to the universities and individual thinkers and searchers." In its new image as an efficient instrument for implementing reforms and modernization in an industrial society, the party appeared more attractive to some middle-class voters, although the CDU taunted that it had merely taken over many of its programs. Under the leadership of conciliatory figures like Willy Brandt, Carlo Schmid, and Fritz Erler, the party intentionally sought to stress that it was prepared to offer a sober and efficient alternative government, which would not radically alter the basis of established domestic and foreign policies.

MINOR PARTIES: The decline of the minor parties proceeded inexorably. Whereas in 1950 almost a dozen political parties had fairly wide following and representation in the Bundestag, by 1960 only three managed to maintain themselves there. The first casualties of political rationalism and the "5 per cent clause" were small regional parties. Some of these, like the Bavarian party (BP), the Center party in Northrhine-Westphalia, and the German party (DP) in Lower Saxony, were for a time aided by the CDU because they were useful in helping to establish majorities on the Land or national level, but they continually declined for lack of leadership and independent programs.[7] Others, like the early Reconstruction Association (WAV), with a base of support in Bavaria, and the Expellees party (BHE), with support in areas where the expellees were concentrated, were special interest parties whose following declined as their constituencies became absorbed into the prosperous German citizenry. Some of these, until the early 1960's, continued to maintain a measure of influence on the Land level but this has not been the

[7] Otto Kirchheimer, "Notes on West Germany," *WP*, VI (1954), 306–21.

case with the extremist parties, like the neo-Nazi Socialist Reich party (SRP)[8] and the Communist party (KPD) which had lost most of their popular support by the time they were declared illegal in 1952 and 1956 respectively. Minor right-wing parties against which this penalty has not been invoked, like the German Reich party (DRP), have also steadily lost influence, as the minor nationalist revival which reached its high point in 1951 to 1952 continually ebbed in the face of official hostility and the present unwillingness of Germans to commit themselves to hoary causes. Some of the rightist parties regrouped themselves in the National Democratic party (NPD) for the 1965 election, but it won only 2 per cent of the vote. Its greater success in local elections in 1966, in which it received 15 per cent of the vote in some cities, aroused surprise as well as anxiety.

The only party which by 1960 had still survived the deadly embraces of the Chancellor and CDU, and the SPD's eagerness to gobble-up odd remnants, was the Free Democrats (FDP). This party constitutes the remainder of what had once been the dominant political force of German liberalism. Its following had shrunk perceptibly during the Weimar Republic, and in 1945 many of its leaders joined either the Christian or Social Democrats, who had come to espouse many of liberalism's fundamental principles. Nevertheless, enough liberals were sufficiently opposed to clericalism or economic planning to provide a respectable following for the FDP which, with support from some industrialists and portions of the Protestant middle class, has continued to attempt to shore-up its position as Germany's "third party." However it failed to throw up leaders of the calibre of its first chairman, Theodor Heuss, who resigned in 1949 to assume the federal presidency. FDP leaders frequently complained that the CDU had stolen most of its program, and in 1956 it broke out of the Adenauer coalition,[9] after which it played an uncertain opposition role for five years. In 1961, it reentered the government, and under its leader, Erich Mende, utilized its pivotal position particularly to further contacts that might lead to reunification.

Viewed as a subsystem endowed with certain tasks to perform to ensure the functioning of the political system as a whole, the German party system has in some respects been strengthened and in some weakened as the result of the changes imposed on it

[8] Otto Buesch and Peter Furth, *Rechtsradikalismus im Nachkriegsdeutschland* (Berlin, 1958).

[9] Gerard Braunthal, "The Free Democratic Party in West German Politics," *WPQ*, XIII (June, 1960), 332–48.

during the two postwar decades. Legalistically, and in terms of identifying themselves with particular role performances, the parties have solidly established themselves; no longer are they the evanescent structures of dubious constitutional status that they were for previous generations of Germans. The reduction in the number of significant parties has allowed the survivors to accentuate their aggregation functions and made possible what seems to be more responsible decision-making by reducing the amount of post-election haggling. The lessening of ideological cleavages has also made possible the formation of a somewhat thicker "cake of consensus," while permitting moderate improvements in the style of political discourse. But these achievements are counterbalanced by certain more or less dysfunctional characteristics and developments. Thus, while the parties have been able to attract fair numbers of ambitious young men to candidacies, the recruitment of talent available at the lower party echelons has remained stable at a rather low level. The consequent low turnover rate among party and government office-holders has strengthened static tendencies. The fact that both the number of parties and the degree of partisan polarization of opinion have decreased has also meant that the public has been offered a choice among fewer alternative policy solutions. To an extent, this has caused nonparty and even nonpolitical organs to become more important forums for deliberations, and has made the established parties appear hostile to the acceptance of nonconformist ideas. Cumulatively, all these factors have caused "input" processes in general and party politics in particular to appear decreasingly interesting from the perspective of the "only-voter" spectator. But they have of course not lessened the activities of the professional lobbyists and other representatives of organized interests vying for resonance from the party politicians for the particular interests they articulate.

ORGANIZED INTERESTS

An analysis of West German interest group structure must take note of one circumstance which causes the situation to differ considerably from that of the United States: in Germany, many special interests are much older than the state, and some, like the Catholic church, even antedate the time when Germans first began to feel conscious of their national identity. In the United States few groups or subcultures reject the main course of constitutional development. The vast majority of them, including even the major religious organizations, developed the bulk of their tradition only after the political institutions had already been established. But in Germany, Bavarian farmers or Catholic Rhinelanders or Hanseatic merchants remain very much aware that their traditions have far deeper historical and institutional roots than do those of the national political system.

A second category of German interest groups makes claims on the loyalty of members and seeks special treatment in public discussion because of factors related to the evolution of the German social system. That system, unlike the American, evolved from a feudal background and in the process of evolution created a tradition of loyalty to "estate" and social class which today still affects the function of some interest groups. A typical example of an antiquated estate claiming privileges for historical reasons were the East Elbian Junkers, who during the Weimar period demanded special subsidies essentially because their forefathers had captured East Prussia from the Poles in the twelfth century. Other old socio-economic groups, like the civil servants and, to a lesser degree, artisans and farmers, continue to this day to make claims for special treatment based at least in part on rights accorded their estate during the feudal or preconstitutional periods. They compete with organizations based on social or class position, like the trade unions, which also continue to appeal both to the loyalty of their members and for recognition in the political process not only because of the specific goals they seek to achieve and the size of their membership, but because they have played an historical role in opening up the full privileges of citizenship for members of their class.

Both of the aforementioned kinds of group still object to being placed on a level with an association of used car dealers or a commercial fishermen's organization. Nevertheless, the newer kinds of narrowly economic interest group set up to achieve pragmatic ends have become more numerous and more important as Germany has disestablished vested privileges to become an industrial society much like the United States. Increasingly, these newer associations with professional staffs, closely knit organizations, and experienced lobbyists rival the older groups in influence. At the same time, many of them have inherited from the older groups the right to participate in the political process by assuming a semipublic character, as administrators of certain kinds of regulations. Thus German chambers of commerce, chambers of agriculture, and the professional organizations have much greater power than most American equivalents, and are in a position to make membership in related interest group organizations obligatory for all clients. All of these factors serve to strengthen the position of the interest groups to the point where they at times emerge not only as powerful claimants on the political parties, but even as rivals, who through their representatives in the legislature and their contacts in the administration will work independently when the parties do not seem adequate instruments for achieving their ends.

The manner in which German interests function politically can perhaps best be brought out through a brief examination of the roles which two of the most important have played in recent years. Though officially neutral, both the Catholic church and the Trade Union Federation have made their sympathies abundantly clear. When asked which groups tend toward which parties, 83 per cent in a German poll associated Catholics with the CDU, only 1 per cent with the SPD; similarly 77 per cent associated the trade unions with the SPD, only 1 per cent with the CDU.[10] During election campaigns Catholic organs give fairly open support to the CDU. Thus the Government Press Office reported in 1957 that, "The main theme for the month of August in the Catholic Church press is the Bundestag election of September 15th. Detailed reports highlight the great achievement of the present government in all domains." In addition Catholic bishops send out pastoral letters which are read to a quarter of the German electorate on pre-election Sunday, with messages like: "Do your electoral duty! Vote only for men and women whose basic Christian principles are well known and whose public activity corresponds to these principles." After the adoption of the Bad Godesberg program, the Social Democrats went to great pains to make themselves appear more acceptable to Catholic clergy and layman. Toward this end they even prepared to make concessions on the principle of publicly-supported denominational schools, which they had long rejected. In 1965 the Socialist-led government of Lower Saxony became the first German Land government to sign a postwar Concordat with the Vatican. Through it the Land pledged itself to promote special Catholic educational facilities from the grade school to the university level and not to allow public communication media to be used for purposes hostile to the Catholic church.

There are of course many hundreds of other interest groups which operate within the German settings. Some of the more powerful ones are the Federation of German Industry, the farmers' organization, the various expellees' groups and *Landsmannschaf-*

[10] Divo Institut, *Umfragen 1957* (Frankfurt, 1958), p. 50.

ten, and the artisans' organizations.[11] At least three hundred of them have offices in Bonn to keep in touch with political developments affecting their interest. The majority, representing industrial and trade associations, operate much like their American counterparts. If anything, however, their role in the political process is more controversial in West Germany than it is in the United States. The reason is that West German acceptance of the principles of a pluralistic democracy is still incomplete. Since many Germans developed their concepts of politics around hierarchical or monolithic models of the state, they are reluctant to concede that the public interest can be adequately defined through the free-wheeling competition of "selfish" pressure groups. There is still strong belief that interest groups should present their requests to the state "from the outside," that is, that they should not directly influence decision-making in the legislature and the administration. However, the organized interest groups are clearly triumphing over their critics. Moreover, the procedures of the federal bureaucracy not only permit interest groups special access but even encourage them to amalgamate in national-level peak associations. Thus the Rules of Procedure binding on all the federal ministries provides that their officials shall deal only with representatives of central or peak associations and not with local interest groups. The provisions regulating which interest groups shall be consulted in the course of the preparations of legislative drafts also provides that consultation shall only extend to associations with a countrywide coverage.[12]

POLITICAL RECRUITMENT

Few factors can sap the crucial self-esteem of politicians more rapidly than the realization that the younger generation is unwilling to follow in their professional footsteps. The memoirs and autobiographies of the leaders of the middle-of-the-road parties of the Weimar period, like Stresemann's, testify how the inability to recruit younger talent contributed to a lessening of faith in their own aims. Political recruitment of course did occur during this period, but dedicated young men were often drawn either directly to parties of the extreme Left or Right or to small "circles" and "brotherhoods" which served as intermediary

[11] Rupert Breitling, *Die Verbaende in der Bundesrepublik: Ihre Arten und Ihre Politischen Wirkungsweise* (Meisenheim, 1955).

[12] Thomas Ellwein, *Das Regierungssystem der Bundesrepublik Deutschland* (Cologne, 1963), p. 392.

recruiting grounds for the nationalist movements. As this development suggests, recruitment is a crucial political process not only quantitatively, in regard to the total participation elicited, but also in regard to the varieties of structures that compete with each other in mobilizing potential political activists.

In the Federal Republic political recruitment has been a function primarily of the political parties and the established interest organizations. In contrast to the Weimar period, structures like the youth "Bunde," paramilitary veterans' associations, and intellectual coteries have not been significant competitors. Moreover, the established socio-economic interest groups have at the lower levels worked primarily through the political parties, rather than overtly against them. Demonstrations by particularly volatile interest groups like the farmers, which were frequently a by-product of unrest in both Weimar Germany and the French Fourth Republic, have been relatively rare. Reunions of war veterans' groups have sometimes been used as forums for extreme statements by unreconstructed officers, but pressure from the Defense Ministry has served to keep them under control. Least controllable have been the expellees' organizations whose members still lay claim to homelands now incorporated into Poland and Czechoslovakia, with the Sudeten-German *Landsmannschaften* the most stubborn and outspoken.

Because most German parties were founded from the top down after 1945, they initially lacked enough qualified members to put forth as candidates for elected office on the lower level. The CDU in particular originally assigned even Bundestag candidacies to prominent interest group representatives who had not demonstrated much party service. In fact, the CDU used to solicit suggestions from interest groups before making up its Land lists for the federal elections. Gradually, as the party has developed more significant party organizations on the local level, this has changed. Now candidates are expected to have held lower-level offices in the party. Thus there is more opportunity to screen them as to background and ability. The SPD has always laid more emphasis on recruiting candidates from among tried and true party members, but in the past this had led to unbalanced candidate lists composed mainly of union secretaries, journalists, and other white-collar employees. One of the party's aims therefore has been to attract a more diversified range of middle-class talents to membership in the party, an endeavor in which it has made gradual progress. Thus for the higher-level positions the recruitment functions of the parties have gradually been increasing, while those of the interest groups have lessened. This is a positive development from other than just functional perspectives. Many of those Bundestag and cabinet members with the most dubious backgrounds and credentials have been the nominees of powerful interest organizations, especially those of the various expellee *Landsmannschaften*.

Since most Germans display a marked resistance to attempts to enroll them as party members, the parties rely heavily on subsidiary organizations, activity in which constitutes only a half-way point to full membership status. The CDU has such an organization in the *Junge Union*, in which sometimes balding "youth" in the 20–40 age bracket discuss policies and figure out how to promote each other to candidacies. More innovating in their stand on issues are the student organizations maintained and subsidized by each of the major parties. These have provided a bridge between the parties and the emerging generation of intellectuals, but they have also frequently bitten the hand that fed them. Thus the Social Democrats in 1961 disowned their student organization, the *Sozialistischer Deutscher Studentenbund* (SDS), which had ignored repeated demands from headquarters that it tone down its radical pronouncements. The party pronounced SDS membership incompatible with party membership and chartered a new organization, the *Sozialistischer Hochschul Bund* (SHB). But by 1965, party headquarters was embroiled in a bitter dispute with this organization as well, and the Christian Democratic and Liberal student organizations, whose secretaries and publications are also heavily subsidized by the parties, have frequently flown in the face of party policies. The German socialization pattern thus provides mechanisms for students to sow their intellectual wild oats as subsidized kibitzers before assuming the responsibilities of organization men within the party fold proper. Their preparation is in some ways less rigorous than that of American politicians-to-be, who, at typical state universities, must display their prowess in organizing float parades, their ability to manage mammoth athletic events, and their acumen in flattering their elders.

The German parties have been least successful in recruiting militants and members to work at the lower levels of the party organization. In fact, the parties have only barely been able to replace members who have dropped out because of age or other factors, as shown by the rather stagnant membership figures of the 1950's and 1960's. In the case of the Socialists, the firmer membership commitment this party has always demanded has been maintained with some success, but for the CDU a very low member-voter ratio has not been significantly improved upon. Thus the average SPD deputy speaks for roughly five times as many party members as does the average CDU/CSU deputy. It has thus become popular in Germany to speak of the SPD as a "membership party" and of the CDU as a "voters' party." It is revealing that the CDU has frequently been able to win national elections without bothering to elicit much lower-level participation, although the SPD's relatively greater success in Land and local elections may be attributed to its more substantial membership organizations.

The SPD party organization, held together by a large staff of paid party secretaries, has often displayed a strong tendency to regard its maintenance as an end in itself, rather than just a mechanism for nominating candidates. Since the late 1950's, this "in-group" has largely followed the lead of Herbert Wehner, the powerful party vice chairman who utilized the power of the central office to push through the ideological transformation of the party over the protests of critics who labeled him an "opportunist." His efforts to force all party units to follow the straight and narrow path created great bitterness. In the spring of 1966, his critics charged in a sensational public attack that Wehner had throttled free discussion and had blocked the channels through which policy recommendations were passed upward within the party. Since Wehner had been largely in charge of the 1965 election campaign, his critics blamed him for the SPD's poor showing. This public attack, which was unprecedented in the SPD's postwar history, seemed to usher in a period in which the SPD, like the CDU, would be severely tested by factional struggles over leadership and policy.

POLITICAL COMMUNICATION STRUCTURES

Political communication processes are shaped by complex interaction patterns between political actors, professionals, and amateurs who define what news is and market it, and the information-consuming publics. In Germany these processes are shaped by some peculiar structural and attitudinal antitheses. Thus a tendency among most German groups and organizations to insulate themselves from the world at large through bureaucratic defenses is countered by the very high value which the society assigns to maintaining an unimpaired freedom to criticize public processes. In addition, a comparatively high level of consumer demand for political news is catered to by media which offer a rather limited variety of communication styles and are focussed on a relatively few centers of political developments. Finally, there is the fact that in Germany a highly centralized political system is "covered" through a relatively decentralized communication system.

Communication styles among the German political elite are still marked by strong defensive reflexes. While political leaders are as elsewhere aware of the need to continually interpret developments to their followers, there continues to exist an almost system-wide tendency to hoard information as a commodity which is potentially classified if not secret. This is evidenced in the business sphere by the tendency of corporations to provide stockholders with only a minimum of information in their annual reports. In the political sphere it is reinforced by remnants of ideological suspicion and by the tendency toward "government by experts." Information does not pass easily from the Government party to the opposition or from the specialist members of a legislative committee to their lay colleagues. Institutions like legislative research bureaus, intended to help the average legislator to better inform himself, are underdeveloped. In order to keep tab on the limited political doings in Bonn, an observer must subscribe to perhaps dozens of partisan and personalized newsletters put out by organizations and inside dopesters. The Federal Press and Information Office towers over the Bundestag to influence information flow toward uniformity. Informal rumor mills which are generated in reaction do not have their output leavened by stories emanating from commercial and cultural centers, which are located elsewhere.

The Occupation period's licensing policy not only gave important positions in the mass media to reliable democrats, but also decentralized the press, establishing all newspapers independently on the local level. The advantages of this system are that Germany has fewer powerful press chains than the United States and Britain, and the larger newspapers tend to have more individual character and editorial viewpoint. The disadvantages are that Germany does not have a powerful "prestige" paper such as *The New York Times* or *Le Monde* and also lacks, for the most part, a national newspaper that is distributed throughout the country. It does however have good regional newspapers, of which the *Sueddeutsche Zeitung* in Munich is the most lively, the *Frankfurter Allgemeine Zeitung* the most sound and the closest to big business, and the *Welt*, published in Hamburg and Essen, the most successful. None of these quality papers have circulations of much over a quarter of a million, and many other good papers do quite well with the sale of less than 100,000. However they are far more important in shaping political opinion than the apolitical tabloid press, which claims a circulation in the millions and thrives on sensationalism on the model of the British popular press. The total circulation of daily newspapers is about seventeen million, a very good showing when compared with Great Britain (thirteen million) or even all of Weimar Germany (fourteen million). Three-quarters of this circulation is distributed to subscribers, so that the pressure to produce sensational headlines is minimized for all but the tabloid papers.

Radio and television have traditionally been public monopolies in Germany, but these media have by no means been simply organs of government propaganda. Their relative independence is due to the fact that they are set up as independent public corporations on the Land and regional level and have been fairly well insulated from pressure by the federal government. As in most European countries, the mass communications directors do not consider themselves bound by the taste of the majority, but present cultural programs of a high level with the purpose of educating the public. The intellectuals in charge of these media are also conscious of a responsibility to educate the public politically, and hence they frequently present politically controversial programs. Despite a continuing increase in the number of television receivers in use (1963: 7.2 million), radio continues to be the most widespread medium, with some 16.7 million subscribers paying dues which provide the bulk of the funds on which the radio networks operate.

The general caliber of political reporting in the German quality newspapers is high, but a comparison with American newspapers suggests some interesting differences. By any supranational standard of newsworthiness, political coverage in both countries is only second-best. But in America it is sports coverage which is of prime importance, while in Germany it is high-brow culture which claims some of the best journalistic coverage. There the tantrums of a big-name theater director will usually edge out the complaints of a minister, if the director's theater is renowned enough. Journalistic coverage of political happenings is biased in a somewhat similar way. Statements issued in and around a few recognized "stages"—the Chancellery, the Bundestag, the party headquarters, and, abroad, the foreign ministries of the major powers—will always receive extensive news coverage and editorial commentary. But developments in, say, local politics, or within interest groups or informal groupings, are given scant notice. German reporters have very little tendency to "dig" for news that is not covered in handouts or official statements—and that is one reason why the periodical following a contrary policy, the newsweekly *Der Spiegel,* has not only been such a success but has also assumed the nature of a political institution.

Germans of only limited education probably get most of their political news and interpretation from either the tabloid press or television, and control of both of these institutions has been sharply contested. Politicians who win the endorsement of tabloids like *Bildzeitung* and *Stern* become known to millions but may invite the hostility of the more responsible press. Control of the television networks has also been sharply contested. The federal government attempted to move into the television field at the expense of the regional public broadcasting systems, but was reprimanded by the Constitutional Court. Later the newspaper publishers, led by the biggest German press lord, Axel Springer, who claimed that advertising money spent through television was undercutting their economic base, sought to force their way into the area of television. In the election year of 1965 they succeeded in getting passage of legislation which forbade public television networks to carry advertising.

STYLE OF POLITICAL LEADERSHIP

Much study has been devoted to what alternatives voters perceive when they prepare to vote, as the Germans have done in five postwar national elections and numerous Land and local ones. For most German voters the party symbols were probably most crucial, particularly during the early period when party identification was reinforced most strongly by ideological and class loyalties. But for large masses of German voters, the name or symbol of the party has been less important than the identity of the Chancellor candidate presented. Somewhat like Roosevelt in the 1930's, Konrad Adenauer became the central figure in electoral contests in the 1950's, with people voting either for or against him. A third electoral image which has at times been presented to German voters in both national and state elections is that of the team, a group of party leaders whose appeal may rest not so much on their individual brilliance as on their ability to pool a quantity of political talents for the conduct of public affairs. The kind of image which the German parties have sought most to project has been largely determined by the character of successive "generations" of leaders who owed their positions to quite different kinds of selection processes.

For more than a decade the style of political leadership in the Federal Republic was set by two self-willed antagonists, Konrad Adenauer and Kurt Schumacher, who ruled their parties with an iron hand, but otherwise represented sharply polarized antitheses. Adenauer was native to the westernmost portion of Germany, Catholic, and the product of a bureaucratic career; Schumacher was born in the easternmost section of the pre-World War I German Reich, an agnostic hostile to established religion, and a life-long agitator and tribune. Where Adenauer thought supranationally, Schumacher sought to return to Germans their national self-respect; where Adenauer was a pragmatist, Schumacher was an ideologue wed to his premises. The altercations between the two which Germans witnessed between 1949 and 1952 were truly as between gladiators, and were climaxed in one instance by Schumacher's temporary expulsion from the Bundestag for calling Adenauer the "Chancellor of the Allies." The past history of the two men—Schumacher had lost an arm in the front lines in World War I and a leg as an aftermath of a ten-year concentration camp stretch under the Nazis; Adenauer had been close to Rhineland Separatists in the 1920's and was also a good friend of Ruhr capitalists as well as Catholic prelates— allowed many to project their most deep-seated conscious and unconscious emotions onto the two contenders.

After Schumacher's death Adenauer continued his sharp and unrelenting style of political controversy when he wanted to talk as a party politician. But when he wanted to talk as a statesman and intimate of world leaders he appeared as the Chancellor who could draw on supraparty loyalties. In neither role were the Social Democrats able to develop a figure who could establish himself as Adenauer's equal. They chose an uncontroversial compromise leader, Erich Ollenhauer, while undergoing the extensive internal remodeling which resulted in the Bad Godesberg program, and were led by him during two disastrous election campaigns. Meanwhile, in the CDU a whole generation of leaders who offered alternative leadership styles—men like Jakob Kaiser, Karl Arnold, Werner Hilpert, and Heinrich von Brentano— shrivelled politically and died physically while the octogenarian Adenauer continued his chosen way. In both parties hard-working and able politicians withdrew to more obscure careers in the

Land governments, where particularly SPD leaders like Ernst Reuter in Berlin, George-August Zinn in Hessen, and Wilhelm Kaisen in Bremen evolved an unspectacular style of leadership that won public recognition, albeit hardly enthusiasm. After a decade Adenauer and his leadership model began to decline in popularity during the Kennedy era. At the time he left office in September, 1963, Adenauer, who had long led German polls as "most-admired Statesman" had actually lost first place in these to the young American president.

Leadership through an experienced team has been offered more by the "ins" than the "outs." After winning two "Adenauer elections," the Christian Democrats resorted to a team image in campaign style only when the Chancellor's popularity was on the wane. Overt dissension during Erhard's first year of office also impeded successful projection of a congenial team image in 1965. By contrast the Social Democrats that year could offer up a "shadow cabinet" whose members blended various forms of experience. Several, like Karl Schiller and Helmut Schmidt, had been Land ministers, one—Gustav Heinemann—was actually Adenauer's first Minister of Interior, one was an insurance executive, several were professors, and a few, like Fritz Erler and Carlo Schmid, had established positive images as leading parliamentarians. But in electoral appeal the SPD team failed to compete effectively against the personal appeal of Erhard.

The Federal Republic has definitely not been a place where young men could quickly introduce new political styles of leadership. The elderly leaders who won control in the 1940's did not promote their juniors easily, and the public got used to associating political maturity with gray hairs. Many "young men in a hurry" got shunted aside, and those who did climb rapidly, like Gerhard Schroeder and Kai-Uwe von Hassell, did not develop much following even within their parties. Those who developed public reputations while still in their thirties or early forties have done so by providing the right kinds of talents at the right time. Sophisticated big-city electorates have been prone to elect energetic young candidates for mayor. Some young politicians have also used the Bundestag to rise to public attention. Rainer Barzel, who rose to the chairmanship of the CDU parliamentary party while Erhard was Chancellor, is outstanding in this respect. After having been variously associated with left-wing and right-wing causes, and the protégé of party leaders as diverse as Karl Arnold and Adenauer, he had gained sufficient experience to function as Erhard's chief parliamentary whipper-in at a crucial time.

It may well develop, however, that by 1969, political leader-ship will rest predominantly with men who gained all of their adult political experience since 1945. The two most likely leading contenders for the Chancellorship nomination then, Barzel for the CDU and Helmut Schmidt for the SPD, were both born in the 1920's and belong to the generation of Adenauer's grandsons. The more senior politicians, who began their careers in the 1920's and 1930's, are increasingly likely to be bypassed. Other younger men are also pushing forward hard. Some, like Gerhard Stolten-berg in the CDU and Ulrich Lohmar in the SPD, have associated themselves with the issue of educational reform. Others, like Hel-mut Kohl in the CDU and Hans-Jochen Vogel in the SPD, have fought their way upward within the context of Land and local politics. These men will be less loaded down by the memories of Weimar and the Nazi period than their elders; whether they have any clearer picture of future goals remains yet to be demon-strated.

BIBLIOGRAPHY

Occupation and Constitution

Almond, Gabriel A., ed., *The Struggle for Democracy in Germany* (Chapel Hill, 1949).

Balfour, Michael, and Mair, John, *Four-Power Control of Germany and Austria, 1945-46* (London, 1956).

Clay, Lucius D., *Decision in Germany* (Garden City, 1950).

Friedrich, Carl J., and Spiro, H. J., "The Constitution of the German Federal Republic," in E. H. Litchfield, ed., *Governing Postwar Germany* (Ithaca, 1953), pp. 117-51.

Gimbel, John, *A German Community under American Occupation* (Stan-ford, 1961).

Golay, John F., *The Founding of the Federal Republic of Germany* (Chi-cago, 1958).

Grosser, Alfred, *Colossus Again: Western Germany from Defeat to Re-armament* (New York, 1955).

Kauper, Paul G., "The Constitutions of West Germany and the U. S.: A Comparative Study," *Michigan Law Review*, LVIII (1960), 1091-1184.

Merkl, Peter H., *The Origin of the West German Republic* (New York, 1963).

Montgomery, John D., *Forced to Be Free: The Artificial Revolution in Germany and Japan* (Chicago, 1957).

Morgenthau, Hans, ed., *Germany and the Future of Europe* (Chicago, 1951).

Oppen, Beate Ruhm von, *Documents on Germany 1945-1955* (London, 1955).

U.S. Military Government, *Documents on the Creation of the German Federal Constitution* (Washington, 1949).

WILLIS, F. ROY, *The French in Germany, 1945-1949* (Stanford, 1962).
ZINK, HAROLD, *The United States in Germany, 1944-55* (Princeton, 1957).

Political Parties

BERGSTRAESSER, LUDWIG, *Geschichte der Politischen Parteien in Deutschland*, 9th ed. (Munich, 1955).
BERTSCH, HERBERT, *CDU/CSU Demaskiert* (East Berlin, 1961).
BRAUNTHAL, GERARD, "The Free Democratic Party in West German Politics," *WPQ*, XIII (June, 1960).
BUESCH, OTTO, and FURTH, PETER, *Rechtsradikalismus im Nachkriegsdeutschland* (Berlin, 1958).
CHALMERS, DOUGLAS A., *The Social Democratic Party of Germany: From Working Class Movement to Modern Political Party* (New Haven, 1964).
EDINGER, LEWIS J., *Kurt Schumacher* (Stanford, 1965).
FLECHTHEIM, OSSIP K., ed., *Dokumente zur parteipolitischen Entwicklung in Deutschland seit 1945*, 3 vols. (Berlin, 1962/63).
FOGARTY, MICHAEL D., *Christian Democracy in Western Europe, 1820-1953* (London, 1957).
HEIDENHEIMER, ARNOLD J., *Adenauer and the CDU: The Rise of the Leader and the Integration of the Party* (The Hague, 1960).
KIRCHHEIMER, OTTO, "Notes on West Germany," *WP*, VI (1954), 306-21.
LANGE, MAX GUSTAV, et al., *Parteien in der Bundesrepublik* (Villingen, 1955).
MERKL, PETER H., "Equilibrium, Structure of Interests and Leadership: Adenauer's Survival as Chancellor," *APSR*, LVI (1962), 634-50.
NEUMANN, SIGMUND, ed., "Germany," in *Modern Political Parties* (Chicago, 1956).
Parteienrechtskommission des Bundesinnenministeriums, *Rechtliche Ordnung des Parteiwesens* (Frankfurt, 1957).
PULZER, P. G. J., "Western Germany and the Three-Party System," *Political Quarterly*, XXXIII (1962), 414-26.
SCHNEIDER, CARL J., "Political Parties and the German Basic Law of 1949," *WPQ*, X (1957), 527-40.
TAUBER, KURT P., "German Nationalists and European Union," *PSQ*, LXXIV (1959), 564-89.

Interest Groups and the Press

BREITLING, RUPERT, *Die Verbaende in der Bundesrepublik: Ihre Arten und Ihre Politischen Wirkungsweise* (Meisenheim, 1955).
DEUTSCH, KARL W., and EDINGER, LEWIS J., *Germany Rejoins the Powers: Mass Opinion, Interest Groups and Elites in Contemporary German Foreign Policy* (Stanford, 1959).
ELLWEIN, THOMAS, *Klerikalismus in der Deutschen Politik* (Munich, 1956).
ESCHENBURG, THEODOR, *Herrschaft der Verbaende?* (Stuttgart, 1955).
HIRSCH-WEBER, WOLFGANG, *Gewerkschaften in der Politik* (Cologne, 1959).
JACOBI, C., "The New German Press," *FA*, XXXII (1954), 323-30.
SPEIER, HANS, and DAVISON, W., eds., *West German Leadership and Foreign Policy* (Evanston, 1957).
SPIRO, HERBERT, *The Politics of German Codetermination* (Cambridge, 1958).
WILLIAMS, EMLYN, "The West German Press," *Gazette* (Leiden), V (1959), 1-10.

4: Political Culture and Political Behavior

The Founding Fathers of the Federal Republic had reason to fear that the institutions they were creating would be hated rather than loved. But these fears proved groundless. The institutions and symbols of the new system very quickly won acceptance by the population. After the early 1950's there was no longer any doubt but that the political structures were coming to be regarded as legitimate by a rapidly increasing majority of the population. When confronted in survey interviews with alternative choices—single-party versus multi-party systems, dictatorial versus parliamentary institutions, and so on—increasing majorities spoke out in favor of those characteristics identified with "Bonn democracy."[1]

SYMBOLS AND SYSTEM AFFECT

While the West Germans accept and largely respect their political institutions, they do not have particular pride in them or derive particular enjoyment from identifying with them. Only 7 per cent of Germans reported feeling pride in their political institutions, compared with 46 per cent of the British and 85 per cent of the Americans.[2] Indeed, patriotic and national symbols are seldom employed conspicuously or spontaneously. It would appear utterly anachronistic if a German theater audience were to sing "Deutschland ueber Alles" after a performance the way British cinema audiences sing "God Save the Queen." The old anthem was readopted in revised form against the wishes of, among others, the first Federal President, who felt its continued use would handicap the attempt to make a fresh start. Perhaps the best judges of German political attitudes are the flag manufacturers. In the Weimar period they did a brisk trade selling both to purchasers who exhibited the republican colors and to the conservatives who exhibited the monarchist black-white-and-red banner. In the Nazi period every German household had to have a good-sized swastika to display on proper occasions. How-

[1] Sidney Verba, "Germany: The Remaking of a Political Culture," in Lucian W. Pye and Sidney Verba, eds., *Political Culture and Political Development* (Princeton, 1965).

[2] Gabriel A. Almond and Sidney Verba, *The Civic Culture* (Princeton, 1963), p. 102.

The Economic and Political Systems: Valuations and Affect

A. Is your standard of living better or worse than prewar?

	1950 %	1954 %	1958 %	1961 %	1964 %
Better	7	18	31	44	56
Just the same	24	29	33	27	20
Worse	64	48	27	15	9
No clear position	6	5	9	14	14
	100*	100	100	100	100*

B. Which is the most important freedom?

	1949 %	1954 %	1958 %	1962 %	1963 %
Freedom of worship	12	16	16	13	14
Freedom of speech	26	32	44	47	56
Freedom from fear	17	17	10	8	10
Freedom from want	35	35	28	17	15
No comment	10	—	2	15	5
	100	100	100	100	100

C. Preference regarding political regime

	1953 %	1956 %	1960 %	1964 %
For democracy	57	67	74	76
For monarchy	11	8	5	3
For authoritarian regime	8	4	2	2
Indifferent/Other	1	1	1	4
No opinion	23	20	18	15
	100	100	100	100

D. What aspects of your country are you most proud of? (1959–60)

	United States %	Britain %	Germany %	Italy %
Political institutions	85	46	7	3
Social legislation	13	18	6	1
Position in world affairs	5	11	5	2
Economic system	23	10	33	3
Character of people	7	18	36	11
Spiritual/religious values	3	1	3	6
Contributions to the arts	1	6	11	16
Contributions to science	3	7	12	3
Physical aspects of country	5	10	17	25
Nothing or don't know	4	10	15	27
Other	9	11	3	21
	158*	148*	148*	118*

* Totals exceed 100 because of multiple responses or rounding off.

SOURCES: A, B, C—EMNID Pressedienst; D—Gabriel A. Almond and Sidney Verba, *The Civic Culture* (Princeton, 1963), p. 102.

ever, manufacturers now report that private demand for the official black-gold-red flag is almost nil. Instead, they make pennants advertising "Bockwuerste" for sausage stands.

If the Germans largely eschew the conventional forms that gestures of national identification usually take, what symbols do elicit their loyalty and pride? It would appear that to a considerable extent Germans have redirected their affect to symbols and structures serving as substitutes for the conventional national political ones. The economic system serves as one important object to which Germans have redirected their affect. The Almond and Verba study shows that many more Germans take pride in their economic system than do citizens of other countries. Whereas this pride can be justified in terms of postwar achievements, the Germans also exceeded other national samples in the pride they take in such factors as "character of the people" and "contribution to arts and sciences," where a displacement effect is more apparent.

The German search for substitute symbols has also gone in the direction of supranationalism. German elite groups in particular have been more and more inclined to identify symbolically with such European and Atlantic structures as NATO, the Council of Europe, and the European Community than they have with such national institutions as the federal presidency and the Bonn Parliament. While it has nowhere become the demand of mass movements, the pressure toward direct election of members of a European parliament has probably been strongest in the Federal Republic, a reflection of the fact that the "nation-state" has been surmounted as *the* unit of political organization in German politics. The trouble is that substitute frameworks have not become fully enough developed. NATO was long regarded by many Germans as more of a substitute *Heimat* than a remote military bureaucracy. The alternative *Heimat* of a United Europe has also in its various organizational guises elicited much commitment. The fact that neither of these structures has matured to the point where it could supply Germans with new passports and identities has nurtured underlying anxieties. Having travelled beyond the psychological confines of narrow nationalism, the Germans do not yet have the security of full membership in a supra-national community. This may be one reason why they attach so much symbolic importance to the visits of representatives of their powerful allies. Few meetings or tours by German politicians elicited anywhere near the enthusiasm and participation evoked by the state visits of such figures as President de Gaulle, President Kennedy, and Queen Elizabeth.

CONSENSUS AND TABOOS

On June 4, 1965, Chancellor Ludwig Erhard emerged from the White House after a lengthy discussion with President Lyndon Johnson. Commenting on plans for regular meetings between the two chiefs of government, Erhard said their purpose would be the strengthening of the Western alliance, "of which our two peoples are the strongest pillars." On the same day a lawyer named Benno Erhard (no relation to the Chancellor, although also a CDU Bundestag candidate) was addressing a Frankfurt jury as defense attorney for one of 18 defendants charged with brutalities as guards and functionaries in the Auschwitz concentration camp, in a trial which at that time was in the course of its eighteenth month. He argued that his client had not physically pushed victims into the gas chambers, but had only "directed" them there through use of a stick.[3]

Skeletons in the Closet

Similar trials were going on all over Germany in the early and mid-1960's. The Eichmann trial of 1961 had been one impetus that caused dusty files to be re-opened. Also contributing to the stepped-up activity of German prosecutors was the realization that the operation of the twenty-year statute of limitations would, in most cases, put an end to prosecution attempts after 1965. Working against this target date, the Central Documentation Office on crimes commited during the Nazi period worked overtime on analysis of available wartime records and in trying to secure supplementary ones, particularly from East Germany and the East European countries. The accused in these trials were not prominent Nazis, but relatively unknown doctors, ex-SS functionaries, and concentration camp guards who had been bypassed in earlier periods and had in the meantime re-established quite normal lives as respected burghers in German civil life. Comfortable German citizens all over the Federal Republic were shocked to find their respected family doctors or neighborhood grocers charged in newspaper reports with playing key roles in the death camps. In one trial a pathetic group of ordinary women in their sixties were put in the dock and charged as accessories to murder because they had followed doctor's orders as nurses in wartime euthanasia camps.

German editors, to their credit, reported the trial proceedings regularly and at length, even though they well knew that this was not the news fare that most readers wanted. The general

[3] *Die Welt*, June 5, 1965.

attitude of public opinion became known when an initiative was taken to prolong the twenty-year statute of limitations so that those accused of acts committed before 1945 could still be prosecuted after 1965. Surveys informed the politicians that over 60 per cent of the population opposed the change essentially because they wanted an end to "denazification," wartime reminders, and other symbols arousing guilt feelings. Also opposed to the extension were some constitutional lawyers who argued that a criminal law alteration with retroactive effect violated the spirit of the Basic Law, and that it was more important to preserve the principle of "government under law" than it was to prosecute a relatively few wartime criminals.

Especially because the issue arose in an election year, German politicians were placed in a dilemma. Elite opinion in allied countries as well as in the Federal Republic strongly urged the extension, and the Bonn politicians knew that if they did not act it would be grist in the mill of the East German propagandists who always sought to link Bonn to pro-Nazi proclivities. At the same time they knew that most of their constituents opposed the measure. For some months the government temporized. Although Chancellor Erhard was in favor of extension, he faced strong opposition within his cabinet, particularly from FDP and CSU ministers. As a consequence, none of the bills favoring extension had received formal cabinet endorsement when they were debated in the Bundestag in March, 1965.

The federal Minister of Justice, Ewald Bucher, who opposed the extension, had to meet not only a complex issue in the spirited Bundestag debate (of which excerpts are printed below) but also to seek to defend the German judicial machinery. In preceding years Communist attempts to bring the West German judiciary into disrepute had been very successful. Such highly placed officials as the federal Attorney General, many prominent judges, and even the chief of the Documentation Center on Nazi Crimes were discovered to have hidden either their membership in the Nazi party or formations, or, more seriously, their participation in wartime Nazi kangaroo courts. The Minister argued that the 6,000 convictions of persons accused of crimes committed during the Nazi period in West German courts (compared to 5,000 convictions before courts convened during the period of Allied Occupation in the three western zones, and 12,000 convictions in East Germany) showed that judicial authorities had not been laggard, and that in fact the extension was hardly needed because proceedings against almost all persons on whom materials were available had already been initiated.

The majority of the Bundestag members, however, had come to feel that the Federal Republic could not afford to leave any margin of doubt that it would carry prosecutions of wartime criminals as far as it constitutionally could. Deputies speaking

---

Delimiting Responsibility for Nazi Crimes

Excerpts from the Bundestag Debate on Extending Statute of Limitations for Murder (March 10, 1965)

BARZEL (Chairman, CDU/CSU Fraktion): . . . The German people did not beget a collective guilt. We have been saying that for twenty years and we will continue to do so. We have always identified with this people, with its whole history and with the honor of German soldiers. That too we will continue to do. We have always delineated cleanly between criminal acts and mistakes in political commitment . . . Only those guilty of crimes must go into court so that the court can determine the question of guilt objectively and finally . . . Mistaken political commitments are another matter. Freedom brings with it the possibility of wrong choices . . . There are no judicial institutions which could determine or measure responsibility for political errors . . .

BUCHER (Minister of Justice, FDP): . . . Then there is the ominous sentence: "We must live with the murderers" . . . I did not mean to say, as I have been accused, that living with a few murderers more or less makes little difference . . . The emphasis was on the word "must." We *must* do so . . . At Munich, when I was studying there, there was a Professor of Public Law—he held doctorates in both law and theology—who prattled to us students during every lecture about the "charisma" of the Fuehrer . . . Well, charisma can account for quite a lot. A man who is endowed with charisma naturally has the power to pronounce death sentences . . . And then came euthanasia, and the next link in the chain was a cleverly and artificially produced film called, "I Accuse." This film was obvious propaganda on behalf of the annihilation of unfunctional human life. Now we bring into court those who carried through these operations by giving injections or pills, and we say—assuming that they are found guilty—"these murderers we will not allow to live among us." But with the Professor, whom we can still meet today, we engage in interesting shop talk, and with the film producer, who is also still around, we talk pleasantly at a cocktail party. But with murderers we don't care to live! . . .

HIRSCH (SPD): This is truly not a matter of denazification, Colleague Unertl. The newspapers reported that you had said in Vilshofen that you were against a renewal of denazification. I can't imagine that you said that.

(DEP. UNERTL: Yes, but also some other things that were not reported.)

That is really not at issue. We are all with you in opposition to a renewal of denazification.

(DEP. UNERTL: Thank God.)

The sole issue is whether the statute of limitations shall be extended for murder . . . All Nazi crimes except murder are now beyond prosecution . . . The only question we must decide is extension of the statute of limitations for murder . . .

ARNDT (SPD): These deeds were not war crimes . . . War crimes are excesses that happen in the heat of battle or when generals or admirals carry things too far . . . The destruction of Dresden was a very great war crime, but it occurred as part of an eager drive for victory. But all that has nothing to do with this. For we weren't carrying out a war against Catholic Action . . . against the Confessional Church, against the feebleminded, against bedwetters, against the mentally ill in sanatoria, and we were not engaged in a war against Jewish women, children, babies, aged or men. This has no connection with war. This was a calculated, cold-blooded murder operation planned with the aid of the entire state machinery . . .

BENDA (CDU): Above all legalistic considerations those who support the motion are moved by the consideration that the moral feelings of a people would be corrupted in an intolerable manner if murders remained unatoned for even though atonement could be imposed . . . We all know that in connection with the events of the last war years Germans were not only criminals but also the objects of crimes. I have nothing against the understandable position of the Expellees . . . who want justice carried through there as well . . . I do have something against possible calculations that where there are such feelings there might possibly also be votes to win.

(*Lively applause from the SPD and deputies of the CDU/CSU*)

. . . Then we naturally get the silly assertions of foreign pressure, then come the anonymous postcards from upstanding German patriots who in all their patriotism forget to sign their letters or post-cards . . .

(*Lively applause*)

Perhaps I will derive some enjoyment from collecting these and similar things received by other colleagues. From these one might be able to deduce considerable insights into the spiritual aberrations that occur within a people—and I repeat this, so that I shall not be misunderstood—which has surmounted the National Socialist experience. There is one thing that is gratifying about these anonymous notes. Our time is not one where people dare say these kinds of things openly. Those who want to say them must hide behind a cowardly anonymity.

(*Applause*)

out in favor of the extension proposals stated that though the pressure of foreign opinion was great, it was not to this that they were yielding but to their concern for Germany's conscience. The Bundestag debate was followed by passage of a cabinet-endorsed bill under which murder charges could be filed for another four years by making the statute of limitations operative only from the creation of the Federal Republic in 1949, and not as of 1945.

The considerable emotions aroused by this issue were caused by a variety of factors, but fear of the revival of neo-Nazi movements in the Federal Republic was not among them. In fact, organizations espousing racialist or Nazi doctrines are much more difficult to locate in Germany than in many other countries—including the United States and Britain. Since the government has been aware that suspicion of the continued existence of strong Nazi sentiment has been one of the main obstacles to re-establishing friendly relations with groups abroad, it has made great efforts to prevent any public utterances that might possibly be interpreted as pro-Nazis, anti-Semitic, or nationalist. Its efforts are supplemented by those of other groups: democratic organizations like the trade unions; interest groups anxious to avoid being branded "pseudo-Nazi"; international organizations of various kinds; and finally, of course the Communists in East Germany, who are eager to find stray evidence of neo-Nazi activity which will fit into their propaganda attacks on the Federal Republic.

Beyond these predominantly informal control mechanisms, the government possesses great additional powers with which to crush determined campaigns by Nazis or totalitarian groups. It has sought to use these powers discreetly, but in 1952 it asked the Constitutional Court to outlaw the neo-Nazi Socialist Reich party, and this step had a marked effect in causing the decline of other neo-Nazi movements of smaller scope. Those that continue to maintain some sort of shadowy existence through the publication of nationalist or anti-Semitic literature, the holding of guarded meetings, and contact with Fascist organizations in other countries are kept under close surveillance by the special police attached to the Offices for the Protection of the Constitution, which are maintained both on the federal and the Land levels.

The Growth of Consensus

Generally speaking, the pattern of political behavior in the Federal Republic in the decade from the mid-1950's to the mid-1960's has been much more similar to corresponding patterns in the United States and Britain than to those of other large continental countries like France and Italy. In Germany, as in the Anglo-Saxon countries, the bulk of public political discussion and controversy has taken place within a relatively narrow sector of the political spectrum. Practically all political spokesmen or commentators, whether in the parties, the press, or even the interest groups, have made evident their acceptance of political democracy, the constitutional framework, and the fundamental structure of a free society. Even before the Communist party was outlawed in 1956, its size and influence had diminished to the point where its role was much closer to that played by the tiny British Communist party than to the Communist mass movements in France and Italy. Even more striking has been the absence of powerful Fascist or right-wing antidemocratic movements, like the neo-Fascist movement in Italy, and the Poujadist party and semi-Fascist cliques which played a significant role in preparing the downfall of the French Fourth Republic.

The programmatic similarities between German parties have been related above all to procedural consensus; they have all accepted without reservation the decision-making mechanism based upon free elections and the parliamentary system. In the course of time, however, they have also narrowed very much the cleavages that used to separate them in regard to principles and policies. Church-State issues have not been too important for national-level politics; they arise mainly on the Land level, but even there controversy has decreased as the result of Social Democratic concessions. The issue of nationalization and state control of industry used to be the subject of a sharp clash of policies, but here too the Socialists' acceptance of the market economy and the CDU's willingness to adopt anticartel and other control measures have narrowed the policy differences. In fact the denationalization of industrial enterprises built up by the state during the Nazi period has proceeded apace with broad interparty agreement. Originally the SPD was skeptical when the federal government began to sell shares in the Volkswagen company to the ordinary public, but the popularity of this step carried it along. Such measures contributed to the further blurring of boundary lines between the haves and have-nots which in earlier periods had nurtured class hostilities. Although not moving as far as does the American federal government in discriminating in favor of home-owners through its tax legislation, Germans have used fiscal and other policies to encourage home ownership and other forms of extending private property. The abundant production of its economy has permitted the Federal Republic to meet most of the material components of its citizen's universe of claims, and this has served to lessen their interests in ideological issues.

The "end of ideology" was associated by Chancellor Erhard in the 1965 election campaign with the slogan-concept, "The Fully Shaped Society." He claimed that a society which had arrived at this stage "no longer consisted of classes and groups which sought to force acceptance of mutually exclusive goals, but had become cooperatively oriented and marked by the interaction of all groups and interests." In this view all German groups had become less conflict-oriented as the result of the series of experiences since 1918, but especially because they had achieved maximal development and recognition in the affluent period of the Federal Republic. A young conservative, writing in the journal *Civis*, emphasized that integration had come about through recognition of social interdependence and not through identification with reified symbols like "Volk" or "Nation." But the growth of consensus was felt by him to have had an especially strong base in the overriding German concern for an efficient economy. "This consciousness of the interdependency of all upon all finds special expression in the focus of all sections of society upon the achievement potential of the entire economy. This consciousness is more strongly developed among us than in such other societies as the French, the Italian or the English ones."[4]

THE CITIZEN AND THE EXPERT

Comparative studies of characteristic national attitudes, such as that by Almond and Verba, have shown that Germans tend to feel more competent as "subjects" than they do as "citizens."[5] Thus they are more likely to carry complaints to local officials in the expectation that they will devise appropriate remedies than to form a civic group which will formulate its own proposals for presentation to local politicians. They are conscious that they have civic rights, but in normal times they will trust "those in charge" to see that they benefit from equal protection of the laws rather than question how decisions are actually made. These attitudes have in part been shaped by the historical tradition of the German *Obrigkeitsstaat* and of the efficient civil service the German rulers developed long before democratization made sig-

[4] Werner Riek, "Erhard's Formierte Geselsschaft," *Civis* (June, 1965), p. 14.

[5] Almond and Verba, *op. cit.*, Chapter VIII.

nificant headway. Though German attitudes have in some respects been changed very greatly from an earlier tendency to be overly respectful to established authority, there does remain a tendency to rely heavily upon the expert in a variety of social and political situations.

The question of who is regarded as an expert in which fields of knowledge or applied arts is of course largely a function of the educational system, and it has long been a German characteristic to leave educational policy to experts in education. There are few equivalents of parent-teacher associations, and local newspapers devote little space to school politics which were mostly laid down in the Land capital. This lack of critical interest is understandable in view of the generally favorable image that Germans hold of their accomplishments in the fields of science and culture, one which has not been rudely shattered by horror stories about children who could not read and write. Difficult performance standards in the academic high schools kept most children from continuing beyond middle or vocational schools, but this evoked little pressure from parents. Working-class families were content to have their children switch from school to the excellent apprentice programs run by industry, and there was limited emphasis on seeking upward social mobility via formal education. Teachers did not carry school questions to the public, partly because they had few serious grievances. As a profession they enjoyed good status and reasonably good pay. In a number of Laender it has even been standard practice to give a special grant to teachers going on exchange programs to the United States because it was felt that they could not maintain their standard of living on the salaries paid American teachers.

Education as a Political Issue

Then, in the 1960's, education suddenly became one of the most talked-about subjects and a hot political issue. Although a similar development occurred in other European countries, the Germans were particularly hard hit by the realization that the rate at which they were producing many kinds of skilled personnel was low compared with other countries. Not only had German scientists won very few top awards like the Nobel prize in the postwar period, but many kinds of technical and scientific skills were in low supply. Critical voices pointed out that very little had been done to attempt to restore Germany's leading position in the social sciences, which had been violently cut short under Hitler. The public thus became generally aware of something the specialists had long known—that Germany's scientific achievements were not up to the reputation developed in an earlier era. Concern also developed about the functioning of the school system. Critics asked how a highly industrialized society could continue to be competitive in an age of automation when the vast majority of its work force concluded their schooling at age fourteen. A study in 1964 showed that only 17.6 per cent of German youth in the 15–19 age group were engaged in full-time schooling compared to 30.8 per cent in France, 32.3 per cent in Sweden, and 66.2 per cent in the United States, while the percentage of young people receiving at least ten years' education was said to be almost four times higher in East Germany than in the Federal Republic. A minority expressed concern not only about the training of experts, but about education for citizenship. Thus there was criticism that the introduction of civics courses in high school curricula was not only belated but ill prepared, since teachers trained in traditional disciplines found it difficult to put the dynamics of social and political processes across to their students.[6]

Educational policy having thus become politically controversial, one of the big issues of the 1965 campaign was whether, and if so, why, the Laender with SPD governments had better educational performance records than those long ruled by CDU cabinets. Education ministers were questioned as to why their school systems were not enabling a larger percentage of students to continue to academic high schools, which in 1964 were still turning out only about 100,000 graduates a year. Reformers questioned the justification for maintaining confessionally separate public schools for Protestants and Catholics at the expense of educational effectiveness. Strong criticism was also levelled at the universities for preserving anachronistic organizations under which there was little coordination between the work of individual professors, inadequate administrative planning, ineffective supervision of student work, and poorly enforced rules regarding programs and degree requirements. German professors, jealous of the dominant decision-making powers of the faculty senates, bitterly opposed a Higher Education Bill in Hessen which aimed at strengthening the power of the University Rektor, an elective position equivalent to the American university president which had been held in rotation by individual professors for terms of one year only. The bill proposed lengthening this period to one of four years, and also restricted the veto powers of the faculty in regard to new appointments. German students, some

[6] Thomas Ellwein, *Politische Verhaltenslehre*.

of whom used difficult study conditions as an excuse to remain "perpetual students" while postponing their degree examinations, were also hit by a decision of the Rektors' Conference to dismiss those who were staying on too long.

Universities and Political Socialization

The controversy over the internal organization of the universities is politically relevant, not only because the German professor is still a widely emulated "culture hero," but also because most students are first socialized politically under the rules of "academic freedom" at the university. It is also interesting because in so many respects the relative positions of both students and professors are the reverse of what they are in the United States, where the student frequently is submitted to rigorous discipline only when he leaves the high school for the university. In Germany, students leave rigorously disciplined study in the Gymnasium for a university life where they are subject to few rules and little guidance. They can choose to hear the professors they please and, because examinations come only after several years, they are free to participate in all manner of activities. This has its effect on student politics which tends to deal with much broader issues than on an American campus (though lately the difference has been lessening). Meetings and demonstrations on behalf of intellectual and political issues are frequent, with the result that many students develop opinions on a larger number of subjects. But since issues come and go quickly, student opinion, though given more plentiful means of articulation than in American universities, seldom brings about concrete reforms. When he finally leaves the university to accept a professional position, the German graduate is likely to find that bread-and-butter politics on the local level does not have much resemblance to the heavy stuff he became used to at the university.

PARTICIPATION AND SUPPORTS

If one were to look at comparative tables in which various forms of political behavior are related to cultural and economic indices, the West German data would in some respects fit into worldwide patterns, but in others it would seem very deviant. Thus Germans exhibit the relatively good command of political information that one would expect from a high-income nation with a developed educational system.[7] But when one probes their attitudes toward

[7] Seymour M. Lipset, "Economic Development and Democracy" in his *Political Man* (New York, 1959).

political symbols, parties, and institutions, the pattern of non-identification that emerges is much more similar to that found in some developing countries where a large peasant sector lacks the communication and other links through which it might identify with the national political system. If one examines data on their participation in civic activities, membership in political parties and clubs, or in informal neighborhood improvement associations, one finds that most Germans seem to be very reluctant to play active roles in public life.[8] Thus, in most West European countries some 10 to 20 per cent of voters are also party members, while in Germany the ratio is only about 3 per cent.

Of course the experience under the Nazis had something to do with producing this phenomenon, insofar as many Germans (and their children) who were led to identify with that regime and its organizations under the prevailing drum-beating later vowed never to take a chance on being made fools of again. But other German traditions, or lack of them, also shaped this pattern. Thus many kinds of structures which in countries like the United States are very successful in eliciting civic participation are either nonexistent in Germany or have quite different traditions. The churches are a good example. In the United States, church membership is entirely voluntary, and all the funds needed for maintaining them are raised through voluntary donations. In Germany, by contrast, the churches are financed through taxes levied by the state on all members who were baptized in a particular denomination and did not officially renounce membership. Thus, because the churches are not dependent on bake sales and the like, they have not become the centers for the kind of auxiliary groups that cluster around a church in the United States and which frequently also form the nucleus of local reform drives of one kind or another. More generally, women's civic and political organizations are almost nonexistent, even though, curiously, the percentage of women among officeholders is not much different from that in the United States and Britain.

The Parties' Finance Problems

The organizations most hurt by the curiously selective pattern of German political participation have been the non-Socialist parties. While the Socialists were able to maintain a strong membership tradition and a respectable 6 per cent member-voter ratio, parties like the CDU and FDP have enrolled barely 2 to 3 per cent of their voters as members. There were usually enough

[8] Wolfgang Hartenstein and Klaus Liepelt, "Party Members and Party Voters in West Germany," *Acta Sociologica* VI, 1 (1962).

to provide candidates for office, but when it came to keeping up local party activity and raising campaign funds these parties were in a bad way. The CDU, for instance, would not have had any difficulty in an election year if it had the same donor-voter percentage prevailing in the United States—some 10 per cent—and if each donor gave perhaps 20 Deutschmarks, or half a day's income. But the dues and voluntary contributions hardly came to a tenth of the required amount. So under Adenauer's leadership the Christian Democrats and the Free Democrats took the seemingly easy way out, and became dependent on continuous subsidies from a political finance Conveyer organization established by the German Federation of Industry, whose funds were derived from assessments levied on business firms through their trade associations.[9]

Happy with the solid electoral victories they kept achieving, the CDU managers gave hardly any thought to their lack of membership base at the grass roots. Then troubles began to pile up. First the Constitutional Court in 1958 threw out as unconstitutional a provision for income tax deductibility which the coalition parties had passed to make anonymous contributions from their business donors less problematic. Furthermore, the Conveyors got into the habit of cutting off funds when they were displeased by the parties' actions. Thus the FDP was cut off without notice when it quit Adenauer's cabinet in 1956. On another occasion the Conveyors cut off subsidies to CDU headquarters after Adenauer had displeased the industrialists by revaluating the currency. As a consequence of these developments, the flow of funds to these parties diminished rapidly to the delight of the SPD which had unsuccessfully sought to make electoral capital out of their state of financial dependency.[10] At this point the parties tried to enlist more of their own members and donors, with little success. The voters had gotten used to having Adenauer run an efficient government from the top down, and they could not understand why his party suddenly needed their help. Businessmen also insisted that they would only contribute if donations were tax deductible and if there were absolutely no chance that news of their financial support ever became public. The trouble with these conditions was that they clashed with the Constitution and the Court rulings.[11]

[9] Arnold J. Heidenheimer, "German Party Finance: The CDU," *APSR*, LI, 2 (June, 1957), 369–85.

[10] Gerard Braunthal, *The Federation of German Industry in Politics* (Ithaca, 1965).

[11] Ulrich Duebber, *Parteifinanzierung in Deutschland* (Cologne, 1962).

Inputs via State Subsidies

As a consequence of these developments, the parties began to view subsidies from the public treasury as an alternative. In doing so, they developed policies which were completely at odds with their ideological commitments. The FDP, which was normally committed to liberal, individualist values, became the strongest supporter of state finance. The SPD, with whose values state finance was reconcilable, took a strongly negative position, since it didn't need the money. The CDU took a wavering position in between, although one of its deputies had taken the lead in introducing a small federal subsidy of DM five million which was shared among the parties from 1959 for "political education" work. After the 1961 elections the Free Democrats demanded increased subsidies as part of their price for entering Adenauer's fourth government and the not unwilling CDU gave way. In 1962 the amount of federal subsidies was raised to DM 20 million, the sum being divided only among the three parties represented in the Bundestag. In 1964 the coalition parties voted an increase once again, this time to DM 38 million. In the meantime most of the Land parliaments and many communal organs followed suit with the consequence that by 1965, well over DM 50 million of public funds was being divided among the political parties annually.

Many critics felt that the parties took all too easy a way around the problem of getting their followers to share a tiny fragment of their prosperity with the party of their choice. Others, particularly the parties not represented in the Bundestag, attacked the distribution formula as unconstitutional insofar as it discriminated against new and small parties. In an interview the CDU treasurer gave to *Der Spiegel* in February, 1965, he sought to cope with some of these attacks:

BURGBACHER: Well, may I ask you how you would organize the financing of a party, if that were your job?

SPIEGEL: On the basis of membership dues.

BURGBACHER: Marvelous! But what would you do if, even though the people vote for you, they refuse to become members?

SPIEGEL: Reduce expenditures. . . . What about contributions without any kind of tax deductibility?

BURGBACHER: Well, and you actually think the contributions would come in. Are you actually of this world, or where do you live? Do you actually think a man would give a contribution if it were publicly reported in the newspaper afterwards? . . .

SPIEGEL: You have explained the poor membership recruitment of the parties by saying that you can't force citizens to become party members. But won't your bill force the citizen to support parties which he actually may be opposed to?

BURGBACHER: If you asked the citizen if he would voluntarily like to pay for all the items contained in the Federal Budget you would hear all kinds of things. We only ask of the citizen that he help to finance the politics whose fruits he reaps. It is only thanks to the policies of these parties that the citizen is able to pay taxes in the first place, out of which they too are to be financed.[12]

POETS IN POLITICS

Observers of the 1965 federal election campaign warm-up were bemused to note that at one point Chancellor Erhard seemed to be fighting his main duel not with the leaders of the SPD but with some of the country's best-known writers. While government leaders in a number of countries might have been tempted to let loose publicly at the wielders of critical pens, Erhard actually counterattacked his critics by name. Thus he dismissed the leading German novelist Guenther Grass, author of the *Tin Drum*, who was conducting an independent speaking tour on behalf of the SPD, as an "intellectual snob" whose drum-beating support he was glad to do without. His comments about Rolf Hochhuth, the dramatist, who wrote some articles critical of postwar German social and economic development, were even more pointed. Rejecting Hochhuth's criticism as "silly stuff," the Chancellor said that he had no more business writing about things he didn't understand than he, Erhard, would have in giving lessons in nuclear physics to Hahn and Heisenberg, two senior German physicists.

Poets, writers, and free-lance critics frequently tend to support radical and critical positions in many countries. A sociologist like William Kornhauser attributes this to the fact they pursue their vocations in less structured settings than, for instance, their fellow intellectuals in academic positions.[13] But writers on the Continent, perhaps more than in the Anglo-Saxon countries, feel that speaking out on vital political issues is not irresponsible pursuit of an unconnected sideline, but constitutes an integral

[12] *Der Spiegel*, February 3, 1965.
[13] William Kornhauser, *The Politics of Mass Society* (Glencoe, Ill., 1959), pp. 186 ff.

part of their professional calling. The German *Schriftsteller*, a professional title more honorific and specific than the English, "writer," tends to feel that his inheritance of the humanistic tradition and the status accorded him in the land of poets and thinkers obligate him to articulate his reactions as an individual to the policies pursued by the established authorities. In the postwar period the urges of the free-lance intellectuals to sound off were reinforced by the feeling that it was their obligation to initiate dialogues on oppressive questions which representatives of the "consensus" thinking dared not open up. It was this kind of drive that produced the indictment of German and Papal responsibility for the wartime extermination of the Jews which was contained in Hochhuth's *The Deputy*. During the 1965 campaign itself Grass came out openly for recognition of the Oder-Neisse line, a policy the parties dared not touch with a ten-foot pole.

One explanation for the willingness of so many Germans to lend an ear to the opinions of intellectuals is that the fare offered them by the full-time politicians became increasingly limited after the SPD, from 1959 on, tended to say the same things as the government parties. As the parties became more institutionalized they became much more selective in their articulation functions, specifically by expelling or shunting aside individuals who represented minority positions within the party and society. Thus the educated public became dependent on receiving critical opinion from intellectuals.

However, when some of Germany's leading writers campaigned personally for the SPD in 1965, it benefitted that party very little. An IFAS survey showed that although 79 per cent of the highly educated had heard of Guenther Grass' campaign, the reaction of the general population was negative. Two-thirds of the respondents felt that writers ought not to mix in politics, thus endorsing Erhard's stand. Two findings were particularly dismaying to liberal intellectuals. The first was that SPD adherents were just about as hostile to "poets in politics" as the more conservative voters. The second was that in the land of "poets and thinkers," fully 68 per cent of adults could not name a single living German writer or poet, while only 10 per cent could name as many as three.

A German Nemesis Figure

No figure has served as a more fulsome target of the intellectuals' attacks than the "negative symbol figure of German democracy," Franz Josef Strauss, the bull-necked Bavarian CSU leader who, in 1962, almost overnight earned the hatred of writers the world over by his crude attempt to suppress the critical voice of *Der Spiegel*.[14] It surprised no one that his name subsequently evoked spontaneous booing at conferences of the Congress on Intellectual Freedom, but more intriguing was the almost visceral reaction toward him that has developed among the kind of German citizen who writes letters to the editor. Seldom in any democratic country has one personality managed to arouse so wide a set of antipathies and anxieties among diverse publics. North Germans see in him the personification of the primitive Bavarian political style they have always scorned. Antimilitarists see in him, partly because of his actions as Defense Minister, an unrestrained advocate of military adventurism who had no scruples about inviting atomic devastation. Those in whom past experiences have left a deep distaste for politicians who overstress emotional appeals have been appalled by the semiphysical compulsion with which Strauss as a speaker seeks to bully his audiences into submission. Those who fear excessive nationalism have been alarmed by statements, such as one given by Strauss' wife to an interviewer, to the effect that Strauss' real foes were "international groupings, in England, and in America, and generally everybody on both sides of the Iron Curtain who are enemies of Germany." Most appalling to many Germans in their image of Strauss is not so much his ruthlessness as his lack of self-discipline, and the thought that he might someday come to power induces nightmares. As an editor of conservative journals has put it: "Although no one says so explicitly, the German public compares this man to Hitler. If he should succeed in returning to Bonn and one day become Chancellor then, according to the nebulous perceptions of the masses, the clock will once again have struck '1933.' "[15]

There is little question but that, compared to the attention paid to the attitudes of other elite and mass sectors, the role of literary and academic intellectuals as political elites in German life has been inadequately explored by social scientists. The politicians on the other hand, have recognized the importance of intellectuals and have made extensive attempts to quiet their fears and win their sympathy. Thus the CDU at its 1964 Congress devoted an extra meeting to a "Dialogue with the Intellectuals," which received far more notice than the Congress itself. The

14 Otto Kirchheimer and Constantine Menges, "A Free Press in a Democratic State?: The Spiegel Case," in W. M. Carter and A. F. Westin, eds., *Politics in Europe* (New York, 1965).

15 Martin Bernstorf, "Wie Maechtig ist Franz Josef Strauss?," *Civis* (May, 1965), p. 18.

SPD, in 1965, sought to associate its name with that of figures in the arts and sciences, but its listing of thirty-five professors who would provide an SPD government with advice and counsel evoked some disavowals from those cited, as well as publication by the CDU of an even longer list of professors who allegedly supported it. The politicians' concern with the good will of the writers aroused speculations that a future government might express its gratitude by supporting outstanding writers with state stipends in a manner similar to that already introduced in Sweden. If this were to become general practice it might, following Kornhauser's analysis, radically diminish the flow of criticism which free-lance intellectuals aim at power-holders.

TO THE HEARTH OF THE
UNKNOWN VOTER

As long as Konrad Adenauer led the CDU as Chancellor-incumbent, the Federal Republic's election campaigns were dry and predictable affairs. Thrice the same drama repeated itself with only minor changes: in 1953, in 1957, and in 1961. A year before the election date the contest looked as if it might have real elements of competitiveness, with surveys showing the opposition Social Democrats favored over the CDU among those prospective voters who expressed opinions. Then, as the campaign intensified, opinion shifted to the CDU as the undecided reacted to the gambits which Adenauer utilized in masterly fashion, so that by election night the CDU was, with 45–50 per cent of the votes cast, either in command of or within sight of an absolute Bundestag majority. Thus, though the Federal Republic was approaching a two-party system on the British model, the element of competitiveness was crucially missing since the SPD seemed cast as a permanent opposition.

In 1965 it appeared to many professionals that this pattern would finally be broken, for many crucial variables had altered. Instead of the stern father-figure of Adenauer, the CDU was this time led into battle by Ludwig Erhard whose more benign personality suggested less forceful leadership as well. A dramatic change had also come over the SPD which, although still led by its 1961 Chancellor candidate, Willy Brandt, had spent the intervening four years in an extraordinary conditioning campaign, and entered the political bout in the belief that it had dismantled its pejorative image as a "radical" and "negative" force. Moreover its team of experienced politicians were confronted by a CDU leadership which had made its internal disputes widely public so that it appeared very likely that many more Germans would this time agree that "it was time for a change." The hardheaded owners of London betting houses offered even money that the SPD would beat the CDU. One leading opinion survey published in the last week of the campaign showed SPD and CDU-CSU neck-and-neck, each with the support of 45 per cent of likely voters.

CDU's Apparent Handicaps

As the CDU, together with its unreliable Bavarian CSU appendage, entered the campaign year, it appeared to most observers that the party had used itself up after sixteen years in office. It was rent by bitter factional quarrels and personal animosities among its leaders. Most harmful was the open vendetta which Adenauer had continued to carry on after unwillingly yielding the Chancellorship to Erhard in 1963. Violating the ground rules of party solidarity in an incredible manner, Adenauer adopted a practice of granting newspaper interviews in which he directly attacked Erhard's general lack of firm leadership and his foreign policy in particular. As he was vigorously joined in his pro-Gaullist criticisms by Franz Josef Strauss, Germany was treated to the spectacle of both chairmen of the two sister parties publicly-attacking the Chancellor who led these parties as government head. After one such "interview war" in November, 1964, the editor of a pro-CDU newspaper reviewed Erhard's record in office in an editorial entitled "The Miserable Ten Months."[16]

During the election year the incohesion in the cabinet and CDU/CSU parliamentary party, as well as Erhard's apparent inability to exert the full powers of his office, became still more evident. There were occasions when he deliberately allowed himself to be outvoted in cabinet decisions rather than assert his constitutional powers of "laying down the guide-lines of policy." Even in his special area of economic policy he could not restrain the Bundestag majority from voting money bills far in excess of available funds. Public awareness of these events was evidenced in survey results showing that those voters who had an opinion as to whether Erhard or Adenauer was the better Chancellor chose Adenauer two to one. But for the majority who had no clear opinion on this, Erhard lost surprisingly little of the popularity which he had accumulated over the years as the "architect of the economic miracle." Furthermore, very little of the poten-

[16] *Die Welt*, November 7, 1964.

tial dissatisfaction with Erhard was transformed into support for his challenger, Willy Brandt. Thus, surveys in the summer of 1965 still showed that when respondents were asked to pick their favorite candidate for Chancellor, not between Erhard and Adenauer, but between Erhard and Brandt, about 50 per cent opted for the former and only about 30 per cent for the latter.

The SPD's Campaign

The Social Democrats were somewhat disappointed that the personal public relations build-up for Willy Brandt had not been more successful. Apparently their tactic of using Brandt's position in Berlin to project an image of suprasectional statesmanship had

ATTITUDES TOWARD ELECTIONS AND PARTY IDENTIFICATION

A. *Feelings about voting and election campaigns*

Per cent of sample who report they:	U.S. %	Britain %	Germany %	Italy %
Feel satisfaction when going to polls	71	43	35	30
Sometimes find election campaigns enjoyable	66	52	28	18
Sometimes get angry during campaigns	57	41	46	20
Sometimes find campaigns silly or ridiculous	58	37	46	15
Never enjoy, get angry, or feel contempt during campaign	12	26	35	54

(Percentages exceed 100 because of multiple responses.)

B. *Party identification*

	Germany %	U.S. %
Convinced party adherents	25.4	35.5
Conditional party adherents	46.3	37.0
Unstable party indentifiers	4.8	14.6
Party adherents and identifiers	76.5	87.1
Nonidentifiers	23.5	12.9
TOTAL	100.0	100.0

C. Willingness to discuss politics

Per cent of sample who:	U.S. %	Britain %	Germany %	Italy %
Sometimes talk politics	76	70	60	32
Refused to report voting preference to interviewer	2	2	16	32
Don't feel free to discuss politics with *anyone*	18	12	32	34

D. Primary group re-enforcement of voting preferences

	PER CENT OF GROUP WHO ANTICIPATED APPROVAL OF THEIR VOTING DECISIONS FROM		
	Family %	Friends and acquaintances %	Colleagues at work place %
SPD adherents if they voted SPD	48	63	76
CDU adherents if they voted CDU	73	55	26

E. Which kinds of elections interest you most? (1964)

Voters in:	Federal elections %	Land elections %	Local elections %	All three %	Little interest in any %
Small communities	25	3	30	18	
Medium-size communities	37	4	19	19	24 21
Big cities	49	3	6	25	17
TOTAL	37	4	18	21	20

SOURCES: *A*—Almond and Verba, *op. cit.*, p. 146; B—Werner Zohlnhoefer, "Parteiidentifizierung in der Bundesrepublik und den Vereinigten Staaten" in Erwin Scheuch and Rudolf Wildenmann, eds., *"Zur Soziologie der Wahl* (Cologne, 1965), p. 133; C—Almond and Verba, *op. cit.*, pp. 116, 117, 120; D—Scheuch and Wildenmann, *op. cit.*, p. 203; E—Fritz Saenger and Klaus Liepelt, eds., *Wahlhandbuch 1965* (Frankfurt, 1965), p. 3-22-5.

caused negative feedback. Some less secure burghers associated Berlin with "danger," while the attempt to live up to his states-man's role caused Brandt to lack spontaneity in public appear-ances. But the SPD commanded many other electoral resources, and it proceeded to marshal these so as to complement the strengths and weaknesses of its top candidate. To strengthen the aura of respectability it had achieved by its adoption of the moderate Bad Godesberg program, it projected a "responsible" campaign style in which free-wheeling attacks were reduced to a minimum. Using a campaign slogan, "Secure is Secure," which was very similar to that of the CDU, the party tried to imply that it would pursue the popular policies of the Adenauer-Erhard period, only with more effectiveness. All of the key members of its shadow cabinet projected a unified policy that had been carefully worked out to appeal to many interest groups, while maintaining an in-herent consistency in sharp contrast to the conflicting policies being expounded within the CDU camp.

The SPD's greatest advantage lay in the fact that a majority of the population perceived it to be better equipped to handle almost all important domestic problems than the CDU. And for the first time such crucial problems as education, scientific growth, and effective regional planning had become important political issues. In many of these areas SPD ministers had performed very well on the Land level, and their records were fully exploited. To carry its message to the voters the SPD fused the volunteer labor of its members with the professional work of paid experts to maximize its audiences. To assure that the membership worked in line with the campaign aims, "programmed texts" were issued which were designed to replace the class-conscious vocabulary of an earlier period with a reformist one. Following the advice of depth psychologists the party also replaced "provocative" or "low-class" symbols and colors (such as red and yellow) on its posters and handbills with "high-class" and "reassuring" ones. Thus the most widely utilized symbol was the one that framed the party initials within a replica of a German automobile license plate, a symbol of prosperity and achievement. Its numerous publications featured the smiles of happy prosperous children rather than frowns of militant workers.

Campaign Style: The Great Reversal

Early in the campaign the CDU leaders became aware that the "embracing" tactic of SPD campaign architect Herbert Wehner was having its effect. By stressing its closeness to the policies of the incumbent government party, the SPD was making itself more widely acceptable. The similarity to earlier CDU campaigns was emphasized still more by the SPD's use of relatively "unpolitical" campaign symbols and techniques. To circumvent this "embracing" tactic the CDU now adopted tactics that seemed to fly in the face of all campaign wisdom. Since Brandt and Wehner were reluctant to attack Erhard directly, the CDU managers now decided to have Erhard go on the offensive. This resulted in much more direct attacks by the "in" candidate on the "out" candidate and party than the other way around, as well as in the man-bites-dog episode in which Erhard personally attacked the poets. But the CDU went even further in violating the rule of "not mentioning your opponent unless you have to." It actually reprinted campaign placards of the SPD on its own handbills. Of course the SPD posters chosen were the ones used in earlier election campaigns, such as those of 1953 and 1957 when the SPD still championed socialization of industry and opposed compulsory military service.

Because of the lack of direct confrontation between the leading candidates, the campaign became diffuse toward the end. The issues emphasized varied according to speaker and locality. The Free Democrats under Erich Mende campaigned on the pledge of continuing the coalition with the CDU but only on condition that Franz Josef Strauss remain excluded from the cabinet. Strauss's unpopularity outside his native Bavaria also led CDU organizations in North Germany to refuse his offers to help in their campaigns, but he used other forums to attack Foreign Minister Schroeder and his alleged subservience to American policy. The general lack of awe felt toward Erhard by young intellectuals was manifested by his reception in university towns like Tuebingen where arrogant students greeted him with such slogans as "More niveau, you're in Tuebingen," and "Once we heard Hegel here, now you." The Socialists made good but unsensational progress by sticking to positive discussion of domestic programs and policies, and Brandt completed an exhausting campaign trip in which his personal reception was apparently highly favorable.

Social Democrats who held moderately good opinions of the political consciousness of their countrymen were encouraged during the last month of the campaign when the Adenauer-Strauss vendetta against Erhard again broke into the open on the question of foreign policy. They reasoned that even the most obtuse voters would recognize that they could not expect stable government from a coalition made up of pro-Gaullist Adenauer and Strauss followers, of "unification first" FDP members, and a moderate pro-Atlantic CDU minority. But cynics maintained that any focus on complex foreign policy issues would serve as a stimulus to drive the undiscriminating marginal voter toward the CDU, even if the issue was largely created by disunity within the CDU-led "team." As it was, the only genuine international crisis in the headlines during pre-election week was the conflict between India and Pakistan, and in his final speeches Erhard did his best to make it appear threatening to Germans.

The Election Returns

When the reactions from West Germany's 38 million eligible voters came in on election night, Sunday, September 19, they showed the following results (comparative 1961 figures in parentheses):

CDU/CSU	47.6%	(45.3%)
SPD	39.3%	(36.2%)
FDP	9.5%	(12.8%)
National Democratic Party	2. %	—
Peace Union	1.3%	(1.9%)
Others	0.3%	(3.8%)
Voting turnout	86.8%	(87.7%)

Most chagrined and disappointed by these results were (1) the public opinion pollsters, (2) the Social Democrats and Willy Brandt, (3) Konrad Adenauer and his supporters, (4) the intelligentsia, (5) the minor parties, and (6) political scientists and electoral experts. Most satisfied with the results were (1) Ludwig Erhard and his supporters in the CDU, (2) the advocates of the continuation of CDU-FDP coalition government, and (3) the FDP.

Ludwig Erhard had reason to feel satisfied because the results showed that the masses of German voters had not been significantly affected by the torrents of criticism directed against him from almost all quarters of politically informed opinion. Moreover, the results paved the way for the continuance of a CDU/CSU-FDP coalition government which he had frequently espoused. For the same reason the FDP also felt satisfied. It had lost one quarter of its 1961 strength, but it had feared much worse. The Social Democrats were the most disappointed of the parties even though statistically they were the largest winners compared to 1961. Not only had the close contest with the CDU not developed, but the party also failed to meet the 40 per cent minimum goal of its remodeling campaign and scarcely narrowed the gap between itself and the CDU. The only groups even more chagrined were the two significant minor parties—the pacifist, anti-NATO German Peace Union which the government accused of receiving Communist support, and the neo-Nazi German Nationalist party which had made an all-out effort to rally extreme rightist elements. Both were the victims of a long-term trend against radical parties and the "five per cent clause" of the electoral law.

Nor was there very much more cheer from many of the reserved sections on the sidelines. Predictions of political scientists that a relatively undramatic campaign with lack of provocative issues and personalities would result in a considerably lower voting turnout were not borne out. Adenauer, who had hoped that a poor CDU showing would be grist in his campaign to force Erhard from the Chancellorship, had to swallow the fact that the CDU did better under Erhard than it had under him in 1961. His chagrin was shared by the intellectuals who interpreted the results, not only as the failure of their "parallel action" campaign on behalf of Willy Brandt, but as a vote for boobery and anti-intellectualism. But by far the biggest prestige loss was suffered by the public opinion survey firms of which the two leading ones, Emnid and Allensbach, had reported a "neck-and-neck" race up to two weeks before the election. Their plea that there had been a last-minute landslide toward Erhard was not widely credited. It is apparent that there are many things about the predispositions and attitudes of German voters that the experts have not firmly ascertained. But, to emphasize the positive, what findings about German voting behavior have gained general acceptance?

FACTORS DETERMINING
VOTING BEHAVIOR

In view of past experiences and the considerable amount of alienation that still characterizes the attitudes of many Germans toward politics, it appears at first sight rather paradoxical that voting participation in the Federal Republic is higher than in the United States and even in Britain. The regularity of turnout in federal elections is astounding, with a variation of less than 2 per cent in

A. Sex, age, and religious structure of party supporters (1961)

Party	Sex		Age			Religion	
	Men	Women	Under 40	40–60	Over 60	Cath-olic	Prot-estant
	%	%	%	%	%	%	%
SPD	52	48	43	37	20	32	61
CDU	39	61	35	41	24	61	37
FDP	53	47	44	38	16	27	66

B. Distribution of votes by region, 1965 (1961 in parenthesis)

Land	Dominant Religious Group	CDU	SPD	FDP	Party with Largest Gain 1961–65
		%	%	%	
Schleswig-Holstein	Prot.	48(42)	39(36)	9(14)	6% CDU
Hamburg	Prot.	38(32)	48(47)	9(16)	6% CDU
Lower Saxony	Prot.	46(39)	40(39)	11(13)	7% CDU
Bremen	Prot.	34(27)	49(50)	12(15)	7% CDU
Northrhine-Westphalia	Cath.	47(48)	43(37)	8(12)	6% SPD
Saar	Cath.	47(49)	40(34)	9(13)	6% SPD
Hessen	Prot.	38(35)	46(43)	12(15)	3% Each
Rhineland-Palatinate	Cath.	49(49)	37(34)	10(13)	4% SPD
Baden-Wuerttemberg	Prot.	50(45)	33(32)	13(17)	5% CDU
Bavaria (CSU)	Cath.	56(55)	33(30)	7(9)	3% SPD
Federal Republic		47.6 (45.3)	39.3 (36.2)	9.5 (12.8)	3.1% SPD 2.3% CDU

C. Party Preferences by Occupation Groups*

	CDU	SPD	Other	No Preference
	%	%	%	%
Self-Employed, Professions	46	18	17	19
White-Collar, Officials	38	39	7	16
Skilled Workers	28	56	3	13
Unskilled Workers	32	48	3	17
(Union Members)	24	61	3	12
Farmers	66	8	9	17
Pensioners	41	36	5	18
Housewives	43	31	4	22

* Based on 1965 pre-election surveys.

SOURCES: A—Max Kaase, "Die Waehlerschaft der Parteien bei der Bundestagswahl von 1961," in Helmut Unkelbach, et al., Waehler, Parteien, Parlament (Frankfurt, 1965), p. 24. C—Press release of September 17, 1965, of IFAS, (Institut fuer angewandte Sozialwissenschaft, Bad Godesberg), which will publish a comprehensive analysis of its 1965 survey data.

turnout between 1953 and 1965. Thus the unexciting 1965 campaign drew virtually the same turnout (86.9 per cent) as that of 1961 (87.7 per cent), in which Adenauer and the Berlin "wall" were burning issues. In fact German voting participation is higher in those (Land) elections which Germans find *least* interesting (about 75 per cent) than in those American (federal) elections which Americans find *most* interesting. It appears difficult to reconcile this with findings which show that Germans derive less satisfaction from going to the polls than do Americans and Englishmen. Part of the difference between the German and American figures is no doubt attributable to the less cumbersome voting regulations and the automatic registration that prevail in Germany as well as Britain. But more important still are the norms that re-enforce the "duty" of voting for most Germans. German researchers have found that a majority of Germans feel that even persons completely disinterested in the outcome of an election should vote in it.[17] The fact that a larger percentage of the older age groups (i.e., 59 per cent of those over 50) feel this way than do younger voters (34 per cent of those under 30) suggests that there may be a psychological carry-over from the sanctions exerted to achieve "99.9% 'Yes' votes" during the plebiscites of the Nazi period. Thus voting participation may be re-enforced by norms of both a pluralist and authoritarian kind.

If one probes for deeper indicators of willingness to assume political commitments—for instance, by examining party identification—clear-cut differences do not become apparent here either. On the verbal level most Germans are just about as willing to express party preferences as are Americans. The percentage of Germans who can be classified as "convinced" party adherents is somewhat lower than in the United States (25 per cent versus 35 per cent), but the percentage of outright nonidentifiers is, all things considered, not that much higher in Germany (23.5 per cent) than in the United States (12.9 per cent). It would appear that to a considerable extent German party identification is a nearly automatic by-product of the factors shaping voting participation. For the majority of Germans, both this and attitudes toward the political system in general are not emotively rooted. Since German election campaigns are less colorful than those in the United States, it might be understandable why a smaller percentage of Germans find them enjoyable. But it is significant that the relationship between negative and positive feelings that campaigns elicit in Germans is much more unbalanced than among

[17] Wolfgang Hartenstein and Guenther Schubert, *Mitlaufen oder Mitbestimmen* (Frankfurt, 1961), p. 39.

Americans and Englishmen (table, p. 102). Even more significant is the fact that over a third of the Germans claim that elections elicit no emotional reaction of any kind whatsoever. This suggests that whereas some Germans still feel very deeply about their political choice, a large group cares even less than relatively apolitical strata in other countries. Indeed, German surveys have found that among those who have not consistently backed one party, the ability to recall past voting decisions is very faulty and inadequate.

Decline of Political Subcultures

Two decades of German postwar political development have led to the gradual lessening of the socio-economic and ideological cleavages that once divided the German electorate into what Gabriel A. Almond has labelled "political sub-cultures." The high degree of polarization of party loyalties on class and religious lines still characterized political behavior in the early 1950's, but the trend since then has been consistently toward diversification of party appeals. Thus the CDU started out as a predominantly Catholic party but soon was able to recruit considerable following among Protestants and even the religiously indifferent. The SPD's progress in supplementing its working-class clientele with middle-class and rural voters has been slower but also consistent so that the religious and socio-economic profiles of the electorates of the two parties have grown more similar.

However, significant differences remain in comparison with voting behavior characteristics in the United States and Britain. In contrast to the United States, the percentage of businessmen, professionals, and other upper-income groups who support the more liberal of the two major parties remains low in Germany, even though it has been increasing. Nor is the religious polarization, which remains very sharp, particularly in Catholic rural areas, usually paralleled in the Anglo-Saxon countries. One curious by-product of this is that the CDU, as the more conservative party, actually gets more support from the very lowest income group than does the SPD. Thus the CDU's special strength lies in groups as diverse as conservative rural and small-town Catholic workers and upper-income urban professionals and businessmen. Geographically it has been strongest in Catholic South and West Germany, but it has also made gains in Protestant North Germany, though it remains weakest in the large cities of the north. The Free Democrats tends to be strong where the CDU is weaker, since it remains the choice of those middle-class and white-collar groups who still regard the CDU as too "Black" (i.e., Catholic).

The groups of voters who remained inaccessible to SPD campaign appeals because they could not possibly vote for the "Reds" has been diminishing since the SPD itself has lessened its identification with what has historically been the color of the revolutionary working class. But conservative farmers, devout Catholics, and businessmen still find it very difficult to vote for the party. More receptive to the party's new look have been white-collar workers, professionals, and civil service employees. But the largest gains achieved by the SPD in the 1965 election were made among the Catholics in cities and industrialized areas, for whom the attractiveness of its socio-economic program was no longer vitiated by its "anti-Christian" reputation. The party increased its share of votes the most in those Laender that were predominantly Catholic, and especially in those—like Rhineland-Westphalia and the Saar—that were also highly industrialized.

However, the electorates of the two major parties, which between them share 85 per cent of German votes, still differ sharply in a number of curious ways. Among these are:

1. The high degree to which the CDU position rests on the disproportionate support of the female vote. Though conservative parties usually find greater favor among women, the extent to which this occurs in Germany is unusual for a secularized, industrial country.

2. The consistent disregard among a portion of CDU voters for the second-level elections on the Land and local levels. This has resulted in a striking but consistent discrepancy between voting results on these levels almost to the point where the SPD has become a permanent "government party" in most Laender and communities, while the CDU has been the "government" party in Bonn.[18]

3. In socio-psychological terms the SPD is viewed as playing a much more functionally specific role for its adherents than does the CDU. This is borne out by the fact that SPD adherents expect more moral support from functionally specific groups like co-workers, whereas CDU adherents expect strikingly more support from their families. For many CDU followers the party fits into a diffuse, traditional environment.[19] This probably explains their lack of motivation for joining it as members, which in turn dis-

---

[18] For a discussion of recent modification of this tendency, see Werner Kaltefleiter, "Waehler und Parteien in den Landtagswahlen 1961 bis 1965," *Zeitschrift fuer Politik*, XII (1965), 111 ff.

[19] Erwin K. Scheuch, "Die Sichtbarkeit politischer Einstellungen im alltaeglichen Verhalten," in Scheuch and Wildenmann, eds., *Zur Soziologie der Wahl* (Cologne, 1965), pp. 169–214.

tinguishes the SPD as a "members' party" from the CDU as a voters' party."

The greater difficulty in predicting voting decisions results from the fact not only that the Germans are rather hesitant about divulging their political preferences, but that many of them are not frank with themselves about how their political choice relates to their basic value systems. Thus the pollsters' failure in 1965 may be in part attributed to the restraint Germans still feel in discussing politics or state party choices. Hence interviewers have a more difficult job than in Britain or the United States. But many voters were probably not even able to be frank with themselves. They wanted to be "good democrats" and as such they knew they shouldn't hold it against Willy Brandt that he had left Germany to struggle against the Nazis, but their qualms nevertheless were registered in the privacy of the voting booth. As patriots they knew that they should admire Brandt's role in Berlin, but deep down they felt that "Berlin" spelled "trouble," while Erhard spelled "prosperity." These problems of the significance of ambiguous symbols and roles constitute imponderables in all free elections, but in Germany still more perhaps than elsewhere.

"WEIGHING" THE VOTES

Some political scientists hold that the nature of a country's electoral law has a crucial impact not only on the nature of the party system but even on voting behavior. To what extent does the West German electoral law explain the trend toward the reduction of the number of parties in the system? Only partly. West Germany has a modified system of proportional representation rather than a majority, single-member district system of the kind used in Britain and the United States. Smaller parties are not automatically discouraged by the electoral rules, since even parties that could not win a single constituency seat can win parliamentary representation via the party lists. But there is one provision in the electoral law that has been very important in discouraging small parties, the "five per cent clause" which provides that only those parties share in the distribution of the "list" seats that receive at least five per cent of the total vote cast.

Under the German system there are an equal number—248 —of constituency and list seats (not counting Berlin). In essence this means that half of the seats are contested and won in single-member districts, but the remaining half are then distributed among the *qualified* parties so as to give each a Bundestag representation proportional to the votes it receives among the "party" ballots that each voter casts in addition to his ballot for the local deputy. This system permits the voter to vote for the constituency candidate of one party and for the "list" of another party, but in fact some 98 per cent vote a straight ticket. This voting system is complex, but improvements in the form of the ballot that were introduced in the 1965 election halted an earlier trend toward an increasing rate of invalid or partially invalid ballots (in 1961; 6.1 per cent).[20]

How seat distribution is worked out can be illustrated by what happened in 1965 in one of the Laender. Thus, in Lower Saxony, 4,036,239 votes were cast for candidates in the 30 Bundestag constituencies, and 4,052,741 votes for the candidate lists submitted by the Land party leadership to fill the 32 "list" seats assigned to that Land. Of the constituency seats, 20 were won by CDU candidates and 10 by SPD candidates; none by candidates of the FDP. Of the party list votes, 45.8 per cent were won by the CDU, 39.8 per cent by the SPD, 10.9 per cent by the FDP, 2.5 per cent by the German National Party, and 1.3 per cent by the German Peace Union. The last two parties did not participate in the sharing of the list seats since they fell short of the five per cent mark. Thus the list seats were shared out among the three leading parties. The CDU was given 9 list seats which, together with the 20 constituency seats, gave it a total of 29; the SPD was given 16 list seats for a total of 26; and the FDP was given 7 list seats for a total of 7. The corresponding figures for all the Laender together gave the following picture for the Fifth Bundestag:

Party	Constituency Seats	List Seats	Total Number of Seats
CDU/CSU	154	91	245
SPD	94	108	202
FDP	0	49	49
	248	248	496

Obviously the FDP would be strongly against changing the present electoral system to one based only on single-member district election since this would mean its death knell. As it is,

[20] Rodney Stiefbold, "The Significance of Void Ballots in West German Elections," *American Political Science Review*, LIX, 2, (June, 1965), 391–407.

voters can support it as a third party without "wasting" their votes. Under the system the only groups whose votes are not "equal" are the followers of the splinter parties receiving less than 5 per cent. In addition, one other group has incomplete representation in the Bundestag—the Berliners. Because of its special status Berlin is represented in the Bundestag by deputies who have advisory votes only. They are named by the West Berlin City Council in relation to the strength of the parties in it, and not directly elected. Inclusion of 22 Berlin deputies (1965: 15 SPD, 6 CDU, 1 FDP) raises the total membership of the Bundestag to 518 members.

BIBLIOGRAPHY

Attitudes, Roles, and Participation

ALMOND, GABRIEL, and VERBA, SIDNEY, *The Civic Culture* (Princeton, 1963).

BRAUNTHAL, GERARD, and DUEBBER, ULRICH, "West Germany," in "Comparative Studies in Political Finance," *JP* (November, 1963), 774–90.

ELLWEIN, THOMAS, *Politische Verhaltenslehre* (Frankfurt, 1963).

HARTENSTEIN, W., *et al.*, "Party Members and Party Voters in Western Germany," *Acta Sociologica*, VI (1962), 43–52.

———, and SCHUBERT, GÜNTER, *Mitlaufen oder Mitbestimmen* (Frankfurt, 1961).

JOHNSON, NEVIL, "State Finance for Political Parties in Western Germany," *Parliamentary Affairs*, XVIII (Summer, 1965), 279–92.

McCLELLAND, D. C., *et al.*, "Obligations to Self and Society in the United States and Germany," *J. Abn. and Soc. Psychol.*, LVI (1958), 245–55.

MOLT, PETER, "Wertvorstellungen in der Politik: Zur Frage der Entideologisierung der deutschen Parteien," *PVS*, IV (1963), 350–68.

NEUMANN, ELIZABETH, ed., *Jahrbuch der Öffentlichen Meinung, 1955–65* (Allensbach, 1965).

POLLOCK, JAMES K., *et al.*, *German Democracy at Work* (Ann Arbor, 1955).

———, and LANE, JOHN C., *Source Materials on the Government and Politics of Germany* (Ann Arbor, 1964).

SCHEUCH, ERWIN, and WILDENMANN, RUDOLF, eds., *Zur Soziologie der Wahl* (Cologne, 1965). This volume contains a number of significant articles, including one on German political attitudes by Scheuch, one on CDU finances by Uwe Schleth, and several 1961 constituency campaign studies.

SCHMIDTCHEN, GERHARD, *Die Befragte Nation*, 2d ed. (Freiburg, 1965).

VERBA, SIDNEY, "Germany: The Remaking of Political Culture," in Lucian W. Pye and Sidney Yerba, eds., *Political Culture and Political Development* (Princeton, 1965).

Campaigns, Electoral System, and Voting Behavior

BARNES, S. H., *et al.*, "The German Party System and the 1961 Federal Elections," *APSR*, LVI (1962), 899–914.

Divo Institut, *Umfragen 1957* (Frankfurt, 1958).

FAUL, ERWIN, ed., *Wahlen und Waehler in Westdeutschland* (Villingen, 1960).

HIRSCH-WEBER, WOLFGANG, and SCHUETZ, KLAUS, *Waehler und Gewaehlte* (Berlin, 1956).

KITZINGER, U., *German Electoral Politics* (London, 1960).

———, "The West German Electoral Law," *Parliamentary Affairs*, XI (1958), 220–38.

KLEPSCH, EGON, *et al.*, *Die Bundestagswahl 1965* (Munich, 1965).

MERKL, P. H., "Comparative Study and Campaign Management: The Brandt Campaign in Western Germany," *WPQ*, XV, 4 (1962), 681–704.

SAENGER, FRITZ, and LIEPELT, KLAUS, eds., *Wahlhandbuch 1965* (Frankfort, 1965).

SPENCER, ROBERT, "Erhard's Dubious Victory," *International Journal*, XXI (1966), 101–109.

UNKELBACH, HELMUT, *et al.*, *Wähler, Parteien, Parlament: Bedingungen und Funktionen der Wahl* (Frankfurt, 1965).

VOGEL, BERNHARD, *et al.*, *Wahlkampf und Waehlertradition: Eine Studie zur Bundestagswahl* (Cologne, 1964).

5: The Policy-making Institutions

THE BONN SETTING

The physical and geographical disposition of capital cities tends to provide clues to the relationships of the political institutions that operate within them. In London, the proximity of the offices of the Prime Minister, most major ministries, and both houses of Parliament—all within a few hundred yards of each other in Whitehall and Westminster—reflects their intimate and subtle interrelationship. In Washington, although offices are more widely separated, there is a symmetry of sorts. Congress and the White House command different parts of the city, the older departments are strung out between them, and the newly powerful military and scientific establishments constitute a suburban outer ring. In the makeshift capital of Bonn the attempt to read symbolic significance into the arrangement of government buildings almost defies imagination, because government came there last and had to build wherever space was available.

The Chancellery does constitute a pivot, with the Parliament buildings a few hundred feet in one direction and the President's mansion about equidistant in the other. The Chancellery and the President's mansion have been developed around what were formerly the mansions of the rich; Parliament is lodged in what was intended to be a teachers' college. But the location of the ministries is hardly indicative of the nature of executive-legislative relationships. They are spread out all over Bonn and the neighboring towns as well. The Press Office and the Foreign Ministry are closest to the Chancellery. The Justice Ministry surveys the scene from a castle on a distant hillside, while the Constitutional Court is over one hundred miles away in Karlsruhe. The Mercedes limousines that transport ministers about town carry special flags, and at the ministry entrances guards check the comings and goings of visitors. Identity cards are also checked at the entrances to the legislature, much more thoroughly in fact than they are when citizens enter or leave the country.

The Bundestag and the Bundesrat are lodged in adjoining series of buildings, the highest of which houses the personal offices assigned to the deputies, one or two to a small room. Good views of the Rhine from the upper floors compensate for lack of a swimming pool.

Some information about the Bundestag chamber will help cast additional light on the peculiar character of German execu-

116

tive-Parliament relations. The chamber has been arranged like the large lecture hall that it might have been, with deputies' seats and desks covering most of the space, except for a raised platform at the front where the ministers and their top civil service aides sit facing the parliamentarians. Members wishing to speak cannot do so from their seats, but have to come to the platform, where they necessarily have to turn their backs on either their fellow parliamentarians or the members of the cabinet. Even the most brilliant orators are hard put to gain the attention of the entire house. The arrangement discourages a free give-and-take and leads speakers to prepare formal lectures. Deputies have called it the worst parliamentary chamber in the world. Many complained that the elevated position of the government bench suggested that the executive had a privileged position.

Encouraged by Bundestag President Gerstenmaier, discussions were initiated in 1959 to renovate the chamber on the model of the British House of Commons, so that the majority and opposition parties would face each other. But considerable difficulties were encountered. The members of the cabinet contended that (unlike British ministers) the Basic Law assigned them a special position quite distinct from their role as leaders of the majority party. This position was based on German practice going back to Bismarck and had been reinforced by a Constitutional Court decision in 1958. Also, the FDP and many members of the SPD feared that such a reconstruction would mean acceptance of a two-party system which they opposed. The reform failed after prolonged negotiations

THE PRESIDENCY

A great problem for political systems born by revolution in hierarchical societies has been the devising of an adequate republican substitute for the figure of the monarch. Even if individual kings were loathed, the institution of the monarchy supplied a tremendously powerful symbol, which a large proportion of citizens needed in order to identify with the state. Many Germans after 1918, conditioned by generations of experience under an *Obrigkeitsstaat* (a state where authority derives from above), missed the security they had symbolically derived from the vestigial lord-vassal relationship. The Weimar Republic's difficulties with this problem were reflected in the fact that its first president, the Socialist Friedrich Ebert, had himself supported retention of the monarchy until just a year before he took office.

Both he and his successor, Hindenburg, who remained a monarchist at heart even while in office, failed to institutionalize the Weimar presidency. In 1949, the Parliamentary Council tried once again, and the office it created has turned out to fit relatively smoothly into the constitutional structure, while at the same time supplying, in the persons of its initial incumbents, likable uncle figures of whom most Germans grew both quite fond and reasonably respectful.

To secure this degree of acceptance, the presidency has been deprived of such important political powers as the power to appoint the Chancellor in times of crisis, the power to issue emergency decrees, and the power to serve as commander-in-chief of the armed forces. Most importantly, its incumbent is not expected to resolve conflicts between the cabinet and the legislature. Rather, his functions are mainly the routine ones of any head of state. He receives ambassadors, issues letters of appointment to officials, judges, and military officers, signs and proclaims treaties and laws, and possesses the power of pardon. But even these actions must be countersigned by a cabinet minister. In addition, he fulfills domestic political functions very similar to those of the British monarch. He proposes Chancellor candidates, appoints ministers on the Chancellor's recommendation, and can dissolve the Bundestag only under specifically outlined situations involving

---

THE FEDERAL PRESIDENT

Article 54

(1) The Federal President shall be elected, without debate, by the Federal Convention. Every German who is eligible to vote in elections for the Bundestag and has reached the age of 40 years shall be eligible for election.

(2) The term of office of the Federal President shall be five years. Re-election for a consecutive term shall be admissible only once.

(3) The Federal Convention shall consist of the members of the Bundestag and an equal number of members elected by the popular representative assemblies of the *Laender* according to the principles of proportional representation.

Article 58

Orders and decrees of the Federal President shall require for their validity the counter-signature of the Federal Chancellor or the appropriate Federal Minister. This shall not apply to the appointment and dismissal of the Federal Chancellor, the dissolution of the Bundestag under Article 63 and the request under Article 69, paragraph 3.

a deadlock between it and the executive. Quite obviously, this job description is different from that appropriate to counterpart offices in the United States or the French Fifth Republic.

The method of the president's election was also designed to provide a figure who would be both fairly widely accepted and insulated from popular influence. The drafters of the Basic Law definitely wanted to avoid the Weimar situation under which a popularly elected president could both campaign for the office and vie with the legislature in his claim to represent the people. They thus provided for his indirect election through a special electoral college made up of all the members of the Bundestag and an equal number of representatives of the Land diets. This *Bundesversammlung* elects the president for a period of five years (compared to a seven-year tenure under Weimar), and an incumbent may be re-elected only once. In 1949, the position went to a figure who very conveniently happened to be both the leader of the third largest party and a story book image of "the other Germany." Theodor Heuss, the first leader of the Free Democrats, was esteemed not only as a liberal politician of the old school but as a writer of essays and belles-lettres. During his ten-year term of office he established an image as an eloquent spokesman for humanitarian values. His re-election in 1954 was almost unanimous, and when he left office in 1959 almost the entire population of Bonn lined the streets to tender him a moving tribute.

It is because neither he nor his successor, Heinrich Luebke, established many constitutional precedents that their records must be evaluated largely in terms of symbolic functions they associated with the office. An important role of the presidency has thus become that of symbolizing continuity of political traditions. Heuss, who had been deeply identified with the cultural movements and democratic politics of the Weimar period, served to link the postwar system to earlier traditions and thus helped to re-establish historical roots. Luebke, who moved to the presidency in 1959 as a compromise choice, has served to perpetuate attitudes of the period of Adenauer, in whose cabinet he had served as Minister of Agriculture. As a Catholic with rural roots, Luebke has tended to moralize with a moderately conservative bias. Thus he has defended traditional educational methods against critics, and in his speeches indirectly supported the continuation of a "hard line" policy toward the Communist bloc. Some have felt that neither his personality nor his intellect qualified him for this high position, but some attempts to prevent his re-election in 1964 came to nought. As head of state, Luebke has developed ties with his opposite numbers abroad. Thus, like Adenauer, he maintained close ties with De Gaulle, even during periods of friction between Bonn and Paris. But his main interest has been in the developing countries, which he has visited extensively. When heads of state of African and Asian countries pay return visits to Bonn, the federal President likes to give them paternal guidance and advice.

But an attempt by President Luebke to throw the potential powers of his office into the bargaining process preceding the formation of a new cabinet was sharply rebuffed in 1965. On that occasion he conceived it as his duty to directly affect the decision-making process within the parties because of the wrangling and division in the CDU. In the week preceding the election Luebke, apparently anticipating the very close outcome the pollsters had forecast, sent an unusual letter to the party chairmen asking them to consult with him before nominating a candidate for Chancellor. After the results were in the CDU chose to ignore this invitation, and the President recognized that Erhard was the only possible candidate. But even then he continued to take a direct hand in the coalition negotiations, particularly by siding with Adenauer and Strauss in pressing Erhard not to rename Schroeder as Foreign Minister. This raised the question of whether, in the case of a conflict between Chancellor and President, the President could refuse to sign a ministerial appointment suggested by the Chancellor. Most constitutional law experts thought the attempt to develop such a veto power unconstitutional, and in the end Luebke wisely decided not to force the issue to a showdown.

Luebke, however, who appeared strongly committed to a negative view of the Erhard cabinet, continued to use his privileged position to snipe at Erhard. In December, 1965, he gave an interview to a Swiss newspaper in which he supported Adenauer's view that the cabinet should be reshaped so as to include the Social Democrats. This constituted a direct and unprecedented challenge to Chancellor Erhard's authority and led to a public clash between the two men at the President's 1966 New Year's reception, at which Erhard told Luebke to cease interfering with his responsibilities.

THE CHANCELLORSHIP

Even convinced democrats have reluctantly come to accept that the German definition of democracy tends to mean "government for the people" more than it does "government by the people."

The German penchant for order and their desire to be given at least a sure sense of direction cause them to place a premium on an individual who can keep firm control of the tiller. It is not only because he unified Germany that Bismarck remains by far the most admired historical German political figure. Despite reservations about his role in retarding progress toward parliamentarism and genuine political democracy, he is still widely regarded as an ideal for German rulers, as was shown in commentaries on the occasion of the one hundred and fiftieth anniversary of his birth in March, 1965.

If in 1948 an outside observer had accused the Parliamentary Council of drafting a Bismarckian constitution tailor-fit to the personality of its presiding officer and second oldest member (who had himself grown up in the Bismarckian era), he would probably have been ridiculed for letting historicism get the better of him. He would have been told that its members had no intention of writing a Bismarckian constitution; that, as presiding officer, Konrad Adenauer had relatively little influence on the important drafting—as distinguished from the polishing—work of the Council, and that it was still extremely problematical whether Adenauer would have a chance at the Chancellorship. The Council concentrated on remedying the faults of the Weimar Constitution. If in the process they created an extremely strong Chancellor, they did so by indirection, for having decided that the president should not have any significant executive powers, power had to be concentrated within the cabinet. As for the cabinet itself, the drafters, since they took the continuation of a multiparty system for granted, feared breakdowns of cohesion of the sort that had occurred under Weimar when ministers were frequently torn between their loyalty to cabinet policies and pressures from the various parties to which they belonged. It was largely to prevent the breakdown of cabinet authority during crises that the Basic Law endows the Chancellor with great powers to maintain executive stability against the legislature, and to impose cabinet cohesion on its ministers.

His position is immensely strengthened by the fact that the Basic Law radically altered the traditional parliamentary practice that a Chancellor and his cabinet must resign if they lose a vote of confidence in the legislature. Instead, it provides that the Chancellor must resign after losing a vote of confidence *only if the legislature at the very same time elects by majority vote someone to take his place.* The adoption of this "positive" no-confidence provision was intended to prevent the kinds of situation in which mutually hostile parties combine to bring down a ministry without being able to agree among themselves on what is to take its place. In practice, its reinforcement of the position of a Chancellor who is also leader of a majority party has made his position virtually impregnable. For it means that as long as he retains control of his party, the legislature is unable to enter a no-confidence vote. On the other hand the Chancellor may, on occasions of his choosing, ask the Bundestag to give him a vote of confidence, but even if he loses he need not resign.

Erhard as Chancellor

Adenauer demonstrated how formidable a power instrument the Chancellorship could be when the incumbent had iron will power, was the formal and effective leader of his party, and the dominant personality in his cabinet. His successor, Ludwig Erhard, showed that the Chancellor could also be a much less influential figure if he lacked the above attributes. It was partly because he felt that his portly Economics Minister did not have a sufficiently developed taste and feel for power that Adenauer fought so bitterly to prevent Erhard's succession to the office. When Adenauer finally did yield it in 1963, he insisted on retaining the chairmanship of the CDU, which he utilized for another three years to snipe at Erhard's conduct of the executive. The incomplete loyalty of Erhard's parliamentary following during this period was illustrated by the votes by which the CDU/CSU parliamentary party nominated him, as well as by the votes by which it and the FDP elected him, to that office. In 1963, 63 of 222 CDU/CSU deputies either abstained or voted "No" on the motion to nominate him. On the formal election motion, 24 of the CDU/CSU–FDP majority abstained in 1963, and 22 did so in 1965, but on the latter occasion he still received 272 votes—a clear majority.

To Erhard much of the spirit and tradition Adenauer had infused into the Chancellery and the federal government were largely alien. His earlier career as a business-school teacher and economic adviser had not provided him with the inside links to the bureaucratic elite that Adenauer had developed through his long career in the Cologne administration. During his fourteen years as Minister of Economics under Adenauer he had focussed his attention predominantly on the economic policy field. There he held firm convictions, but not in many other policy areas. As an adherent of modified laissez-faire principles, he was inclined also to let decisions mature by themselves in a free marketplace of political ideas, so that his style was in sharp contrast to Adenauer's characteristic attempts to force through his own opinions. As a nominal Protestant, Erhard also did not share some commitments of his staunchly Catholic predecessor. Thus he did not give an automatic preference to stressing cultural affinities with the Catholic countries of Western Europe as did the Rhinelander Adenauer, for whom the alliance with France fitted into an historical tradition going back to Charlemagne. Since he had written with pride of Germany's postwar comeback in world markets, he was not inclined to allow purely Continental commitments to threaten Germany's political and economic relations with the wider Atlantic and overseas world. These differences in the personal predilections of the two men were not the sole cause of the foreign policy disputes in which they became embroiled, but they played an important role. Contributing to their cool relations was the fact that, in 1965, the 90-year-old Adenauer looked upon the 67-year-old Erhard as a prodigal son who was neglecting the family inheritance. The "family" harangues they engaged in, such as the two-hour disputation in the sickroom of the dying Heinrich von Brentano, the Federal Republic's first Foreign Minister, had many of the elements that one finds in the dramas of García Lorca.

In this situation even a stronger-willed individual than Ludwig Erhard might have had difficulty in "laying down guidelines of policy" which would firmly shape the destinies of the nation. As it was, Erhard's exploration of the powers of his new office were wary and cautious. He sought to divide responsibility by giving other ministers more influence, and put more effort into bringing about consensus within the cabinet than Adenauer had done. But the test came on issues such as those posed by the recognition of Israel and the extension of the statute of limitations, on which the cabinet remained deeply divided. Here Erhard often became the prisoner rather than the leader of his cabinet, and there were even occasions when it was publicly announced that he had allowed his colleagues to outvote him. Nor did Erhard strive to strengthen his position by building up a body of highly competent and loyal personal advisers either in the Chancellery or outside, a device used by most heads of government. Rather he sought to cope with the manifold duties of the Chancellor largely with the aid of the same few individuals who had served him earlier in the Ministry of Economics. Of these the most important was Ludger Westrick, whom Erhard put in charge of the Chancellery with the rank of Minister. But the latter developed into very much less an *éminence grise* than had his predecessor, Hans Globke, who for fifteen years had had a dominant voice in the selection and promotion of senior bureaucrats throughout the government.

Game theory concepts may be applied to point up the differences between the original Adenauer model of the Chancellorship and the one employed by Ludwig Erhard. Thus, inherently the office can be regarded as having been designed by architects who had reason to regard politics as a zero-sum game, as an instrument to assure the victory of the Chancellor's "friends" over his "enemies." The rules provide him with means, if needed to completely shut out the opposition from the decision-making process, and to force his party subordinates, ministers as well as parliamentarians, to choose between accepting his policies and taking the chance of losing their offices. Because of his personality and optimistic economic philosophy, Ludwig Erhard, however, tends to view politics as a positive-sum game, that is, a game in which enlightened participants will make rational choices that will allow all players to increase their "gains." From this point of view power plays and personal preferment do not appear as rational techniques, for if a leader were to seek to increase his bargaining advantage by, say, filling half the cabinet positions with men personally beholden to him, he would gain only a short-term, artificial advantage. And indeed, in reality there is hardly a member of the Bonn cabinet who can be regarded as anything like an "Erhard man." Possibly no major government leader has taken less advantage of the patronage power inherent in his office.

THE MINISTERS

Parliamentary government developed with the acceptance of the convention that the executives in charge of government departments ceased being chosen on their merit as the king's civil servants, but were chosen because they enjoyed the confidence of party majorities in Parliament. In accordance with the rule that "the powers of the Crown must be exercised through ministers who are members of one or the other Houses of Parliament and who command the confidence of the House of Commons,"[1] a clear line was drawn in Britain between politicians and civil servants. One could either enjoy the tenure and pension rights

[1] Albert Dicey, *Law of the Constitution*, 10th ed. (London, 1960), p. 431.

of a permanent civil servant, in which case one could not hope to become a minister, or one could go into Parliament with the hope of becoming a minister, but retain office for only so long as one's party remained in power. One could not switch back and forth between the two careers. In Imperial Germany, where parliamentary government was never fully established, this distinction was never drawn. The situation has changed very slowly from Bismarck's time, when practically all the "state secretaries" fulfilling ministerial roles were really civil servants responsible only to the Chancellor, who was himself the chief civil servant and only incidentally accountable to the Reichstag. In the Weimar period, though ministers were drawn predominantly from the ranks of parliamentarians, they were reluctant to relinquish the pension rights and other privileges arising from the fact that under public law they had much the same position as did civil servants. In 1930 a special law had to be passed to make it evident that ministers were not covered by *all* the civil service regulations. But the distinction between parliamentary ministers and civil servants still remains difficult for the German legal mind to grasp, and a constitutional law text published in 1954 had to devote a paragraph to informing law students that ministers do not *have* to be recruited from among civil servants.[2] Nevertheless, their salaries, as well as that of the Chancellor, remain tied to civil service scales. The former receive one and one-third times (presently about 1,200 dollars a month), the latter one and two-thirds times the salary of the top civil service bracket, plus expense allowances.

Under the parliamentary system, of course, ministers function in at least two major capacities, as part of the collective decision-making machinery of the cabinet and as the politically responsible heads of their individual ministries. As a collective decision-making instrument, the German *Bundesregierung* has always functioned quite differently from the British cabinet. Thus the former is a much less exclusive body since its meetings are attended not only by all the ministers (whereas in Britain only some attend regularly), but also by all the nonparliamentary state secretaries who are the heads of each ministry's bureaucracy. Partly as a consequence of this, the meetings of the German "cabinet" are much less confidential. The degree to which the various members share in decision-making has varied tremendously under such different personalities as Adenauer and Erhard, with the latter apparently more willing to use the formal voting pro-

[2] Fritz Munch, *Die Bundesregierung* (Frankfurt, 1954), p. 123.

cedure the cabinet rules make provision for. In neither case, however, has there necessarily been any close connection between the size of the ministry that a minister is personally responsible for and his importance in the cabinet. Thus the ministers of Post and Transport actually have the largest number of subordinates, but this does not make them politically powerful.

The five most politically important ministries may be those of Foreign Affairs, Economics, Finance, Defense, and Interior. Of these, two, Finance and Interior, have very important jurisdiction but a limited administrative substructure, since most of the field administration for these areas is carried out by the Land ministries. Other ministries that are important because of their role in drafting legislation and policy recommendations on significant matters are the ministries of Justice, Agriculture, Labor, and the Ministry for All-German Affairs. Finally there are a group of ministries that administer more specialized kinds of welfare programs, such as the Ministries of Housing Construction, Refugees, Family Affairs, Health, and International Development Aid. Small ministries in charge of contact to the Bundesrat, the limited federal role in science and education, and the supervision of public properties (Treasury), complete the list, although there are also several ministers without portfolio. As a consequence of the hard bargaining preparatory to the formation of successive cabinets, the number of cabinet ministers has become consistently larger under both Adenauer and Erhard.

But the bitterest struggles occur sometimes not so much over how many ministries each party is allocated, but over whether particular men shall remain in office. This was the case in 1965 when the coalition bargaining opened with strong demands on Erhard from two wings of his potential coalition. Thus the FDP, which had taken most credit for forcing Strauss to resign from the Defense Ministry in 1962, insisted that it would not tolerate his return to any cabinet office. The CSU and the Adenauer wing of the CDU, on the other hand, insisted that both Foreign Minister Schroeder and Minister of All-German Affairs Mende be removed from their ministries. While all this was being shouted from the rooftops, the politicians concerned insisted hypocritically that of course they did not in any way intend to impinge on the Chancellor's constitutional right to name whomever he pleased.

Since he realized that the attacks on Schroeder were really directed at him, Erhard wisely insisted on not yielding Schroeder's post even to the combined demands of the chairman of the CDU, the CSU and the federal President. To make this decision palatable to the CDU/CSU, Erhard agreed, however, that the FDP party leader, Erich Mende, who as Minister of All-German Affairs had pursued a policy of developing "small step" contacts to East Germany, be shifted to another ministry. He also agreed that the CSU and the FDP would both get four ministries each. However, in the final interparty bargaining, the FDP stood firm on its insistence that it would only join the cabinet if Mende remained at his post. After some days of crisis Erhard yielded the point to the great chagrin of Strauss and the CDU. In order to restore the balance somewhat, Erhard got the FDP to sign a statement that they would discontinue their attacks on Strauss, and he also offered to let the CSU have an additional ministry. As a final sweetener it was arranged that Strauss could announce that Erhard had offered him an important ministry, but that he had decided, "under the circumstances," not to accept the offer. As a result of the negotiations the second Erhard cabinet, installed in October, 1965, had the following party make-up, in addition to the Chancellor and his major-domo, Westrick:

CDU Ministers		FDP Ministers	
Foreign Affairs	Schroeder	All-German	Mende
Interior	Luecke	Finance	Dahlgruen
Economics	Schmuecker	Housing	Bucher
Labor	Katzer	Development Aid	Scheel
Defense	Von Hassel		
Transportation	Seebohm	CSU Ministers	
Refugees	Gradl	Justice	Jaeger
Family Affairs	Heck	Agriculture	Hoecherl
Science	Stoltenberg	Post	Stuecklen
Health	Schwarzhaupt	Bundesrat	Niederalt
Without Portfolio	Krone	Treasury	Dollinger

THE BUNDESTAG

Organization

Like the United States Congress, but unlike the House of Commons, the Bundestag has as its presiding officer an active party leader of the majority party. The office of Bundestag president is endowed with a good deal of formal dignity—the members rise when he enters the chamber—and its incumbents have in the main been men respected by their colleagues both for their outstanding intellectual capacities and their strong will power.

Both Hermann Ehlers, who died in 1954, and his successor, Eugen Gerstenmaier, were kept busy presiding over frequently unruly Bundestag sessions, supervising the modest legislative bureaucracy, and maintaining reasonably cordial relations between the legislature and the executive. The internal machinery of the chamber is run in a fairly decentralized manner on the basis of rules which the Bundestag has inherited from the Reichstag. Most important decisions regarding committee assignments, the scheduling of debates, etc., are made on the basis of broad agreement by the party leaders. The instrument through which they function is called, not very appropriately, the "Council of Elders," and includes the president, the three vice-presidents (representing the three major parties), and a number of delegates sent by each of the parties.

The Deputy

The average German deputy is considerably more difficult to describe than his American equivalent. He might be a prominent businessman who was prevailed upon to go into politics when his local CDU was looking for candidates, or a man who had spent twenty years as a labor union secretary before being nominated by the SPD, or a teacher or journalist in either party,

---

THE BUNDESTAG

Article 38

(1) The deputies of the German Bundestag shall be elected by the people in universal, free, equal, direct and secret elections. They shall be representatives of the whole people, not bound to orders and instructions and subject only to their conscience.

Article 39

(1) The Bundestag shall be elected for a term of four years. Its legislative term shall end four years after its first meeting or on its dissolution. . . .

Article 43

(1) The Bundestag and its committees may demand the presence of any member of the Federal Government.

(2) The members of the Bundesrat and of the Federal Government as well as the persons commissioned by them shall have access to all meetings of the Bundestag and its committees. They must be heard at any time.

---

or a farmer sent by the farmers' organization into the CDU to look after their interests, or the executive secretary of a trade association, or an official who had entered the civil administration through political channels, or frequently a lawyer, doctor, or intellectual. The greater variety of types is due to the fact that in a traditionally class- and group-conscious country most interest groups want to be represented by "some of their own," and the parties take care to include candidates with all kinds of background and expertise.

SOCIO-OCCUPATIONAL COMPOSITION OF BUNDESTAG (in percentages)

Occupations, Social Group	All Bundestag Deputies	CDU Deputies	SPD Deputies
Government officials and employees	22.3	22.7	23.1
Professions: lawyers, doctors, journalists, clerics, etc.	20.5	17.5	25.1
Employees of political parties and labor unions	16.1	9.6	28.1
Entrepreneurs, executives, business association officials	15.5	16.7	8.4
Farmers and farm organization representatives	11.5	18.3	1.5
Small businessmen, artisans	6.0	8.0	3.5
White and blue-collar workers	5.6	4.8	7.4
Housewives	2.5	2.4	2.9
TOTAL	100.0	100.0	100.0

NOTE: Based on data for 1961–65 Bundestag.

SOURCE: Wolfgang Zapf, "Sozialstruktur deutscher Parlamente," in Fritz Saenger and Klaus Liepelt, eds., *Wahlhandbuch 1965* (Frankfurt, 1965).

As the accompanying table makes evident, the largest single group, in the Bundestag as a whole as well as in both major parties, is composed of officials on leave from positions on the various levels of government. The importance of this group is much greater than any similar phenomenon in Anglo-American parliaments, and reflects the overlapping of administrative and parliamentary careers that has always been possible in Germany. But the civil servants' bloc is not quite as cohesive as the figures might suggest, as many in this group are basically party politicians who achieved *Beamten* status in the postwar period. The second largest group, composed of members of the professions, is even less homogeneous and cohesive. It is of rather similar significance in both major parties, though the SPD has relatively more journalists and the CDU relatively more lawyers.

The four next largest occupational groups in the table tend to be more directly representative of their organized interest groups, and their differential distribution within the parties is significant. Secretaries and officials of political parties and labor unions constitute the largest single category of SPD deputies, reflecting the high degree to which that party has depended on union support as well as the candidature preference it has frequently given its own party organizers. In the CDU/CSU parliamentary party, a more significant part is played by businessmen and farmers, frequently represented by officials of their trade associations, who play a key role in shaping economic policy in the specialized Bundestag committees. It is not surprising that the broader interest-group appeal of the CDU is reflected among its deputies, since nominations—especially those on the Land lists—are made up with "representativeness" high in mind. To many Germans a legislature composed predominantly of members of one profession, as the American Congress is dominated by lawyers, would seem odd. But that is because they would identify lawyers primarily as members of the professional middle class, not as a group whose profession has socialized them into the roles of brokers and middlemen.

Only some German Bundestag deputies devote themselves as undividedly to their jobs as most American congressmen are obliged to. This vital group, however, includes the key party chairmen and secretaries, and the leading committee chairmen. Many other deputies also hold political or administrative positions—as mayors, chairmen of county councils, or board members of public authorities—which cause them to spend a good deal of time away from Bonn. This accumulation of offices is a peculiar German problem, arising in part because of traditions and also because those who achieved party status soon after the war had "inside" positions from which to ward off competitors for the best nominations. Finally, there are a fairly considerable number of deputies who manage to carry on private business and professional careers on a part-time basis.

Partly because the individual deputy has a rather narrow range of functions and limited voting freedom, legislative roles and behavior have been much less intensively studied in Germany than in the United States. Because of the diverse ways in which they entered or were sent into the Bundestag, the deputies' conceptions of their parliamentary roles probably varied greatly in the earlier period, and have become more uniform as the road to a Bundestag nomination has become more standardized. Aside from the socio-economic composition, considerable study has been devoted to the turnover among Bundestag members. Curiously, a study of the Fourth (1961–65) Bundestag showed that almost one-quarter of the members were first-, second-, third- and fourth-termers, respectively. In 1965 a concerted effort was made to rejuvenate the membership by persuading more elderly veterans to retire. Consequently the average age declined from 52.4 to 50.7 years. A comparison of the age groupings in 1961 and 1965 showed that the number in the category 44 or younger had increased from 121 to 159, while the group 65 and older declined from 49 to 28.

The Fraktionen

The most important components of the Bundestag are undoubtedly the *Fraktionen*, the parliamentary parties with at least fifteen members. The tradition of party unity and discipline is strongly embedded in German tradition, and it is customary for the individual deputy to be very active within the party and its discussion groups. On most important matters party caucuses meet first to decide what the party position should be, and then appoint spokesmen to present their position in the plenary session. Work in the committees is less under direct party supervision, but most committee members, who owe their position to the fact that they were selected by their Fraktion, frequently carry out instructions from the party. The parties also tend to vote uniformly on roll-calls, though there is some difference between the behavior of the different party groups. The Socialists have inherited a strong informal tradition of party discipline, and their deputies very seldom fail to vote in accordance with the party position as determined by the party majority. The Christian Democrats, representing a far wider variety of interests within a much looser party framework, have always declared that they do not impose party discipline. But even their rules provide that a deputy who believes he cannot follow the party position must announce this fact beforehand, and on matters on which the leadership places high priority, such as most foreign policy issues, the Christian Democrats have in fact voted almost as much as a unit as the Socialists.

In Germany, as in Britain, there has been considerable

criticism of the position to which such party dominance relegates the deputy:

Do not individual responsibility and conscience . . . wilt under the majority decisions of the parliament and the parties? Does not the real position of the deputy stand in crass contrast to the Constitution, according to which he is bound neither by instructions nor directives, but by his own conscience? Would it not suffice—so often one hears the sarcastic refrain—if the parties were represented by only one deputy apiece, empowered to cast a vote corresponding to the strength of the party? Would not this fully satisfy the functions of parliament?[3]

Essentially, the argument is between those who adhere to the nineteenth-century concept of the deputy as someone elected to help make national decisions on the sole basis of his personal judgment and those who believe that in an age of mass electorates democracy can only function rationally through cohesive parties that rely on party discipline to carry out election programs. In Germany, the "individual responsibility" argument has frequently been used by groups who wanted to impede the acceptance of parties as instruments of increasing democratization.

Despite the weight of the Fraktion leadership, there is considerably less uniformity of voting than there is in the House of Commons, where the parties almost always vote as a unit except in the rare instances when "the whips are off." One of the results of the lack of an organic tie between cabinet and majority party has been the fact that, except when pressure from the Chancellor is really strong, the majority party does not feel itself automatically bound by the wishes of the cabinet. Thus on many domestic matters the CDU Fraktion has frequently been at odds with the official government position, attacked its own ministers, and even introduced bills in direct competition with those introduced by the cabinet. Since in practice there is no such thing as a vote of confidence, the government's stability is not impaired if it fails to have its way, and the matter is usually argued out until a compromise is reached which is satisfactory to a Bundestag majority. On occasion it even happens that a cabinet bill is passed through the Bundestag with the support of the official opposition parties, and against the votes of a majority of the government party.

The Committees

Most of the Bundestag's real legislative work is done in committees. Here, as in most other aspects of legislative procedure,

[3] Klemens Kremer, *Der Abgeordnete* (Munich, 1953), p. 10.

the German example lies halfway between American and British practice. In Britain, the traditional cabinet dominance and the cabinet's fear that standing legislative committees would develop into dangerous competitors, both to the party leaders on questions of policy and to individual ministers as originators of legislation, caused the trend toward the development of specialized standing committees to be nipped in the bud. According to British practice, the parliamentarian is supposed to be a jack-of-all-trades and not an expert trying to compete with the civil servants, whom, as minister, he may one day have to direct on questions of broad policy, not detail. In the United States, under the separation of powers, no such inhibitions have prevented congressmen from attempting to become sufficiently expert to trip up the bureaucrats whenever possible. The committees have emerged as powerful centers, where interest groups frequently reject or rewrite bills submitted by the executive agencies. Germany combines the British deference toward executive initiative with something like the American tendency toward expertise. Thus the parties try to fill their committee places with experts, many of them ex-officials and interest group representatives who can compete with the civil servants in their own technical and legal language.

Comparative statistical evidence bears out the importance of committee and party meetings in the German legislative process. Thus in 1954 the British House of Commons, where committee and party meetings do not play a very large role, did the bulk of its work in 170 plenary sessions which totalled 1,408 hours. The same year the French National Assembly, which spent more time in committee meetings, met in plenary sessions 132 times for a total of 796 hours. The United States House of Representatives, which also did the bulk of its work in committee, held 123 plenary sessions that year for a total of 533 hours. The Bundestag, however, went furthest in concentrating work in committee and party meetings. Its plenary meetings, usually held on only two days a week when the Bundestag was in session, numbered only about fifty-five. However for every plenary session, the Bundestag that year held no less than twenty committee and nine party meetings.[4]

Legislative and Control Functions

The Basic Law allows the executive to compete with both houses of the legislature in introducing bills, and in fact most legislation originates with the ministries. The German legislator has more of

[4] "Wie die Parlamente Tagen," *Das Parlament*, December 12, 1960, p. 11.

an opportunity to toss bills into the hopper with some hope that they will become law than his British equivalent, who has to draw lots for such a chance, but even so he finds it hard to compete with the civil service bill drafters, who have all the authority and resources of the ministries at their disposal. Thus of the 483 laws passed in the four years of the Second Bundestag (1953 to 1957), seven originated in the Bundesrat, 126 were introduced by Bundestag members, while 350, or almost three-quarters, were submitted by the cabinet. In fact, so much do Germans identify the legislative functions with executive dominance that reports that the cabinet has sent a bill to the legislature are frequently headlined in German newspapers as, "Cabinet Decides To Pass Traffic Law," thus causing the unsophisticated reader to take passage by Parliament as almost a matter of course.

LEGISLATIVE PROCESS

Article 76

(1) Bills shall be introduced in the Bundestag by the Federal Government, by members of the Bundestag or by the Bundesrat.

(2) Federal Government bills shall first be submitted to the Bundesrat. The Bundesrat is entitled to state its position on these bills within three weeks. . . .

Article 77

(1) Federal laws shall be passed by the Bundestag. After their adoption, they shall, without delay, be transmitted to the Bundesrat. . . .

(4) [In regard to bills where the Bundesrat has only a suspensory veto] Vetoes adopted by the majority of the votes of the Bundesrat . . . may be rejected by a decision of the majority of the Bundestag. Should the Bundesrat have adopted the veto by a majority of at least two-thirds . . . the rejection of the Bundestag shall require a majority of two-thirds. . . .

Article 81

(1) . . . the Federal President may, on the request of the Federal Government with the consent of the Bundesrat, declare a state of legislative emergency with respect to a bill, if the Bundestag rejects the bill although the Federal Government has declared it to be urgent. . . .

(2) If the Bundestag, after the state of legislative emergency has been declared, again rejects the bill or passes it in a version declared by the Federal Government to be unacceptable, the bill shall be deemed to have been passed insofar as the Bundesrat consents to it. . . .

This in fact would be true in only a few areas. In most, especially where important interest groups have managed to rouse their followers both in and outside the majority party, cabinet bills do not always have an easy passage, as a few examples from the 1960 legislative session show. At the beginning of the year, Finance Minister Etzel announced that the budget could stand no more than a 4 per cent pay increase for government employees. The civil service organizations denounced this as altogether insufficient, and the opposition parties immediately announced they would press for a 9 per cent increase. In the Interior Committee, most of whose members possess civil service background, a majority, including the CDU chairman, altered the cabinet bill in line with the 9 per cent figure. But some weeks later in the plenary session, the same CDU committee chairman, having in the meantime consulted his party leaders, introduced a motion on behalf of the CDU calling for a 7 per cent increase, and this was finally passed. During the same period the Labor Minister was having a difficult time with his bill to reform the medical insurance system, which called forth violent opposition from both the trade unions and the medical associations, and split the CDU so badly that even the Chancellor's personal intervention failed to bring about an acceptable compromise.

The Bundestag has had great difficulty in developing proper techniques and styles through which to exercise control over the policies of the cabinet. The concept of the proper role of the Opposition as a critic of the government has proved especially difficult to establish. "There is unfortunately little need to substantiate the fact that in the Federal Republic there exists no special demand for being shown various sides of a question," writes the author of a leading German government text. "There is more preference for exclusive emphasis on one side which appears to indicate pursuit of a firm and clear policy." This prejudice against the political critic was probably accentuated by the activity of the first "generation" of leaders, when Schumacher consistently opposed almost every major policy backed by Adenauer. Also responsible, as the discussion of the Bundestag chamber illustrated, is Germany's lack of that tradition which in Britain is symbolized by the fact that the Leader of Her Majesty's Loyal Opposition possesses an official title and a salary. The Social Democrats gradually grew tired of being regarded as unfruitful nay-sayers, and in line with their general reorientation after 1959, changed their parliamentary tactics as well as their over-all strategy. In an effort to emphasize their "positive" contributions they often limited criticism to questions of implementation rather than policy, and they came to vote against government measures almost as infrequently as they had once voted for them.

The parties do present, of course, alternative views in debate, which Bundestag rules allow to occur during discussions of the budgets of relevant ministries and on the basis of interpellations introduced by thirty members. Since plenary sessions occur relatively seldom, there is not enough time for many large-scale debates in the course of a year. When they do occur, the speeches made have usually been weighed extensively in party committees beforehand, which hardly makes for spontaneity. Enough parliamentarians have taken the trouble to develop forceful speaking styles so that the general level of debating has improved somewhat, and the galleries are better occupied than they used to be. With few exceptions, however, the function of debates in controlling the government by rousing concern and resonance in the general public is still limited. "The prestige of parliament is not great enough for its debates to have a great influence on the shaping of popular opinion, and consequently the government parties don't take them terribly seriously."[5]

A control instrument used frequently in the United States but very rarely in the Federal Republic is the special investigating committee. Its potential for staging pseudo-trials in which personal reputations form the targets of sensational charges has even more unpleasant memories for Germans than for Americans. A number of these committees have been set up to investigate several postwar scandals, but their sensational work reminded many observers of ill-fated precedents during the Weimar Republic. Disliked everywhere, the demagogue is still the nemesis of German politics.

More enthusiasm has been developed for the adaptation to the German settings of a peculiarly British parliamentary institution, the question hour. It was introduced experimentally in the 1950's, when it occurred only once a month. A 1960 rule change provided for question hours at the beginning of each plenary meeting, allowed written questions to be submitted as late as the day before, and permitted supplementary questions. Since this development coincided with a period during which the Bundestag sought to reassert some prerogatives that had wilted under Adenauer, the question-hour soon achieved dramatic as well as in-

[5] Thomas Ellwein, *Das Regierungssystem der Bundesrepublik Deutschland* (Cologne, 1963). p. 138.

formative functions. Ministers and state secretaries, the top-level civil servants who unlike their counterparts in Britain may answer queries for their ministers, were frequently cracked over the knuckles if their responses were deemed evasive or condescending. As it has developed in the Bundestag, the question-hour has, however, not preserved its British character of a series of "happenings" which, whether their value is dramatic or informative, are characterized by their brevity. Although questions are initiated by individual deputies, there is a tendency for the whole party to want to get into the act on issues that are highly political. Thus some question-hours have dealt with only one topic, with dozens of deputies volunteering supplementaries on a series of closely-related subjects. In one question-hour in May, 1965, for instance, State Secretary von Hase of the Press Office was interrogated about spending DM 200,000 of government funds to place unsigned pro-Erhard advertisements in 500 daily newspapers four months before elections. In the course of a half-hour exchange, von Hase was questioned on the same issue no less than thirty-eight times by twelve deputies from all three parties.

THE BUNDESRAT

The second chamber in the German Parliament is unique, in that it is the only one in the world which is in effect a continuous congress of state (Land) ministers who vote in accordance with the instructions of their governments. This throwback to an

---

THE BUNDESRAT

Article 50

The *Laender* shall participate through the Bundesrat in the legislation and the administration of the Federation.

Article 51

(1) The Bundesrat shall consist of members of the Governments of the *Laender* which shall appoint and recall them. Other members of such Governments may act as substitutes.

(2) Each *Land* shall have at least three votes; *Laender* with more than two million inhabitants shall have four, *Laender* with more than six million inhabitants shall have five votes.

(3) Each *Land* may delegate as many members as it has votes. The votes of each *Land* may be cast only as a block vote and only by members present or their substitutes.

organizational form similar to that of the princes' chamber of Imperial Germany resulted from efforts to build up the Laender so as to prevent a return to the German tendency toward ultimate centralization of power in the national government. As presently constituted, the Bundesrat consists of forty-one members of Land cabinets, five each from the four Laender with populations of more than six million (Northrhine-Westphalia, Bavaria, Lower Saxony, Baden-Wuerttemberg), four each from the three Laender with between two and six million inhabitants (Rhineland-Palatinate, Schleswig-Holstein, Hessen), and three each from the three small Laender with less than two million (the Saar, Hamburg, Bremen). In line with the legalist, single-will doctrine that it is unreasonable that a state should at one and the same time have two contradictory wills, the Land votes must be cast as a unit, which means that in cases where Land governments are based on coalitions (as most are), they are usually cast in line with the policy of the strongest Land party.

The Basic Law assigns the Bundesrat much greater legislative power than its Weimar predecessor possessed. Its approval is required for all constitutional amendments, and for all federal legislation affecting the administrative, taxation, and territorial interests of the Laender, rather a broad category. With regard to all other kinds of legislation it can enter a suspensive veto, which, however, can be overridden by an equivalent majority of the Bundestag. In addition to this impressive (by continental European standards) potential legislative authority, the Bundesrat approves federal government ordinances, shares in the election of judges to the Constitutional Court, and possesses considerable reserve powers in the case of serious conflict either between the executive and the Bundestag or the federal and Land governments.

The very nature of its make-up insures that the overwhelming share of Bundesrat work is done in committees. Almost all Bundesrat members are Land ministers for whom the Bundesrat role is a secondary one to which they attend in the course of brief visits to Bonn once or twice a month. By the time they arrive proposals have already been worked out in committees, and in 99 per cent of all cases where only one committee report is presented, this is adopted by the plenary session.[6] Obviously, the question of *who* writes the committee reports is more crucial here than in perhaps any other legislative chamber. The answer is that although Bundesrat members occasionally participate in

[6] Karlheinz Neunreither, "Politics and Bureaucracy in the West German Bundesrat," *APSR*, LIII (September, 1959), 716.

committee sessions, the bulk of committee work is done by their alternates, who are not politicians but permanent Land civil servants. In view of the fact that the upper chamber has at most three weeks to consider legislation submitted by the government (and frequently much less), the Land ministers have extremely limited opportunity to form judgments other than those based on the recommendations of their civil service advisers. Indeed, a German law professor has written that, "In the committees . . . there is in process of growth a tight world of its own . . . in which the permanent civil service and changing delegates from the Land ministries are in their own metier, the world of a bureaucracy with its own laws."[7]

However, seen within the traditional German context, the Bundesrat provides an ideal meeting-place where federal and Land officials can work out differences regarding federal legislation— as well as federal ordinances based on legislation—affecting their respective spheres of responsibility. Though it seems complex, this arrangement provides for a rational division of labor, while also introducing checks to unlimited power; the Bundesrat may be viewed as "providing a stage for the antagonism between the *Land* and the Federal bureaucracies, while at the same time forcing them to some kind of advantageous cooperation."[8]

In effect, the Bundesrat has sought to reinforce its delicate position by utilizing its constitutional powers only halfway and its legislative prerogatives largely under camouflage. It has sought to avoid being caught between the powerful party machines by, for instance, placing the elections of its presiding officer "above politics," rotating this honor according to a fixed scheme. On the whole, it adopted the coloration of the nonpartisan bureaucrats who are officially only its assistants. "A kind of exaltation of the administrative functions of the Bundesrat has taken place, while its political functions are more or less disparaged."[9] In line with bureaucratic aversion to public controversy, it has shunned frank conflict with the Bundestag (only one or two, usually minor, laws a year fail because of its negative vote) and instead seeks to get its way in the secret councils of the inter-chamber Conference Committee. The Bundesrat tends to call the Conference Committee into effect whenever it does not want to assent to a law, but even there the Land ministers argue less

[7] Werner Weber, *Spannungen und Kraefte im westdeutschen Verfassungssystem* (Stuttgart, 1951), p. 91.

[8] Neunreither, *op. cit.*, p. 726.

[9] *Ibid.*, p. 728.

on the merits of the issue than on "grounds of administrative infeasibility."[10] Thus the Bundesrat "obscures its political intentions by cloaking them in recommendations of a technical character so that they will be more readily endorsed by the relatively inexpert lower house. Staff members of Bundesrat Committees claim that this procedure is highly successful."[11] As best they can, the Land representatives try to protect the interests of the Land government against the increasing encroachment of the federal government, since they do not want to be relegated exclusively to the position of carrying out federal laws. At times the Laender even engage in some adroit horse-trading which angers the national party leaders. But this kind of Bundesrat action makes the headlines only very occasionally. On the whole, its policy of "obscuring political issues in administrative forms,"[12] has, in effect, turned it into a sort of federal-Land administrative council which is remote from the public (polls have shown that only one out of nine Germans know what the Bundesrat is) and insulated from the major political currents of the day.

PROVISIONS FOR DEADLOCKS

Adenauer's dominance over his party and cabinets together with the CDU's strong numerical position have all but shielded the Federal Republic from the kinds of crises the Weimar Republic experienced as a result of deadlock among differing branches of the government and other breakdowns in the decision-making machinery. The Constitutional Court, whose role is discussed in Chapter 7, has played an important part in arbitrating conflicts over constitutional powers between governmental organs. However, with a change in the constellation of political forces, it is quite possible that situations will develop which cannot be resolved by the normal techniques. The Basic Law includes special provisions for a number of such situations.

One of these (Art. 63) provides for the situation that arises when the president's nominee for the Chancellorship does not succeed in getting the requisite support of an absolute Bundestag majority. If another candidate can get the support of an absolute majority, he is elected. If, however, the Bundestag remains deadlocked for two weeks, another ballot is called for, and the president has the discretion of either appointing the candidate with

10 *Ibid.*, p. 722.
11 *Ibid.*, p. 724.
12 *Ibid.*, p. 728.

the largest number of votes (even if short of a majority) or of dissolving the Bundestag. Provision for the use of the dissolution power is made in regard to one other kindred situation (Art. 68). If a Chancellor loses his political support in the Bundestag and is defeated on his own motion of confidence, he may within twenty-one days ask the president to dissolve the Bundestag and call new elections. Thus, while the opportunities for dissolving the Bundestag are limited, they do exist under these specified conditions.

The Basic Law also provides for a variety of techniques through which decisions of particular organs may be overridden or the abuse of power checked. Thus the president may be impeached by one-fourth of the members of either the Bundestag or Bundesrat "for willful violation of the Basic Law or any other Federal Law" (Art. 61). He may then be tried, and if found guilty, removed by the Constitutional Court. A Constitutional Court decision can of course also be overridden by amending the Constitution, which, however, requires an absolute two-thirds majority in both houses of the legislature (Art. 79). In conflicts between the federal government and the Laender relating to the manner in which the latter administer federal legislation or allegedly violate federal law, it is the Bundesrat which has the decisive voice (Arts. 37, 84). With its consent the federal government may send out commissioners to give direct instructions to the Laender bureaucracy.

Though normally not endowed with very significant political powers, both the presidency and the Bundesrat may have key roles to play in case of a prolonged deadlock between Chancellor and Bundestag. When the Bundestag refuses to pass a piece of legislation which the federal government declares to be "urgent" and when the powers of dissolution under Article 68 are not used, the president and the Bundesrat may, at the request of the cabinet, declare a so-called "state of legislative emergency" (Art. 81). In this situation the Bundestag can in effect be deprived of its legislative powers for a period of up to six months, during which time approval by the Bundesrat suffices to enact legislation.

BIBLIOGRAPHY

Political System

ELLWEIN, THOMAS, *Das Regierungssystem der Bundesrepublik Deutschland* (Cologne, 1963).

WILDENMANN, RUDOLF, *Macht und Konsens als Problem der Innen-und Aussenpolitik* (Bonn, 1963).

142 — THE FEDERAL REPUBLIC

Legislature

ESCHENBURG, THEODOR, *Der Sold des Politikers* (Stuttgart, 1959).

GLUM, FRIEDRICH, *Das Parlamentarische Regierungssystem in Deutschland, England, und Frankreich* (Munich, 1950).

JOHNSON, W., "Questions in the Bundestag," *Parliamentary Affairs*, XVI (1962), 22–34.

KIRCHHEIMER, OTTO, "The Composition of the German Bundestag," *WPQ*, III (1950), 590–601.

———, "The Waning of Opposition in Parliamentary Regimes," *Social Research*, XXIV (1957), 127–56.

KRALEWSKI, WOLFGANG, *et al.*, *Oppositionelles Verhalten im ersten Deutschen Bundestag, 1949–1953* (Cologne, 1963).

KREMER, KLEMENS, *Der Abgeordnete* (Munich, 1953).

LOEWENBERG, GERHARD, "Parliamentarism in Western Germany: The Functioning of the Bundestag," *APSR*, LV (1961), 87–102.

MARKMANN, HEINZ, *Abstimmungsverhalten der Parteifraktionen in deutschen Parlamenten* (Meisenheim, 1955).

NEUNREITHER, KARLHEINZ, "Politics and Bureaucracy in the West German Bundesrat," *APSR*, LIII (September, 1959), 713–31.

———, *Der Bundesrat* (Heidelberg, 1959).

PIKART, E., "Probleme der deutschen Parlament spraxis," *Zeitschrift fuer Politik*, IX (1962), 201–11.

PRITTIE, TERENCE, "The German Federal Parliament," *Parliamentary Affairs*, X (Spring, 1955), 235–39.

PINNEY, EDWARD L., *Federalism, Bureaucracy and Party Politics in Western Germany: The Role of the Bundesrat* (Chapel Hill, 1963).

RITTER, GERHARD A., *Deutscher und Britischer Parlamentarismus* (Tuebingen, 1962).

STAMMER, OTTO, *et al.*, *Verbaende und Gesetzgebung: Die Einflussnahme der Verbaende auf die Gestaltung des Personalvertretungsgesetzes* (Cologne, 1965).

STEFFANI, W., "Funktion und Kompetenz parlamentarischer Untersuchungsausschuesse," *PVS*, I (1960), 153–76.

Executive

ALLEMANN, FRITZ RENE, *Bonn ist nicht Weimar* (Cologne, 1956).

ALTMANN, RUEDIGER, *Das Erbe Adenauers* (Stuttgart, 1960).

ESCHENBURG, THEODOR, *Staat und Gesellschaft in Deutschland* (Stuttgart, 1956).

HEIDENHEIMER, ARNOLD J., *Adenauer and the CDU: The Rise of the Leader and the Integration of the Party* (The Hague, 1960).

HERMENS, FERDINAND A., *The Representative Republic* (Notre Dame, 1958).

HISCOCKS, RICHARD, *Democracy in Western Germany* (London, 1957).

KNIGHT, MAXWELL E., *The German Executive, 1890–1933* (Stanford, 1952).

LOEWENSTEIN, KARL, *Political Power and the Governmental Process* (Chicago, 1956).

SCHMIDT, HANNELORE, "Die deutsche Exekutive 1949–1960," *European Journal of Sociology*, III–IV (1962–63), 166–76.

SPEIER, HANS, and DAVISON, W. P., eds., *West German Leadership and Foreign Policy* (Evanston, 1957).

WEYMAR, PAUL, *Adenauer* (New York, 1957).

The Administrative System

GERMAN OFFICIALDOM

The shaping influence which any branch of government will have on political traditions will depend not only on its position of power vis-à-vis the other branches of government, but also on the degree to which it can influence patterns of behavior in everyday life. The average American is of course aware of the existence of bureaucrats in Washington and the state capitols, but, except during times of war and depression, his contacts with officialdom are apt to be limited. Many of the government employees whom he does encounter, such as the school principal, the county clerk, or the agricultural field agent, may themselves be only vaguely aware of their place in an official hierarchy outside of their local office. Whether for good or bad, this is a reflection of the fact that as a result of competitive, individualist values and great decentralization, American public servants have never gone very far toward creating an *esprit de corps* of their own. In Germany this situation has traditionally been very different. There, the administrative branch is the oldest of existing political institutions, and for a long time in Prussia its members even considered their experience and impartiality a sufficient substitute for a formal constitution.

It has been well remarked that "in dealing with the 'civil service' in Germany one is dealing with a concept which is vastly wider than that used by most other countries."[1] Under German law the employees of all public law institutions, communities, counties, and public facilities are all part of an integrated body of public officials, a body that includes not only administrators and government clerks, but also teachers, railroad conductors, and the men who read the gasometers. All vie for the status and security of the *Beamte*, the professional civil servant with tenure. Also, the inhabitants of most German provincial towns will more frequently be in contact with officials of the central government bureaus, which, in contrast to American practice, tend to be dispersed all over the country. Moreover, civil service ranks and titles have for generations dominated German middle-class society to such an extent that German businessmen used to compete with each other in philanthropy and public spiritedness in the hope of being granted the honorary title of "Com-

[1] Brian Chapman, *The Profession of Government* (London, 1959), p. 67.

mercial Counsellor"—a title that would lift them onto a social par with the higher officials. And civil service salaries remain to this day an almost universal measuring rod, with everyone from the Chancellor down receiving compensation pegged to the pay of a specified Beamte rank.

The status of its officials, its interpenetration with society, and its reputation of incorruptibility long allowed the German administration to claim the position of a preferred instrument for making political decisions. Many Germans, no matter how opposed they might be on principle to the hierarchical traditions of the administration, still cannot help feeling a greater confidence in its ability to make the correct, impartial decision than in the ability of remote, party-influenced parliamentarians. Thus, whereas in the United States bureaucrats tend to seem more remote than local politicians, in Germany the reverse is true. German citizens are in close contact with the administrative apparatus, not only because of the large number of services that are traditionally state run (railroads, utilities, health services, etc.), but also because most aspects of economic and social life tend to be supervised by officials. This was particularly true of the immediate postwar period, which was not ideal for the Allied attempt to convert the administration into a bulwark of local democracy. The element of localized decision-making which the Americans in particular tried to develop was resisted by officials who believed that only a system based on hierarchical coordination could provide rational and equitable allocation of resources.

FEDERAL AND LAND FUNCTIONS

As a result, particularly after the creation of the Federal Republic, the German administrative system tended to reshape itself in order to conform to earlier patterns. The creation by the Allies of strong Laender bureaucracies did not deter this trend; even under the Empire effective, centralized control had been achieved without greatly expanding the size of the national administrative apparatus. Until the Nazi period, the bulk of administrative functions had remained with the Laender, and indeed a good part of the Land administration's tasks consisted of executing Reich laws. Both the national government and the Laender preferred a system under which the Reich exercised the bulk of legislative power, while the Laender retained control over administration. This allowed the greatest degree of uniformity in basic policy with a considerable amount of latitude in local application. The national administration consisted in part of ministries for the few areas in which the Reich had exclusive jurisdiction, but mainly of authorities who acted as top level planning and supervisory agencies in fields where actual administration was carried out by the Laender. Of course the national government set up norms to which the Land administrations had to conform concerning both internal structure and organization, and thus a maximum of uniformity was achieved.

Administration in the Federal Republic is set up in much the same way. The staff of most federal ministries is relatively small; only the Foreign Ministry, the Finance Ministry (in part), the post office, and the federal railroads possess their own administrative substructure. For the rest, administration of federal programs is carried out by the Laender either as a matter of traditional prerogative, or as a service rendered at the special request of the federal government. There are thus four different ways in which administration is carried out: (1) execution of federal laws by federal administration, for example, the railroads and the post office; (2) execution of Land laws by Land administration, for example, the police and education authorities; (3) execution of federal laws by Land administrations as a matter of right, for example, labor and social welfare offices; (4) execution of federal laws by Land administrations at the request of the federal government, for example, the agencies maintaining the Autobahnen and waterways. The over-all effect of this kind of arrangement is that though an overwhelming share of public expenditure is spent on programs based directly or indirectly on federal legislation, the greatest proportion of civil servants work for the Laender administrations. Thus, if one excludes the railroads and the post office, only about 10 per cent of public officials work for the federal government, about a third are in the employ of local government, and well over one half belong to the Land administrations.

How do the Germans avoid the kind of problems encountered by the United States in such areas as Southern state enforcement of federal voting guarantees or civil rights laws? The fact is that the federal administration has extensive control over Land administration of federal laws. Where the Laender administer federal laws, the federal government may issue binding administrative regulations, may demand the rectification of inadequacies, and may send agents to investigate cases. As a last resort, it may, with the approval of the Bundesrat, force the Laender to comply; the Basic Law provides that the federal government or its commissioner shall have the right to give orders to all Laender and their authorities.

These relationships give Germany a much more uniform kind of administrative system than someone acquainted with the American type of federalism might expect. The tendency toward uniformity leads the Laender officials to accept federal administrative regulations as a framework even when there is no obligation, that is, in relation to the administration of their own Land laws. Such regulations must have the approval of the Bundesrat, which, however, seldom opposes them. On the contrary, all the Land governments conceive it in their own interest to accept such federal regulations, so as to achieve the greatest amount of administrative homogeneity and to avoid haphazard differences between the Laender. After considering this development, some Germans have come to the conclusion that administrative rationalization has "led the *Laender* to derive their powers from the Federal Government and its laws, just as much as the counties and the cities derive theirs from the *Land* governments and their laws. They are as much subject to Federal supervision as the cities and the counties are to Land supervision."[2]

FINANCE AND TAXES

Anyone surprised to find that the Basic Law includes a discussion of the beer tax should consider that in Germany the national government's share of taxes had not only increased steadily at the expense of the Laender and communities (from 40.3 per cent in 1913, to 67.6 per cent in 1928, to 78.5 per cent in 1937), but had reached a climax in the Nazi wartime experience, when no less than 95 per cent of taxes were collected by the national government. The authors of the Basic Law (and the Allies) were determined to halt this trend and not only took great pains to specifically allocate tax sources, but also sought to prevent overlapping revenue claims and to spell out responsibility for tax administration. The result is a "finance constitution," which is so well integrated that a German expert labeled this section of the Basic Law "as the specifically Prussian contribution to a constitutional liberal-democratic state, which otherwise bears more the hallmarks of Rhenish-Bavarian influences. It is surely no accident that the intellectual father of the finance constitution is a former Prussian finance minister."[3]

[2] Heinz Kreutzer, "Bund und Laender in der Bundesrepublik Deutschland," in O. K. Flechtheim, ed., *Bund und Laender* (Berlin, 1959), p. 20.
[3] Karl M. Hettlage, "Die Finanzverfassung im Rahmen der Staatsverfassung," *Veroeffentlichungen der Vereinigung der deutschen Staatsrechtlehrer*, XIV (1956), 13.

As a result, the Basic Law not only allocates exclusive tax powers, but also provides for the sharing of taxes utilized concurrently by both federal government and Laender. Thus the sources of the federal government's revenues include custom

ADMINISTRATION

Article 35

All Federal and *Land* authorities shall render each other mutual legal and official assistance.

Article 83

The *Laender* shall execute the Federal laws as matters of their own concern insofar as this Basic Law does not otherwise provide or permit.

Article 84

(1) If the *Laender* execute the Federal laws as their own concern they shall regulate the establishment of the authorities and the administrative procedure insofar as Federal laws consented to by the Bundesrat do not otherwise determine.

(2) The Federal Government may, with the approval of the Bundesrat, issue general administrative rules.

(3) The Federal Government shall exercise supervision to ensure that the *Laender* execute the Federal laws in accordance with applicable law. For this purpose the Federal Government may send commissioners to the highest *Land* authorities and, with their consent or, if this consent is refused, with the consent of the Bundesrat, also to the subordinate authorities.

Article 87

(1) The foreign service, the Federal finance administration, the Federal railways, the Federal postal services, the administration of Federal waterways and shipping . . . the administration of the Federal defense forces shall be conducted by a direct Federal administration with its own administrative substructure.

Article 106

. . . . .

(3) Receipts from income tax and corporation tax shall accrue . . . to the Federation and the *Laender* in a ratio of 35 per cent to 65 per cent.

(4) . . . The requirements of the Federation and the *Laender* in respect of budget coverage shall be coordinated in such a way that a fair equalization is achieved, any overburdening of taxpayers precluded, and uniformity of living standards in the Federal territory ensured.

receipts (DM 3.4 billion), excise taxes like tobacco (DM 4.2 billion) and coffee (DM .7 billion), but most importantly a 4 per cent turnover tax on most business transactions (DM 19.2 billion) and corporation and income taxes (DM 11.7 billion). Federal and Land corporation and income taxes are administered uniformly with proceeds being divided in the ratio of thirty-eight to sixty-two between the federal and Land governments. They provide the major source of Land revenue (DM 22.7 billion) and are supplemented with sources like the inheritance and beer taxes. Local government is dependent on the Laender for many services, such as education and police, but derives its own taxes from sources that include the real estate tax (DM 1.86 billion) and local business taxes (DM 8.77 billion).[4] Of total tax receipts, the federal government initially *collects* about 60 per cent, the Laender about 25 per cent, and the communities about 15 per cent. In the renegotiation of how the receipts shall be allocated among the various governments, the federal government has a potentially strong position.

Most Germans were appalled at the suggestion that they follow the American practice of allowing the various governmental levels to administer concurrent tax powers independently. Hence, as hitherto, the federal and Land finance administrations are closely integrated for purposes of collecting income and corporation taxes. The chief Land finance officials who administer the collection of these taxes are chosen jointly by the federal and Land Finance ministries, while their salaries and the costs of maintaining the collection machinery are also shared. As the State Secretary of the Finance Ministry has put it:

Today we have one income tax, with two partial claimants, with a split administration active as a Land administration for the Land part, and as a Federal agent for the Federal part of the tax. This is curious enough. But if we had adopted the other method, we would have had two distinct income taxes collected by two claimants, as in the United States where 35 of the 48 states collect their own income taxes parallel to the Federal one. As to the retarded and economically dubious nature of such a double and unequal taxation of income I need not comment here. . . ."[5]

Even with uniform tax rates, the richer and more industrialized Laender command much higher per capita revenue receipts than do the poorer ones. To the Germans, the limited

[4] Amounts collected in 1962.
[5] Hettlage, *op. cit.*, p. 24.

way in which United States federal subsidies try to bridge the great gap between state tax resources in, say, New York and Mississippi, seems quite inadequate. Thus one of the major roles of the German federal government is to attempt to equalize the tax resources in the various areas. This is accomplished directly through the federal budget, insofar as it provides for welfare payments and subsidies to refugees, expellees, and war victims, who are cared for by the Land administrations. But in addition to this "vertical" equalization, the West Germans also have a "horizontal" equalization program, under which the richer Laender must contribute a certain proportion of their tax receipts for redistribution to the poorer ones. The table on this page shows how this worked out in 1955.

The result of this program, supplemented by others, is to provide throughout the Federal Republic something very close to uniformity in the matter of public services and administration, even on the Land and communal level.

THE CIVIL SERVICE

As mentioned previously, the core unit of the German civil service is the Beamte, a permanent professional civil servant who has achieved his position only after passing through rigorous

		PER CAPITA LAND TAX INCOME AS PER CENT OF FEDERAL AVERAGE	
Land	Subvention and/or contribution	Before horizontal equalization	After horizontal equalization
Northrhine-Westphalia	−DM 259.9 Mill	117.2	110.0
Baden-Wuerttemberg	− 105.5	110.8	104.8
Hessen	− .8	97.2	97.1
Bavaria	+ 82.0	83.5	87.1
Lower Saxony	+ 126.5	77.0	84.9
Rhineland-Palatinate	+ 71.6	74.7	83.6
Schleswig-Holstein	+ 174.0	62.3	93.7
Hamburg	− 81.3	171.5	152.7
Bremen	− 6.6	141.3	137.1
TOTAL	+ 454.1 Mill −		

training periods and examinations. Not all public servants are Beamten. Those who are simply public employees (*Angestellten*) or manual workers (*Arbeiter*) may be ineligible for Beamten status because of the lowly function of their jobs, the temporary nature of their employment, or because they lack some of the specific qualifications which allow Beamten to claim lifetime tenure and pensions. Such pensions range from a minimum of 35 per cent of regular pay after ten years' service to 75 per cent of regular pay after thirty-five years' service. Within the public service as a whole there are four broad grades—the regular, middle, superior and higher services. For the middle and superior grades, which include everybody from secretaries, through inspectors, to supervisory officials, requirements include a training period of from one to three years, with subsequent examination. For the higher service, requirements include the completion of university studies (usually in law), passing of the *Staatsexamen*, and a three-year training period climaxed by the passing of a second broad state examination.

In return for security and high social status, the Beamte has traditionally been bound by a code of behavior whose premise is that, unlike other salary earners, he must as the representative of the state at all times exhibit exemplary behavior and self-sacrifice. Thus it was long widely accepted that those who entered into the Beamten status voluntarily limited their civil rights. The Beamte must be ready to take over nonpaid side work, change his place of residence, or work up to twelve hours above the

DISTRIBUTION OF PUBLIC SERVICE CATEGORIES BY LEVEL OF GOVERNMENT, 1963

	EMPLOYED BY			
Category	Federal government	Laender governments	Local and county governments	Total
Beamte and Judges	67,757	552,606	119,289	738,652
'Angestellte'	84,662	295,374	260,218	640,254
'Arbeiter'	90,722	101,769	186,415	378,906
TOTAL	243,141	949,749	565,922	1,758,812

SOURCE: *Statistisches Jahrbuch fuer die Bundesrepublik Deutschland 1964* (Stuttgart, 1964), p. 442.

regular weekly norm, which at forty-eight hours weekly is considerably higher than in most countries. In addition, he is bound not only to exercise correct and conscientious behavior on the job, but also to behave in private life so as to command the respect and confidence which his profession requires. The Beamten Law also enjoins him to look after the "reputation of members of his family," which in a commentary is held to include assuring "modest behavior by his spouse." The provision that he is allowed to accept gifts only with the permission of his superiors was ignored, in the course of the 1950's, by a fair number of federal officials who seemed to be under the impression that methods which prevailed in business life should also apply in the public service. A sizable number of prosecutions, particularly against members of the Finance, Defense, and Traffic ministries, but including also a case in the federal Chancellery, served to stem this minor wave of corruption. The German public did not react with as much indignation as it once might have, a reflection of the fact that the Beamte is no longer considered infallible. Many civil servants blame this loss of prestige on the fact that official salaries, especially in the higher grades, have failed to keep up with the general trend. In 1954 a civil service paper claimed that the buying power of the salary of a *Ministerialdirektor* was only half what it had been in 1910. Since then some considerable increases have been made in the salary scale.

The denazification and other reforms carried through by the Allies in the postwar period aroused a considerable amount of righteous indignation among dismissed officials, who held that their basic right to lifelong tenure had been arbitrarily violated. They claimed that the Allied action was illegal under German law and sought not only reinstatement but back pay. Of the fifty-three thousand civil servants removed in the Western zones, only about one thousand remained permanently excluded through German official action.[6] Most of the rest were gradually taken back into various official agencies, and the others enlisted the civil servant's associations to put great pressure on the Bundestag to enact legislation in their favor. They were known as the "131'ers," after the article of the Basic Law which provides that the status of civil servants who lost their jobs after 1945 was to be settled by law. There were basically two categories in the post-1945 group: (1) those dismissed because of Nazi activity and (2) those officials who had previously served in the Eastern sec-

6 Taylor Cole, "The Democratization of the German Civil Service," *JP*, XIV (February, 1952), 7.

tions of Germany now outside the Federal Republic's boundaries. The law which the Bundestag passed in 1951 neatly evaded the political problem involved by lumping the two groups together and giving their members priority in reinstatement to public positions as well as generous retirement options. A Constitutional Court decision of 1954, however, indirectly rapped the civil service over the knuckles. The Court found that the thorough nazification of the civil service had in effect turned the service into a tool of the Nazi regime. While recognizing that Article 131 bound the Federal Republic to provide some sort of care, it held that dismissed officials had no automatic right to reclaim positions in what was essentially a new postwar employment situation. However in practice few were denied a fresh start. In the Foreign Office, for instance, those officials who had been dismissed for anti-Nazi activities fared quite well after 1949. But on the other hand, of the majority who had retained their positions in the Hitler era, "only a few were actually rejected because of concessions they made to National Socialism."[7]

In addition to attempting to remove Nazis, the Allies had also sought to democratize the German civil service by breaking down its caste structure so as to allow the admission of "outsiders" who possessed qualifications other than the traditional legal training or long service on lower levels of administration. The Americans regarded the caste structure of the civil service as a fossilized remnant from the period of absolutism, whose strong *esprit de corps* perpetuated undemocratic and reactionary political values. They felt that the special status held by the Beamte led not only to dangerous claims of privilege against outside criticism, but also to internal administrative stratification which tended to perpetuate irrational methods of administration.

German reaction to this criticism was predominantly hostile. Beamten spokesmen argued that it was no accident that the Americans saw eye-to-eye on this problem with German Socialists. "American liberalism, with its trend toward a minimization of the state, has found common ground with Marxists who want to 'socialize' the Beamtentum. Both want to do away with the remnants of class rule and to achieve a 'classless society.'" The Americans were said to be badly misguided in seeking to destroy in Germany what they themselves were trying to foster at home:

[7] Samuel Wahrhaftig, "The Development of German Foreign Policy Institutions," in Hans Speier and W. P. Davison, eds., *West German Leadership and Foreign Policy* (Evanston, 1957), p. 32.

a feeling of dedicated service among public employees. They were held to be ignorant in failing to realize that the legal prerequisite for German Beamten was made necessary by the continental type of legal system. "American officials do not seem to recognize that case law was abandoned in Germany in the 17th century. This may be deplorable, but adoption of the Roman law system requires for its application the legally trained civil servant."[8]

Only a minority of Germans, mainly "outsiders," agreed with a liberal Stuttgart lawyer who argued in reply that the German Beamte was still excessively concerned with carrying forward his former rulers' role as "carriers of the state's honor." He called for the abolition of the "marriage-like vow of fidelity through which the Beamte dedicates his entire service to the state," as well as for the abolition of distinctions between Beamten and other civil as well as private employees, and a de-emphasis of pension privileges. "The high premium placed on the generous pension forces the Beamte to make do with unsatisfactory or dishonorable working conditions, for no matter how much he disagrees with the legislator or his superiors he dare not leave his job, thereby forfeiting pension rights for which he has worked for years."[9] Such arguments, however, failed to prevail in the Bundestag, where strong Beamten organization influence caused the adoption of a new Beamten Law which embodied no really fundamental reforms. The traditional internal stratification, the difficulties facing entrance by noncareer applicants, and the emphasis on perpetuating the distinct character of the Beamtentum through pension and other privileges have been modified in only minor ways. One of the few concessions consists of the creation of Personnel Committees which check the qualifications of noncareer applicants and review complaints from individual civil servants. Intended to open up personnel policy-making to some degree, their make-up does not, however, indicate that the claims of nonprofessionals would meet with strong support. On the federal level, the Personnel Committee is made up of the president of the Government Accounting Office, the personnel chiefs of the Interior and Finance ministries, three representatives suggested by the two leading civil service organizations, and one

[8] Ernst Kern, "Berufsbeamtentum und Politik," *Archiv des oeffentlichen Rechts*, LXXVII, 108.
[9] Otto Kuester, "Zur Frage des Berufsbeamtentums," *Archiv des oeffentlichen Rechts*, LXXVII, 364.

appointee of the federal president. The federal Personnel Committee has only advisory powers, but its equivalents on the Land level sometimes make policy directly.

To some it appears that postwar reforms have left the German civil service fundamentally unchanged as an institution. Thus an English student of comparative administration wrote in 1959 that "the German public official's status is unique in western Europe" because the German respect for the expert causes him to be placed on a pedestal and idealized to a far greater extent than he is in other countries. Even in somewhat monarchic and Germanic countries like Sweden, Denmark, Austria, and Holland the public official may be "trusted, respected, and in some ways reluctantly admired," but unlike his German colleague he is "not assumed to have a monopoly on political wisdom nor to typify all that is best in the national character."[10]

The traditional elite character of the German civil service is seen as one of the factors that might make the German model applicable to the problems of certain developing countries, for some of whom—like India, Ghana, and Nigeria—a well-trained civil service helped perform some of the tasks of nation-building that their equivalents did in Germany. The federal division of powers on the German model may also be an attractive model for such countries since "it allows the central regime to keep control over policy-making while the constituent states administer the central mandates. In the face of powerful centrifugal forces, new nations may find that administrative federalism offers an attractive solution to some of their thorniest political problems."[11]

In Germany itself, however, much of the old pride and interest in administrative achievements has declined. Upon returning to Germany in the mid-1960's, the outstanding scholar of administration, Fritz Morstein Marx, observed that the degree of public interest in administrative achievements was hardly greater than in most developing countries. He found that the standard of German bureaucracy fell short of the image held by experts abroad, who admired the efficiency it had displayed in earlier eras.[12] No longer an instrument which knows only one hierarchy of values, the civil service has had to accept the fact that political parties, interest groups, and other organizations will not tolerate

[10] Chapman, *op. cit.*, p. 310.

[11] Herbert Jacob, *German Administration since Bismarck: Central Authority versus Local Autonomy* (New Haven, 1963), p. 214.

[12] Fritz Morstein Marx, "Verwaltung in auslaendischer Sicht," *Verwaltungsarchiv* LVI (April, 1965), 106.

being denied legitimate influence on official decision-making. Those who idealize the civil service as an aloof elite unbiased by party, class, or religion seem to be fighting a losing battle, as other hierarchies and bureaucracies effectively contest its pre-eminence.

BIBLIOGRAPHY

BRECHT, ARNOLD, "Personnel Management," and MOTT, RODNEY L., "Public Finance," in E. H. LITCHFIELD, ed., *Governing Postwar Germany* (Ithaca, 1953), pp. 263–93, 326–60.

CHAPMAN, BRIAN, *The Profession of Government* (London, 1959).

COLE, TAYLOR, "The Democratization of the German Civil Service," *JP*, XIV (February, 1952), 3–18.

ESCHENBURG, THEODOR, *Staat und Gesellschaft in Deutschland* (Stuttgart, 1956), pp. 760 ff.

HERZ, JOHN, "Political Views of the West German Civil Service," in HANS SPEIER and W. P. DAVISON, eds., *West German Leadership and Foreign Policy* (Evanston, 1957), pp. 96–135.

JACOB, HERBERT, *German Administration since Bismarck: Central Authority versus Local Autonomy* (New Haven, 1963).

KREUTZER, HEINZ, "Bund und Laender in der Bundesrepublik Deutschland," in O. K. FLECHTHEIM, ed., *Bund und Laender* (Berlin, 1959), pp. 1–21.

SAINTONGE, R. A. CHAPUT DE, *Public Administration in Germany* (London, 1961).

7: The Judicial System and the Constitutional Court

Even more than other Continental peoples accustomed to a codified law structure, the Germans tend to see in the body of law a unified system which covers all possible contingencies arising out of the frailty of man in human interaction. While the citizens of more pragmatic political cultures, like those of the Anglo-Saxon countries, tend to utilize the machinery of law only after having exhausted less formal means of settling disputes, such as compromise and arbitration, the continental European, convinced of the rightness of his case, will go to court as a matter of course. He sees in the judge not a fallible fellow human seeking to decide between conflicting claims and precedents, but an expert trained to apply detailed code provisions and an aloof representative of an abstract justice.[1] Writers, social philosophers, and a surprisingly large number of average Germans have tended to agree with Hegel when he wrote: "How infinitely important, how divine it is, that the duties of the state and the rights of the citizen, just as the rights of the state and the duties of the citizens, are legally determined."

The adoption of the modern German civil law code occurred at the end of the nineteenth century, a century later than in France. It was the fruit of stupendous labor by many legal scholars who paid intensive attention to problems of classification and arrangement. As a result the code, though more useful than the French in that the information it provides is more exhaustive, has a very elaborate and complicated structure.[2] Those who use it have to be thoroughly trained. In the course of their training, generations of German law students have been immersed in the ideological assumptions on which the code is built. Implicit is the premise that the written law is self-sufficient, and that the codes, together with the statutes through which they are implemented and amended, constitute a key capable of deciding all problems that come before the court. Judges are supposed not to seek answers outside the provisions of the written law. This orientation nurtured and accentuated a positivist tradition which had led German legal scholars to emphasize that the law is what the sovereign says it is. Since German jurisprudence has

[1] Herbert Spiro, *Government by Constitution* (New York, 1958).
[2] Max Rheinstein, "Approach to German Law," *Indiana Law Journal*, XXXVI (1959), 546 ff.

tended to emphasize that sovereignty rests with the state (in contrast to the French, who emphasized the role of the nation), justice and the interests of the state became difficult to dissociate.

For want of constitutional traditions or other expressions of community consensus, the Germans were more and more inclined to universalize the philosophical principles of law. This produced magnificent writers of jurisprudence, but it also encouraged super-positivist trends which tended to produce rules of constitutional law so "pure" that their relationship to the facts of social and political reality grew increasingly remote. Thus, in the upheaval preceding the advent of nazism, democratic legal philosophers found their theories inapplicable to the seemingly obvious political problems at hand. Later many judges and lawyers saw no in-compatibility in remaining at their posts as long as the legal frame-work was left standing, even though hollowed out by the Nazis with the substitution of their own arbitrary decrees.

THE JUDICIARY

German judges are very different from their American and British peers not only in their legal philosophy, but also in their training, their professional standing, and the role they play in the decision-making process. In contrast to the Anglo-Saxon countries where judgeships are usually awarded to mature lawyers after successful careers in private practice, German judges get their practical training solely within the judicial administration. At the conclusion of their studies, German law students decide whether to go into the regular civil service, private practice, or the judiciary. If they decide for the latter they must be prepared to go through a prolonged period of preparatory service, examinations, and probationary service, similar to that expected for the highest grades of the civil service and stretching over a period of seven to eight years. Then, in their thirties, they are given lifetime appointments. They are then at the bottom of the judicial hierarchy as local judges with salaries of about three thousand dollars a year, and they can hope for eventual promotion to the highest regular judicial appointments on the Federal High Court, whose members are paid about eight thousand dollars.

Partly because of the very large numbers of judges required to staff the many different kinds of German courts (there are more than five hundred judges in the city of Hamburg alone), the average German judge has in no way the exalted position of his British colleague. He is, at all but the highest levels, very much like a civil servant, dependent upon the Justice Ministry for promotion within the hierarchy, and imbued with a spirit and tradition very much akin to that of the regular civil service. He has been characterized as seeking to clothe himself in anonymity, to hide his person behind his office, to insist that it is the "court" and not the "judge" which proclaims the verdict. Influenced by the traditional teaching that the judge should minimize his own role in the judicial process, he seeks conscientiously to apply the written law and does this with exacting objectivity. He "administers" the law; he does not "proclaim" or "find" it. However, in contrast to the Weimar period when many judges allowed their reactionary biases to distort equitable legislation, the administration of justice in the Federal Republic has left little ground for fundamental criticism, although not all courts have punished high ranking Nazis with sufficient severity.

GERMAN COURT STRUCTURE

The West German court system differs from the American most significantly, in that (1) the regular courts are paralleled by an array of specialized and administrative courts; (2) questions of constitutional law are decided by still another series of courts; and (3) although there are both Land and federal courts, these are integrated into a single hierarchy. The Laender court systems include the lower courts and the middle echelon courts of appeal, while federal courts stand at the apex of both the regular and the various administrative and special court systems. Thus the regular courts have four levels, of which three are built into the Land system and the highest is on the federal level. At the lowest level, there is the district court (*Amtsgericht*) which has jurisdiction over the less important criminal and civil cases. The next highest court, the *Landgericht*, has original jurisdiction over more significant cases and acts in an appellate capacity for district court cases. The *Oberlandesgericht*, the highest regular court within the Land judiciary, is made up of separate senates for civil and criminal cases and has only an appellate jurisdiction. Finally, the highest court of the regular court system is the High Federal Court (*Bundesgerichtshof*) at Karlsruhe, where close to one hundred judges adjudicate nonconstitutional problems arising from the lower courts in all the Laender, and seek to preserve a uniform pattern of decision-making throughout the Federal Republic's regular court system. In addition to exercising wide appellate jurisdiction, the High Federal Court, whose members are named jointly by federal and Land authorities, exercises original jurisdiction in cases involving treason. The widespread Communist espionage activity and other consequences of the division of Germany cause them to be kept quite busy on this score.

In addition to the regular courts and the constitutional courts (discussed below), there are the special courts, which have been well developed on the continent to deal exclusively with controversies relating to administrative decisions, labor-management problems, and other enumerated areas. Most important are the *administrative courts*. These handle all manner of questions arising out of decisions made by administrative organs on both the Land and federal level. Individuals feeling ill served by administrative action can ask the court to review whether the regulations were properly applied in their case. Similarly, civil servants who feel that their claims to promotion, tenure, and pensions have been ignored may ask these courts to review the decisions of their superiors. Basically, the administrative courts are supposed to serve as a check on the bureaucracy, but since much German rule-making is based on administrative decree rather than on legislation, the administrative courts hear many kinds of controversy that would go before regular courts in other countries. Other kinds of special courts include the *labor courts*, which deal with questions related to collective bargaining agreements, working conditions, and the prerogatives of labor and management; the *social security courts*, which deal with cases arising out of the administration of welfare legislation; and the *finance courts*, which deal mainly with problems of tax law administration. All of these special court systems parallel the regular courts in that they have lower courts on the Land level with final appeal centered in a federal administrative court, federal labor court, etc.

THE GROWTH OF JUDICIAL REVIEW

While the regular and special courts are all based on foundations well established before 1933, the Federal Constitutional Court with its sweeping powers of judicial review is only as old as the Basic Law, and its equivalents on the Laender level are also postwar innovations. In view of their traditional respect for legalistic forms of decision-making, one might have expected the Germans to have long ago created a judicial organ which would play a role analogous to that of the United States Supreme Court, but until 1933 a number of factors impeded such a development. Some German lawyers and legal scholars, sharing as they did the continental code law tradition, believed a court to interpret the Constitution unnecessary, since they thought that a skillfully wrought body of constitutional and code law would suffice to settle all conflicts if administered by a trained regular judiciary. Others tended to deny that constitutional law had any special position, arguing that both Constitution and statute were manifestations of the will of the same legislative power.[3] Finally, democrats of the Weimar period were inclined to regard the judiciary as a reactionary clan, not only in Germany but the world over. This impression was, if anything, reinforced by their study of the role of the conservative United States Supreme Court in American politics in the period around the turn of the century. The drafter of the Weimar Constitution had said that his plans for introducing judicial review in 1919 had been opposed by the Social Democrats mainly because they were horrified by the "notorious practice of the U.S. Supreme Court."[4]

By 1949, the perspective of German democrats had undergone considerable change. For one thing, still looking at the American model, they saw from the record of the New Deal Court that progressive judges could deal with social problems in the spirit of the times. But more important was the imprint left by European experience. Not only in Germany, but also in other code law countries like Italy and Austria that had experienced totalitarian or authoritarian regimes, the old legalist belief that good laws would by themselves assure good government was seriously undermined. Recalling that Hitler had come to power without seriously violating the letter of the law, Germans now were more willing to experiment with techniques that would make the Constitution, the law, and the courts into more effective control mechanisms to preserve democratic systems. This entailed giving up the old positivist belief that the realm of law was sharply separated from the realm of politics. It also entailed a dismissal of the idea that sound law was virtually self-executing. Finally it entailed acceptance of the need for institutions which could (1) effectively supervise the judiciary's interpretation of constitutional norms; (2) interpret the Constitution flexibly and yet in line with the liberal democratic spirit which gave birth to it; and (3) possess the power

[3] G. Dietze, "Judicial Review in Europe," *Michigan Law Review*, LV (1957), 564.

[4] *Ibid.*, p. 557.

to enforce a consistent reading of the Constitution on the other branches of government. If the list of functions had ended here, then the powers of judicial review later vested in the Constitutional Court would have been no wider than those exercised by the United States Supreme Court. But the politicians who had observed the agonies of the Weimar system saw additional functions which had to be fulfilled. These included (1) a power which could prevent deadlocks between the various governmental organs by arbitrating their claims to jurisdiction; (2) a power which could exercise great discretion in preventing anticonstitutional forces from using constitutional rights to overthrow the system; and (3) a power which could grant quick and effective relief to individuals whose constitutional rights were infringed. All of these powers came to be concentrated in the Federal Constitutional Court.

THE FEDERAL CONSTITUTIONAL COURT: ROLE AND POWERS

In their effort to prevent abuse of the powerful positions on the Constitutional Court, the West Germans devised a complex and revealing election procedure. Even though bestowing such vast constitutional powers on a court, the Germans showed their incomplete confidence in the political commitment of their judges by providing that only six of the original twenty-four places be filled from the ranks of professional federal judges. Other candidates were to be drawn from the ranks of legally trained candidates in the universities, the legal profession, the administration, and politics. This effort to prevent the development of a rigid "council of elders" was further reinforced by the provision that, except for the career judges (who are given lifetime appointments), most of the members of the court were to be appointed for a maximum period of eight years, with staggered terms to allow for the continued influx of new members.

No political organ is given as decisive a voice in the nomination process as that of the American president. The German procedure works as follows: initially the federal Ministry of Justice provides a list of (1) all federal judges who are eligible for elevation to the Court and (2) all other persons nominated for constitutional judgeships by the federal government, political parties, and Land governments. From these and other candidates, elections are then made, alternately by a Bundestag committee and by the Bundesrat. Elections require a two-thirds majority.

In contrast to American practice, the Court is not set up as a single body, but is divided into two equally large senates which meet together in plenary session only when there are problems of deviating decisions. These occur rarely, primarily because the legislature sought to avoid overlapping by assigning each of the senates a distinct area of jurisdiction. However, due to political pressures and a misestimation of the number of different kinds of cases that would be forthcoming, the initial division of responsibility included in the 1951 law resulted in a gross

CONSTITUTIONAL COURT

Article 92

Judicial authority shall be invested in the judges; it shall be exercised by the Federal Constitutional Court, by the Supreme Federal Court, by the Federal courts provided for in this Basic Law and by the courts of the *Laender*.

Article 93

The Federal Constitutional Court shall decide:

1. on the interpretation of this Basic Law in the event of disputes concerning the extent of the rights and duties of Federal organs or of other participants endowed with independent rights by this Basic Law or by the Standing Orders (Rules of Procedure) of a Federal organ;

2. in cases of differences of opinion or doubts on the formal and material compatibility of Federal law or *Land* law with this Basic Law, or on the compatibility of *Land* law with other Federal law, at the request of the Federal Government, of a *Land* Government or of one-third of the members of the Bundestag;

3. in case of differences of opinion on the rights and duties of the Federation and the *Laender*, particularly in the execution of Federal law by the *Laender*, and in the exercise of Federal supervision;

4. on other public law disputes between the Federation and the *Laender*, between different *Laender* or within a *Land*, unless recourse to another court exists;

5. in all other cases provided for in this Basic Law.

Article 100

(1) If a court considers a law unconstitutional, the validity of which is relevant to its decision, proceedings must be stayed and, if a violation of a *Land* Constitution is involved, the decision of the *Land* court competent for constitutional disputes shall be obtained and, if a violation of this Basic Law is involved, the decision of the Federal Constitutional Court shall be obtained. This shall also apply if the violation of this Basic Law by *Land* law or the incompatibility of a *Land* law with a Federal law is involved.

imbalance in the workload of the two senates. Thus, after four years' operation, the First Senate had received 2,893 cases while the Second had received only 29. The figures somewhat exaggerate the imbalance, since the First Senate handled the bulk of minor constitutional complaints, but the distortion was still great. A partial redistribution was brought about by a 1956 Amendment Act, but by 1959 the First Senate still had a backlog of cases almost thirty times as large as the Second. Therefore, acting on powers granted it under the 1956 Amendment Act, the Court itself initiated a further redistribution which became effective in 1960. As a result, the First Senate is now virtually limited to dealing with most complaints of infringement of civil and constitutional rights, with the Second Senate responsible for most other kinds of cases. Some groups have expressed the desire that the Constitutional Court be reshaped into a one-chamber court, but there remain groups and parties opposed to such a step for fear of concentrating too much power in the hands of a Court majority. Political considerations have also caused considerable wavering with regard to the total size of the Court. The original number of twenty-four judges was felt to be excessive, and in its 1956 Amendment the legislature provided for a reduction to a sixteen-member group. But the deadline for fully implementing this change was subsequently postponed.

The multiple functions of the Constitutional Court, plus factors arising from its role within a code law system, make even a summary description of its jurisdiction complex. Perhaps one might start with its powers related to *judicial review of legislation*. Here the Germans distinguish between the Court's exercise of "concrete" and "abstract" review jurisdiction. "Concrete" review occurs when the Court is asked to rule on constitutional questions arising as aspects of an actual controversy being adjudicated in lower courts. Applicants for concrete judicial review of legislation are regular lower courts, which *must* submit problems of constitutionality that they encounter in the process of adjudication. Applicants for "abstract" judicial review may include organs of federal and Land governments contesting the constitutionality of legislation or the constitutional interpretations of other agencies even without reference to a particular case. In addition, "Everyman" may complain if he believes that enacted legislation (as distinct from the way in which laws are administered) directly infringes on his constitutional rights.[5]

A few examples may illustrate how these powers are used.

[5] Ernst Friesenhahn, "Verfassungsgerichtbarkeit," in *Handwoerterbuch der Sozialwissenschaften*, XXIX (Stuttgart, 1960), 83–91.

A case involving abstract review of legislation was initiated by the Socialist Land government of Hessen in 1957, based on the allegation that a federal law which allowed contributions to political parties to be written off as tax deductible was unconstitutional because it violated the constitutionally guaranteed equality of political parties. Applying sociological jurisprudence, the Court found, on the basis of scholarly and empirical evidence, that some parties received much larger contributions than others from business groups favored by these provisions. It reasoned that enforcement of the provisions would indeed cause those parties close to business interests to be unduly favored and declared the applicable provisions of the tax laws to be unconstitutional because they violated the Constitution's equality clause.[6] In another case, the Land government of Baden in 1951 challenged federal legislation that was to merge several southwest German Laender into the new Land of Baden-Wuerttemberg. Baden argued that the Basic Law so fortified the position of the Laender that they could not be abolished without the majority approval of all relevant sectional groups, but the Court ruled that territorial reorganization could be carried out, even against the will of a majority of the population in one affected unit.[7] In another case, the 1956 Federal Electoral Law was challenged by a small party on the grounds that the provisions that only parties receiving 5 per cent of the total vote were eligible for Bundestag seats violated the equality principle. However, the Court held, in this and similar cases, that such provisions were justified even in the face of constitutional equality provisions because splinter parties prevented an "orderly handling of affairs," and that the legislature could legitimately discriminate against them in this manner.[8]

A second distinct function of the Court arises out of its constitutional power to *decide disputes concerning the extent of the rights and duties of the federal and Land organs, as well as parties functioning within them.* Many cases coming to the German Court under this heading would probably be dismissed as "political cases" if brought before the United States Supreme Court, but the German Constitutional Court must accept them, and is drawn directly into the area of partisan political conflict. Thus in 1958

[6] *Entscheidungen des Bundesverfassungsgerichts,* VIII (Tuebingen, 1952–60), 51 ff.

[7] Gerhard Leibholz, "The Federal Constitutional Court in Germany and the 'Southwest' Case," *APSR,* XLVI (1952), 723–31.

[8] Taylor Cole, "The West German Federal Constitutional Court: An Evaluation after Six Years," *JP,* XX (February, 1958), 294.

when the Socialists were fighting against atomic rearmament, the federal government came to the Court with a plea to prevent the Socialist-dominated Land government of Hamburg from carrying through a popular referendum on the question at the Land level. In this case the Court, siding with the Adenauer government, ruled that the Hamburg action was unconstitutional since matters relating to questions of defense and foreign policy were exclusively the business of the federal government.[9]

But perhaps the most important decision shoring up Laender powers was handed down by the Court in 1961 in the Television case. The issues in this case were rather parallel to those in the famous American case of *McCulloch v. Maryland*, but it was decided the other way. It arose out of an effort by the federal government to break the Laender's control of radio and television by instituting a federal network on a nation-wide basis. Chancellor Adenauer in 1960 singlehandedly chartered just such a network with instructions to begin operations the next year. Attacking this attempt to expand the federal government's functions by a *fait accompli*, the Socialist-led Laender carried the case to the Constitutional Court, which in its decision rapped the Chancellor sharply over the knuckles. It ruled that through his action the federal government had violated the Constitution in manifold ways, most importantly by ignoring the provisions of Article 30, which specified that state functions not assigned to its jurisdiction remained automatically within the jurisdiction of the Laender.[10]

A third broad function of the Constitutional Court arises from its powers to *decide on petitions charging infringements of the constitutionally guaranteed basic rights of individuals*. These relate to the substantive and procedural guarantees of the Bill of Rights (Art. 1–19) whose provisions are "binding as directly valid law on legislation, administration and judiciary" (Art. 1). In order to encourage Germans to feel that the Constitution was a close and living guarantor of civil rights, the German legislature went out of its way to allow citizens who feel their rights violated by actions (such as acts of legislation) against which there is no alternative route of appeal, to complain to the Constitutional Court directly. Their submission involves neither court costs nor even the participation of legal counsel—indeed, an ideal situation for Hans Everyman to bring his woes to the direct attention of the country's highest tribunal!

[9] *Entscheidungen des Bundesverfassungsgerichts*, VIII, 124 ff.
[10] *Entscheidungen des Bundesverfassungsgerichts*, XII, 205 ff.

The legislators might have foreseen that in a country as legalist as Germany such generous provisions would bring the Court a flood of complaints. Petitions have come in at the rate of over five hundred a year, and they have made up about 80 per cent of all items brought before the Court. Many complaints have been of a nuisance variety. Petitions have contended that police regulations relating to the closing of bars constituted infringements of the right of assembly, while prostitutes have argued that regulations against "loitering" conflicted with guarantees relating to the right to freedom of occupation and the right to choose one's place of work.[11] Serious complaints have also come in, and account for about half of all the Constitutional Court decisions. But the problem of weeding out serious from "freak" complaints has imposed a serious strain on the Court's work, especially since it does not have the United States Supreme Court's selective power based on a discretionary granting of writs of *certiorari*. Since 1956, however, the Court has been permitted to defend itself against the flood of constitutional complaints by the setting up in each senate of three-man committees which can by unanimous vote dismiss complaints unless decisions in the case will either help clarify a question of constitutional interpretation, or prevent the appellees from being exposed to a great and otherwise unavoidable disadvantage.

In still another role, the Court has the power to *deprive groups and individuals of normal constitutional rights if they engage in enumerated kinds of antidemocratic and anticonstitutional behavior*. This role of the Court as a kind of constitutional police-judge came into play in particular in two cases involving the outlawing of antidemocratic parties. The first of these arose as a consequence of the initial success achieved by extreme nationalist, neo-Nazi groups in the period immediately after the Allies' licensing requirements for the founding of political parties were dropped. The Socialist Reich party (SRP) included among its leaders men closely associated with the Nazi regime who copied Nazi agitation tactics in order to whip up antidemocratic sentiments among voters, particularly in sections of North Germany. Organized in a conspiratorial manner, the SRP made startling gains, winning 11 per cent or more of the popular vote in some Land and communal elections in 1950 to 1951. After having gathered evidence of the party's internal make-up and its public slogans, the government presented to the Court a motion to outlaw the party as unconstitutional, in line with the applicable pro-

[11] Cole, *op. cit.*, p. 288.

visions of the Basic Law. The Court acceded to this motion in its decision of October, 1952.

The second case, involving the Communist party, was submitted by the government at the same time, but a decision was delayed for over four years. One difficulty encountered in this case was that while the relevant Basic Law clause had been clearly intended to hinder the growth of neo-Nazi parties, its application to a party like the Communists was not self-evident. Communist delegates had helped to write the Basic Law, and

BASIC RIGHTS

Article 1

(1) The dignity of man shall be inviolable. To respect and protect it shall be the duty of all state authority.

(2) The German people therefore acknowledges inviolable and inalienable human rights as the basis of every human community, of peace and of justice in the world.

Article 3

(1) All men shall be equal before the law.

(2) Men and women shall have equal rights.

(3) No one may be prejudiced or privileged because of his sex, descent, race, language, homeland and origin, faith or his religious and political opinions.

Article 5

(1) Everyone shall have the right freely to express and to disseminate his opinion through speech, writing and illustration and, without hindrance, to instruct himself from generally accessible sources. Freedom of the press and freedom of reporting by radio and motion pictures shall be guaranteed. There shall be no censorship.

Article 8

(1) All Germans shall have the right, without prior notification or permission, to assemble peacefully and unarmed.

(2) For open air meetings this right may be restricted by legislation or on the basis of a law.

Article 14

(1) Property and the right of inheritance shall be guaranteed. The contents and limitations shall be determined by legislation.

(2) Property shall involve obligations. Its use shall simultaneously serve the general welfare.

Communist ministers had served in West German Land governments as late as 1948. But with the increasing tension between the
East and West German regimes, the Court found itself "unable to
avoid rendering a decision in the face of continuing pressure
from a government with its eye on both internal and foreign
policies." Basing its decision on extensive materials seized in successive raids on Communist party headquarters, the Court decided
that the Communists' campaign could, in the total perspective,
be interpreted in only one way: "It is the result of a planned program of agitation which seeks to expose the constitutional system
of the Federal Republic to slight and contempt . . . and to shake
the people's confidence in the values it has created." In its decision
of August, 1956, the Court thus added the Communists to the list
of banned parties.[12]

The Constitutional Court has several other functions, including powers (1) to make decisions on constitutional questions
arising out of election proceedings; (2) to decide whether parts
of international law are binding on Germans; and (3) after im-
peachment by a legislative body, to try the federal president and
federal and Land judges on charges of having violated the Constitution. It also had the power to give advisory opinions, but
this was ended in 1956. The Laender constitutional courts adjudicate in questions relating to the Land Constitution in much the
same way as the Federal Constitutional Court. But their powers
and significance are far more limited because decisions and precedents on the federal level dominate decision-making procedures
on the lower levels.

THE COURT AND THE POLITICAL
SYSTEM

Whenever a court is set up as a third branch of government there
will be those who will question its right to make vigorous use of
its powers so as to overrule the political decisions of constitutional
organs elected by the people. There is likely to be disagreement
between those who argue on behalf of a policy of "judicial
restraint" and others who expound a doctrine of "judicial dynamism."

Some German constitutional law experts soon began to cry
alarm that the Court was using its powers with too much

[12] Edward McWhinney, "The German Federal Constitutional Court
and the Communist Party Decision," *Indiana Law Journal*, XXXII (1957),
295–312.

abandon. In discussing the Court's decisions in 1954, one law professor took the Court sharply to task for allowing itself to express opinions about historical developments under the Nazi regime.

The great judicial art of moderation, the traditional judicial wisdom of saying only what is necessary for the decision of a particular case, seems not to stand in particularly high regard in our highest Court. Rather, there is a tendency toward elaboration and pedagogic explanation which is not suitable. . . . It is never the task of a court, not even of a constitutional court, to enunciate historical lessons which are not pertinent to the case, or which are at least not necessary. . . . The Constitutional Court should remain what it was created: our highest Court, the protector of the Constitution. But it should not regard itself as *Praeceptor Germaniae*![13]

Other critics attacked the Court's concept of its role as being one of building up the Constitution by handing down opinions which would form a substantial philosophical structure on which its successors, as well as other political organs, should seek to build. "The real task of a constitutional court is not . . . to set up abstract rules for interpretation, but to bring concrete differences to a peaceful solution, and, by checking the validity of norms, to secure general respect for the permanent constitution."[14]

Other criticism blames the Basic Law, rather than the judges, for the Court's deep involvement in the making of so many political decisions. The Court is seen as having to exercise "vast functions in the regularization of political dynamics far beyond the practice of most other constitutions. . . . In many instances in which, in other political civilizations, the compromise of conflicting interests is left to the natural dynamism of political forces (parties, state organs, public opinion), in Germany it is the judges who are called upon to decide. . . . One may well speak of a judicialization of political dynamics."[15] One deplorable effect of this "judicialization" is that the Court's wide powers have been a factor in retarding general acceptance of a body of political, as distinct from legalistic, "rules of the game." It will be seen from the kinds of cases brought to the Court, particularly under the second category enumerated above, that a political party or gov-

---

[13] Otto Bachof, "Beamte und Soldaten," *Oeffentliche Verwaltung*, VII (1954), 226.

[14] Ulrich Scheuner, "Das Bundesverfassungsgericht und die Bindungskraft seiner Entscheidungen," *Oeffentliche Verwaltung*, VII (1954), 647.

[15] Karl Loewenstein, "Justice," in E. H. Litchfield, ed., *Governing Postwar Germany* (Ithaca, 1953), p. 262.

ernment organ can usually find a constitutional law "handle" through which to bring almost any political dispute to the Court. This means that in Germany a political party or a government organ that is defeated on a particular issue as a result of a parliamentary vote or even an election tends not to reconcile itself to this defeat. Rather, convinced of the rightness of its position, it will engage in prolonged legal proceedings before the Court, in the hope of perhaps overthrowing the earlier decision or at least deriving some political benefit from a Court ruling on a technical point. So much of the prestige of the British Parliament rests on the fact that a decision of Parliament is final and can be reversed only when the electors turn the opposition into the government party. In Germany, the legislature is frequently regarded not as the final arbiter whose decision can only be changed by the voters, but as a trial arena for arguments which may eventually be submitted to the Constitutional Court.

However, as Professor Taylor Cole wrote in 1958, "There does not appear to be any major pressure group in Germany which seeks to restrict the jurisdiction of the Court, and there are increasing evidences of growing popular support and appreciation of its work."[16] The Germans, as yet incompletely adjusted to the idea that in a pluralistic democracy decisions are made by groups and not by a fictional all-embracing state, welcome the presence of a strong reviewing power. Commenting that interest group pressure frequently causes laws to be more "ad-hoc commands in favor of a certain group than a well-balanced rule promoting the common weal," a member of the Court has written that it is "quite natural" that the judiciary should be called upon to exert a countervailing effect on behalf of "the individual and the whole community."[17] This argument might seem quite alien to an Englishman, but familiar and reasonable to an American. Germans, like Americans, although for different reasons, favor the idea of an arbiter who can curb irresponsibility on the part of the political power-holders in the executive and the legislature.

"It may be that a Supreme Court should not act as the 'school board' of the nation, but there are dangers too, in allowing unbridled political majorities to act as the ultimate electoral determinants of the nation." Evaluating the German Constitutional Court from this perspective, McWhinney believes that the Constitutional Court acted wisely in moving slowly toward a more

[16] Cole, *op. cit.*, p. 305.
[17] H. G. Rupp, "Judicial Review in the Federal Republic of Germany," *Amer. Jl. of Comp. Law*, IX (1960), 46.

activist position. "The political consolidation that this policy of hastening slowly allowed the court to achieve, the gathering of group confidence as a collegial body, and the increasing technical sophistication as a constitutional tribunal, were all necessary to the sophisticated outcome and public acceptance of the resolutely activist role that the court ventured on in later years."[18]

BIBLIOGRAPHY

BAADE, H. W., "Social Science Evidence and the Federal Constitutional Court of West Germany," *JP*, XXIII (1961), 421–61.

COLE, TAYLOR, "The West German Federal Constitutional Court: An Evaluation after Six Years," *JP*, XX (February, 1958), 278–307.

DIETZE, G., "America and Europe, Decline and Emergence of Judicial Review," *Virginia Law Review*, XLIV (1958), 1233 ff.

Entscheidungen des Bundesverfassungsgerichts, (Tuebingen, 1952–date).

FELD, W., "German Administrative Courts," *Tulane Law Review*, XXXVI (1962), 495 ff.

KIRCHHEIMER, OTTO, Political Justice: The Use of Legal Procedure for *Political Ends* (Princeton, 1961).

LEIBHOLZ, GERHARD, "Der Status des Bundesverfassungsgericht," *Das Bundesverfassungsgericht* (Karlsruhe, 1963).

——, *Politics and Law* (Leyden, 1965).

LOEWENSTEIN, KARL, "The Bonn Constitution and the European Defense Community Treaties," *Yale Law Journal*, LXIV (1955), 805–39.

——, "Justice," in E. H. LITCHFIELD, ed., *Governing Postwar Germany* (Ithaca, 1953), pp. 236–62.

McWHINNEY, EDWARD, *Constitutionalism in Germany and the Federal Constitutional Court* (Leyden, 1962).

NADELMANN, K. H., "Non-Disclosure of Dissents in Constitutional Courts: Italy and West Germany," *American Journal of Comparative Law*, XIII (1964), 268 ff.

RHEINSTEIN, MAX, "Approach to German Law," *Indiana Law Journal*, XXXVI (1959), 546 ff.

RUPP, H. G., "Judicial Review in the Federal Republic of Germany," *Amer. Jl. of Comp. Law*, IX (1960), 29 ff.

WEYRAUCH, WALTER O., *The Personality of Lawyers: A Comparative Study of Subjective Factors in Law, Based on Interviews with German Lawyers* (New Haven, 1964).

[18] Edward McWhinney, *Constitutionalism in Germany and the Federal Constitutional Court* (Leyden, 1962), p. 69.

8: Functions of Land and Local Government

GERMAN FEDERALISM

Many characteristics of the relationship between West German Laender and the federal government will seem unusual to a reader who thinks of federalism in terms of the American model. That the Laender pass much of their legislation in accordance with federal "framework laws," that the Land bureaucracy carries out both Land and federal administration, and that the Land ministers participate directly in the shaping of federal decisions through the Bundesrat—all these are indices of the very significant differences between the American and German varieties of federal structure. In fact it has frequently been asked whether the German arrangement can be really classified as "federal" at all. A leading British student of federalism, Professor K. C. Wheare, is among those who have answered the question in the negative. Following American practice, Wheare argues that the true principle of federalism is based on a division of power in which "the general and regional governments, are each within a sphere, coordinate and independent."[1] In view of the aspects of German federal-Land relationships which have already been examined above,[2] he comes to the conclusion that the German system is not really federal, but constitutes instead a special example of a decentralized unitary state.

Critics have contended that Wheare's true federal model contains too much of an ethnocentric bias in favor of the example of the United States and other Anglo-Saxon countries. Thus one critic argues that: "The rigid requirement of the mutual independence of the executive and legislative institutions of both levels is at best a product of historical circumstances, and not an indispensable part of a general definition of federalism." The German arrangement, according to this point of view, is characterized by coexistence and voluntary cooperation leading to a functional separation under which the federal government is assigned the bulk of legislative power while the states exercise most administrative powers. Hence the West German arrangement is seen as an example of "executive-legislative federalism."[3]

[1] K. C. Wheare, *Federal Government*, 3d ed. (London, 1953), p. 11.
[2] See above, pp. 136–40, 144–46.
[3] Peter H. Merkl, "Executive-Legislative Federalism in West Germany," *APSR*, LIII (1959), 732–41.

Whatever the terms employed, the discussion of the merits of the American and German types of federalism continues unabated. A German politician who holds an office for which, from the American point of view, there is little justification, the federal Minister for Bundesrat Affairs, von Merkatz, in 1958 reaffirmed his faith in the native model. "I know on the basis of my own observations in the United States, that the system there is constantly criticized for its lack of any kind of systematic base. Our principle of the close interdependence of the Federal government and the Laender has developed historically and has throughout proved its worth."[4]

The origins of the German arrangement lie in the compromise through which the German Empire emerged under Prussian leadership. "It was painful enough for the non-Prussian states to see the symbols of political power move to Berlin; but they were considerably more apprehensive at the thought of Prussian administrators setting up offices of the national administration in their cities and towns. So they attempted to preserve their integrity by restricting the new national government as much as possible to the new political center, Berlin, and insisting that policy emanating from this center should be administered wher-

---

LAND AND LOCAL GOVERNMENT

Article 28

(1) The constitutional order in the *Laender* must conform to the principles of the republican, democratic and social government based on the rule of law within the meaning of the Basic Law. In the *Laender*, counties and communities, the people must have a representative assembly resulting from universal, free, equal and secret elections. . . .

Article 30

The exercise of the powers of the state and the performance of state functions shall be the concern of the *Laender*, insofar as this Basic Law does not otherwise prescribe or permit.

Article 31

Federal law shall supersede *Land* law.

Article 70

(1) The *Laender* shall have the power to legislate insofar as this Basic Law does not confer legislative powers on the Federation.

---

[4] Ossip K. Flechtheim, ed., *Bund und Laender* (Berlin, 1959), p. 51.

ever possible by local officials."[5] The question of whether the individual states could prevent themselves from becoming over-shadowed under this arrangement depended mainly on their ability to guard their tax revenues and to maintain a strong political position.

Under the Empire the states retained control over the bulk of direct taxes, but during the Weimar period the Reich took important state taxes over for its own use, and during periods of crisis the Laender were dependent on Reich funds to keep their administrations going. Politically, the problem of equilibrium was crucially affected by Prussian predominance in terms of power and population. The Prussian kings who inherited the Imperial mantle had tended to dominate the national scene, but at least they respected the formal rights of the lesser kings and princes. After 1918 the kings and princes were removed, but Prussia remained the German Land which had more population than all the rest of Germany put together. This fact, together with the strong centralist bias of the Weimar Constitution, tended to weaken the functioning of federal institutions during the inter-war period. When Hitler abolished the Laender in 1934 their political significance had already all but disappeared.

The determination to break up Prussia was one of the few important points on which the Allies were in agreement in 1945. But in the formation of new Laender each of the occupying powers followed its own inclinations. In the south the Americans re-created Bavaria and combined smaller territories to form the Laender of Hessen and Wuerttemberg-Baden, both of which had some historical traditions. On the left bank of the Rhine the French combined the former Bavarian province of Palatinate with parts of Hessen and Rhenish Prussia to form Rhineland-Palatinate. The British combined other formerly Prussian areas to create the large and heavily industrialized state of Northrhine-Westphalia, while further to the north they shaped other ex-Prussian areas to make the Laender Lower Saxony and Schleswig-Holstein. Together with the two city-states of Hamburg and Bremen and (since 1956) the Saar, these constitute the Laender of the Federal Republic. The attachment of the population to their Laender varies considerably, growing less intense as one moves from south to north. Polls have shown that only one out of four West Germans would be upset if the Laender were abolished. In 1954 to 1955 the people of Lower Saxony were four to one in favor of

[5] Karlheinz Neunreither, "Federalism and the West German Bureaucracy," *Political Studies*, VII (1959), 235.

dissolution, those of Northrhine-Westphalia two to one, and those in Bavaria split one to one. If there are any genuine state's rights advocates in Germany they tend to be the Bavarians.

LAND POLITICS

For the most part the structure of the Land governments closely resembles that of the federal government. They are based on the parliamentary system, and (except for Bavaria) they have a uni-cameral legislature (*Landtage*). Elections to the Landtage are made on the basis of varying Land election laws, all of which, however, embody modifications of the principle of proportional representation. The executive is composed of a minister-president and a cabinet, but the powers of the former are considerably more limited than are those of the Chancellor in Bonn. Land cabinets usually are fairly small, and the ministers are appointed by the minister-president on the advice of parties participating in the government. Because the prime function of Land governments lies in administration rather than in policy-making, the parties represented in the government tend to nominate leaders with administrative experience for the cabinet positions. The latters' salaries are pegged at a specific fraction, 70 per cent, of the salaries of federal ministers. Since these in turn are fixed in relation to prevailing civil service scales, the salaries of both civil service and political decision-makers on both federal and Land levels are closely linked.

Many Land ministries constitute positions of considerable power, especially those relating to areas where the federal government plays a relatively small role. This holds true, for instance, for the Land ministers of the interior, who set down policies for the police, and the Land ministers of education and culture, who are instrumental in handling perennial "hot" issues like those dealing with the question of whether public schools should be maintained on an integrated or denominational basis. Since the Catholic church presses for the maintenance of separate public schools for Catholic and Protestant, school controversies frequently break out, and Land ministers of education can quickly become very well known indeed. However the bulk of the work of other ministers tends to revolve around more prosaic problems of how to administer policies which are basically determined in Bonn.

Despite this, Land politics have by no means been just a haven for those who can't succeed on the federal level. For one thing, the fact that the Laender existed for several years before the federal government caused the former to attract many of the most able politicians as well as some of the best civil servants. Many of these politicians stayed on at the Land capitals, and they, in turn, have been able to encourage the progress of potential younger successors by smoothing their way to prominence on the Land level. The concentration of talent has been particularly evident among Socialist Land politicians, since these have never even been given an opportunity to assume office on the federal level. Some of the ablest SPD politicians—such as Max Brauer and Wilhelm Kaisen, the Lord Mayors of Hamburg and Bremen, August Zinn, the minister-president of Hessen, Waldemar von Knoerringen, the leader of the Bavarian Socialists, and Willy Brandt, the mayor of Berlin—have made their names on the Land level.

No parallels can be found in American state politics to figures like Altmaier and Zinn, who in 1966 were close to completing two continuous decades as heads of their Land cabinets. Even in one-party states, which these two Laender resemble as regards voting results, American state governors are faced by obstacles like constitutional limitations on re-election and the challenges of ambitious young men in primary elections. These limitations are much less operative in Germany. Because they are party- rather than candidate-centered and because they work through a parliamentary system, German election laws place few limitations on the tenure of an individual politician. In this they reflect the attitude of most Germans who see no reason to remove an able man from office just when he has accumulated considerable experience. Challenges from young men are also relatively rare, because party organizations are so strong that an individual or clique can rarely cause an upset in a nomination struggle at a party convention or parliamentary caucus. Moreover, since Land politicians are guided largely by administrative norms, scandals which might have been used against incumbents have also been infrequent, except perhaps in Bavaria. Thus the younger generation who began their political careers in the postwar period have had to make haste slowly. They carried off their earliest successes in the FDP, where the elderly generation was squeezed from leadership in many places already before 1960. But in both the CDU and SPD the pressure from the younger politicians in the 30–40 age bracket became particularly intense in the mid-1960's. With age cohorts lending each other assistance it proved possible to deny renomination to many venerable Landtag and Bundestag representatives so as to make room for fresh blood.

In many Laender, government changes have been more frequent as the result of changing coalition arrangements. During his period of dominance Adenauer sought to force all CDU Land parties to leave coalitions with the SPD, and in the mid-1950's most Land cabinets were either composed on the "Bonn pattern" or SPD-dominated.[6] In the 1960's something of a reverse trend set in, so that all kinds of party coalitions may now be found on the Land level. The FDP, for instance, was in 1965 allied in three Laender with the Social Democrats and in four with Christian Democrats. There were also several Land cabinets where the SPD and the CDU formed the government. The recruitment pattern for Land ministers might surprise those American students of British politics who are startled that British MP's often run in constituencies in which they do not even reside. In Germany even Land ministers are brought in to their job from another Land because of their expertise. Their lack of grass-roots political support is little handicap since the party provides all the support they need, while intimate knowledge of the structure of a particular Land is less necessary because so many aspects of administration are uniform throughout the country.

Although Land parliaments have the same four-year term as the Bundestag, Land election dates do not coincide with federal elections. Rather they occur one or two at a time at different dates. This contributes to lower voting turnouts and different voting patterns than are evident in the federal elections. Thus the Social Democrats, until the mid-1960's, consistently obtained better results in Landtag campaigns, mainly because their voters were more disciplined than the marginal CDU voters who were brought out by Adenauer's appeal but often did not bother to vote in Land elections. Over time, however, the Landtag elections have mirrored the same trend toward a two-party system that has become evident on the federal level. Thus, whereas the combined CDU and SPD share of the Northrhine-Westphalia Landtag vote in the early 1950's amounted to 69.2 per cent, it had risen to 89.7 per cent in the mid-1960's. In Bremen and Schleswig-Holstein, predominantly Protestant Laender where the CDU was originally weakly established, the change in the corresponding figures is even more significant, from 48.1 per cent to 83.5 per cent, and from 47.3 per cent to 84.2 per cent respectively. Although they held out longer on the Land than on the federal level, small and especially regionally based parties have gradually disappeared even from the Landtag. Except for several north German Laender,

[6] Arnold J. Heidenheimer, "Federalism and the Party System: The Case of West Germany," *APSR*, LII (1958), 809–28.

the FDP has also lost much of the strength it showed in the early Landtag elections.

Bavaria constitutes the only significant regional phenomenon in German politics, and even that isn't as distinctive as it used to be. Thus quite a few of the numerous smaller parties which twenty years ago ran candidates only in Bavaria have disappeared since. However, the Christian Social Union, the Bavarian affiliate of the CDU, remains as a token that Bavaria is different. The CSU is the only Land branch of any of the three major branches which bears a name different from that of the Federal party. It also boasts that its party organization is independent from that of the Federal CDU, and maintains a Bundestag *Fraktion* which is not integrally a part of the CDU. For many years this Bavarian independence was relatively nominal, but after Franz Josef Strauss became leader of the CSU he emphasized its distinctiveness in order to establish a personal power base. Thus CDU Chancellors have been forced to bargain for CSU support for cabinets just as they have with other coalition partners. The internal politics of the CSU are notable particularly for the bitter factionalism that prevails. These provide plenty of color and are reported widely in the newspapers of other areas where Land politics are less dramatic.

LOCAL GOVERNMENT

Though many German cities can look back to periods of medieval splendor when they counted among the leading political powers in Germany, today (except for the city-states of Hamburg, Bremen, and West Berlin) they owe their status to the Laender just as American cities owe theirs to the states. Because of the diversity of regional development there has been considerable variety in the kind of governmental forms adopted on the municipal level. The Rhineland cities, for instance, under Napoleonic influence developed a very centralized system (which might best be called the *dominant mayor* pattern) under which mayors elected by the city councils for terms of twelve years were unchallenged heads of the city administration while also serving as presiding officers of the city councils. Chancellor Adenauer held this kind of position as Buergermeister of Cologne from 1917 to 1933. In the Prussian areas of North Germany, by contrast, the municipal government was based on the *Magistrat* type, in which executive power lay in the hands of a plural board of magistrates elected by the council, who at the same time served as the upper house of a bicameral municipal legislature. In South Germany yet another system prevailed (the *council* type) under which the city council, made up of the elected members and the chief city administrators, was a unified organ responsible for both legislation and administration. All three of these systems included the figure of the Buergermeister, but he had much less power under the latter two systems. In their own way, the Nazis wrought uniformity through the German Municipal Government Act of 1935 which abolished all elections on the local level. Mayors and city councillors were appointed after consultation between local and national Nazi leaders and the Reich Ministry of Interior, and became agents of the Nazi party and the national government.

The postwar period was characterized by a tendency to return to the pre-Nazi system, modified however by an attempt on the part of the occupying powers to break up undue concentrations of communal power. The British, especially, sought to reduce or abolish the power of the mayor and magistrates by splitting the political and administrative functions of the chief local officials and vesting all executive and legislative power exclusively in the council (on the British model). They abolished the magistrate boards, reduced the mayor to the position of chairman of the city council, and centered administrative powers in a nonpolitical city manager (*Gemeindedirektor*) who was made responsible to the elected city council. This *council-manager* system has prevailed in Northrhine-Westphalia and Lower Saxony. Schleswig-Holstein, on the other hand, returned to a *Magistrat* system, but a weakened one under which this collegial executive is no longer also a second legislative chamber, while its members are subject to recall by the city council. Most cities in Hessen operate with the same system. The French also tried to get the Germans in their zone to abandon the dominant mayor form (even though it had been inspired by Napoleon), but they were less successful, and Rhineland-Palatinate reinstalled the dominant mayor system in 1948. Fewer problems were encountered in South Germany where the Americans found the old council system to be acceptable in terms of distribution of powers. Thus in Bavaria and Baden-Wuerttemberg, elected city councils combine legislative with executive powers while a mayor, elected either by the council or the citizens, is the chief administrative officer responsible to the council. This *council-mayor* system is distinguished from the system prevalent in Northrhine-Westphalia and Lower Saxony by the fact that the mayor and not the city manager is the main bearer of administrative responsibility. In addition to these four types of West German city government, there is also the system prevalent in Hamburg, Bremen, and West Berlin, which combines the functions of municipal and Land governments. In these cities the council elects a collegial executive, the *Senate*, which is headed by a governing mayor.

West German county government in rural and small town areas varies in roughly the same manner as does city government, that is, according to regional patterns. The leading organs here are the county council (*Kreistag*) and the county director (*Landrat*). In some areas the Landrat is more politician than administrator, and in others he combines the two functions. The German tradition of interdependence, which inclines to squeeze county directors into the state official hierarchy and to integrate local administration into the Land system, tends to limit the degree of self-determination that local government can achieve. Although the county directors have become more autonomous as the result of postwar reforms which caused them, in the main, to be either appointed or elected on the county level, the Laender have substituted indirect supervision for the direct hierarchical controls they once possessed. The principal control mechanisms that the Laender now use are (1) reserving policy decisions to Land agencies, (2) establishing standards for staffing county agencies, (3) staffing offices of the county director's office with Land civil servants, (4) increasing the county's dependence on Land grants-in-aid, and (5) assigning functions to specialized field units that remain under direct ministerial control.[7] In any case, the cities are financially dependent on the Land treasuries. The kind of equalization which operates horizontally among the Laender, operates vertically among communities, with the Land holding the purse-strings. The average German city is dependent on Land subsidies of varying sorts to cover about a fifth of its budget. In the early 1950's the cities were angry that the Laender were not equitably sharing increases in tax revenues. As a result of their pressure, the federal Parliament in 1956 amended the Basic Law (Art. 106) to strengthen the communities' claims to certain kinds of taxes, and to provide for some sort of fixed key for the division of Land tax receipts between Land and municipal treasuries.

The desire of local government advocates that cities and counties be placed on an equal level with the federal and Land governments by greater constitutional recognition of their role as a "third power" in administration has, however, not been fulfilled. Indeed, local government authorities have not yet succeeded in

[7] Herbert Jacob, *German Administration since Bismarck* (New Haven, 1963), p. 185.

getting many of the Laender to abolish what they regard as the obsolescent middle-echelon district administrations. These subsidiary Land government offices exist in all the Laender except the city-states and Schleswig-Holstein, and, among other duties, supervise communal police, education, and public health activities which are carried out with the support of Land funds. The communal politicians argue that these organs are undemocratic, since they are not directly responsible to any parliamentary organ, and are largely unnecessary in that their functions could be transferred to the Land ministries and communal governments. However the orthodox German view continues to differentiate between the higher claims of the "state" (the Land) and the communities. "The state has not become merely a 'holding corporation' for the communities and the communities have not taken over the role of the state. There has been a democratization of administration on all levels, insofar as free elections for the local and state legislatures are guaranteed . . . and in that these exercise a control over the administration. But the state is superior to the communities integrated within it, as its legislation, administration and legal system prove."[8]

BIBLIOGRAPHY

BRECHT, ARNOLD, *Federalism and Regionalism in Germany* (New York, 1945).

FLECHTHEIM, OSSIP K., ed., *Bund und Laender* (Berlin, 1959).

HEIDENHEIMER, ARNOLD J., "Federalism and the Party System: The Case of West Germany," *APSR*, LII (1958), 809–28.

MERKL, PETER H., "Executive-Legislative Federalism in West Germany," *APSR*, LIII (1959), 732–41.

NEUNREITHER, KARLHEINZ, "Federalism and the West German Bureaucracy," *Political Studies*, VII (1959) 232–45.

PETERS, HANS, ed., Handbuch der kommunalen Wissenschaft und Praxis, 3 vols. (Berlin, 1956–59).

REICH, DONALD, "Court, Comity and Federalism in West Germany," *Midwest Journal of Political Science*, VII, 3 (August, 1963), 197–228.

VARAIN, HEINZ, *Parteien und Verbaende: Eine Studie ueber ihren Aufbau, ihre Verflechtung und ihr Wirken in Schleswig-Holstein 1945–1958* (Cologne, 1964).

WELLS, ROGER H., *The States in West German Federalism* (New Haven, 1961).

WHEARE, K. C., *Federal Government*, 3d ed. (London, 1953).

[8] Erich Becker in Hans Peters, ed., *Handbuch der kommunalen Wissenschaft und Praxis* (Berlin, 1956), I, 118.

PART THREE
COMMUNIST EAST GERMANY

9: One-Party Rule and Its Instruments

THE "OTHER GERMANY"

Most citizens of the Federal Republic find it difficult to "place" the political unit to their immediate East. Although the territory, as distinct from the regime, is accepted as German, there then arises the question of what to call it. Is it to be regarded as "East Germany," as common foreign parlance would have it, or would this not suggest German acceptance of the permanent loss of the Oder-Neisse territories now attached to Poland? Hence West German authorities always refer to "Central Germany" or the "Soviet zone" when talking about the Democratic Republic. Secondly—whether East or Central Germany—is the territory between the Elbe and Oder to be regarded as a state? Formally at least, West Germans refuse to so regard it since their government claims to speak for all Germans and considers itself the only legitimate government in Germany. By 1965 this position, judging by the standard of diplomatic recognition, was still supported with varying degrees of enthusiasm by most of the non-Communist world. The German Democratic Republic, in turn, claims that it is at least as legitimate as the Bonn government, and is supported by all the Communist states. The resulting impasse epitomizes the lack of progress on the question of German unification during the period from 1950 to 1965.

When examined from the point of view of formal milestones of political development, the two hostile German states seem at first sight to show some parallels. Both evolved from Occupation status in 1949, both achieved formal sovereign status in 1954 to 1955, and both have set up military forces which have become integrated with those of their respective power blocs. But though these parallels should not be lost sight of, they tend to obscure characteristics which indicate completely different patterns of development. The sharply contrasting evolution of social and economic structures in the two states has already been described and analyzed (see Chapter 2). Their political systems are so different that meaningful comparison is difficult. Whereas the Federal Republic has revived and reinvigorated liberal democratic political institutions to create a stable parliamentary regime on a constitutional basis, East Germany has uprooted "bourgeois" political institutions and developed instruments to facilitate increasingly totalitarian rule by a Communist party which seeks to turn the rump-state into a proletarian dictatorship.

CAMOUFLAGED ONE-PARTY STATE

Like the other East European Communist-dominated states, the German Democratic Republic (DDR) conceives of itself as a "People's Democracy" at an intermediary stage of development toward a genuinely socialist state on the Marxist-Leninist model. Its rulers believe themselves to be some distance yet from the goal since not all the means of production have been collectivized and because remnants of nonworking-class elements still exist. But these elements have become increasingly insignificant. The East German Communists claim legitimacy for their incomplete proletarian dictatorship by virtue of the numerical and political dominance of workers and peasants. As the result of the elimination of "class enemies" and "reactionaries" and the pushing forward of collectivization, the Communists came to declare (in 1952) that they were beginning to lay the groundwork for a "Socialist" order and later (in 1958) that this groundwork had been completed. These progress reports were made in the context of a theoretical Leninist timetable, but they serve also as rough milestones of the institutionalization of totalitarian characteristics within the political system.

According to its official ideologists, the German Democratic Republic is the first state in German history in which the working class possesses power. "For the first time in the history of the German people the talents and capacities of the broad masses can develop freely. There has developed a powerful increase in the awareness, initiative, activity and work-discipline of the workers, farmers and other productive citizens."[1] Such bombastic language betrays the debt which the East Germans owe to the ideologists

---

[1] From 1957 DDR law relating to local government, cited in Bundesministerium fuer Gesamtdeutsche Fragen, *Unrecht als System: Teil III, 1954–58* (Bonn, 1958), p. 11.

of Soviet communism, and indeed the Soviet influence has been overwhelming. Not only did the political officers attached to Soviet Occupation agencies facilitate the Communist rise to dominance, but the leading figures of the regime received extensive training in Soviet party schools, and in times of crisis Soviet advisers have stood by with advice (and sometimes orders), while Soviet troops and tanks have been available to discourage dissenters. If Communist institutions have been imposed with somewhat less brutality and in more disguised form than in some of the other "people's democracies," this has been due less to moderation on the part of the German or Russian Communists than to the fact that the exposed geographical position of the Democratic Republic limited the amount of pressure which could be applied at any one time. This factor has also dictated the continued use of a constitution which formally provides for a multi-party parliamentary system and other democratic devices. But even the continued existence of "non-Socialist" parties, which in reality completely follow the Communist lead, does not disguise the fact that the Democratic Republic is a totalitarian one-party state. The ruling party calls itself—for reasons which will be explained shortly—the Socialist Unity party (SED).

The Communists make no bones about the fact that the state is essentially an instrument to advance the policy of the party. Assuming as they do that the working class is the legitimate ruler and that the SED executes policy on its behalf in line with Marxist socio-historical laws of political development, the Communists have little difficulty in convincing themselves that "the decisions of the party constitute the highest scientific generalizations derivable from political practice."[2] That their workers' and farmers' state is led by a Marxist-Leninist party they regard not as convenient fact but as irrevocable law. The SED party statutes, adopted in 1954, recognize this manifest destiny by declaring that the party is the force not only supervising all other social and political organizations, but also dominating the governmental apparatus of the state. In its instructional material the party even tells its younger members that in the governmental machinery "not even a single decision is taken without reference to the guiding directions worked out by the party."[3] It is because the SED regards itself as the center of state power and acts accord-

[2] A 1956 speech of SED Central Committee functionary, cited in Bundesministerium fuer Gesamtdeutsche Fragen, *op. cit.*, p. 19

[3] A 1956 collection of SED teaching materials, cited in Bundesministerium fuer Gesamtdeutsche Fragen, *op. cit.*, p. 15.

ingly that an analysis of the functioning of the formal political organs of the Democratic Republic must necessarily be preceded by a study of the origins and organization of the party and the means at its disposal to maintain tight control over both society and state machinery.

The relationship between the party and the governmental apparatus is the most vital link in the totalitarian system, and it is not a simple one. The party does not merely make decisions and leave it to nonpolitical bureaucrats in the administration to carry them out, nor does the party apparatus as such try to run everything. Rather, the party exercises power indirectly in a number of ways. It sets the policies which the administration is to carry out, but it sends its *own* members—above all politically reliable and if possible technically qualified—into the administration to supervise their execution. Then, periodically, the work of the functionaries in the government machinery is reviewed and criticized by party organs to make sure that the decisions were really followed through in spirit as well as in letter. Moreover, since it is a totalitarian party which seeks to reshape the entire social structure according to its ideological dictates, the party must also make sure that its "line" is not only adhered to by important power-wielders, but permeates as much as possible into every nook and cranny of the social structure. To this end it manipulates a vast network of subsidiary social and political organizations whose efficiency must also be supervised. These vast responsibilities, as well as the even vaster ones involved in running a planned economy, must be met by a party whose cadre of active militants makes up perhaps as little as 1 per cent of the population.[4] To understand how the party developed sufficient power and discipline for this task and why it chose the pace and means that it did, it will be useful to review the party's postwar evolution and its changing role in what was originally the Soviet Occupation zone.

POST-1945 POLITICS IN THE SOVIET ZONE

The key to an understanding of political developments in East Germany lies in an understanding of the relationship between German Communists and the Kremlin. Paradoxically, while most of the leading German Communists spent the bulk of the war period in Soviet Russia, they were for the first three postwar

[4] Ernst Richert, *Macht ohne Mandat* (Cologne, 1958), p. 148.

years under specific instructions *not* to attempt to copy the Soviet example at home. Although installed in influential positions in the Soviet-occupied zone, the German Communists did not advocate either the radical abolition of private property, or the establishment of a one-party system, or any other innovation introduced during the early years of the Soviet Russian regime. Instead, there was talk of a specifically German road to socialism, which seemed to entail almost no demands for a class dictatorship, a relatively moderate amount of socialization of the economy, and a readiness to cooperate with other political parties. In an effort to attract a mass following, the Communists opened the party doors very wide. Even a knowledge of Marxism was not considered a prerequisite. "Who can expect honest anti-Fascists to be schooled in Marx and Lenin after twelve years of Fascist dictatorship," said the party strong-man, Walter Ulbricht.[5]

In contrast to the Soviets' plans to quickly transform the East European states into "peoples' democracies," they originally seemed to have no such intentions for their zone of Germany. In a sense, the Soviet Union did take seriously the plans for the eventual establishment of an all-German government, as vaguely laid down in the inter-Allied Potsdam agreement. Therefore they wanted in the Soviet zone not a separate, Communist state, but a beachhead from which to influence developments in all of Germany. They were excessively confident that under the conditions of general devastation large masses of Germans would embrace communism if it appeared in a reasonably attractive guise, and they were hopeful of being able to use their influence as an Occupation power and in the Allied Control Council to shape political development in an indirect rather than overt manner.

Hence the political system of the Soviet zone during the years from 1945 to 1947 displayed many characteristics of a democratic parliamentarianism resting on a plural party system. Democratic political institutions were established on the communal level, the newly created Laender were given legislatures based on open elections just as they were in the Western zones, and anti-Nazi politicians of almost all kinds were encouraged to take an active part in politics. Political parties were licensed earlier than in the other zones and given considerable encouragement, funds, and party newspapers. While the Communist party (KDP) was the first to be established in June, 1945, the Social Democrats (SPD), the Liberals (LDP), and the Christian Democrats (CDU) were allowed to initiate formal activity shortly thereafter. The

[5] Walter Ulbricht, *Die Entwicklung des deutschen volksdemokratischen Staates, 1954–1958* (Berlin, 1959), p. 34.

leaders of the new parties were of course subject to screening by Soviet political officers, but initially this process was little different from that in the Western zones. The parties were also quite free to spell out their programs.

However, as the Communists realized toward the end of 1945 that their hope of emerging dominant from the first Soviet zone elections stood little chance of realization, they called first for the putting forward of joint Communist-Socialist candidates in the forthcoming elections and then for a complete merger of the two parties. Among Western zone Socialists, where Kurt Schumacher had already become dominant, this proposal was sharply rejected, but in Berlin and particularly in the outlying areas of the Soviet zone Socialist functionaries led by Otto Grotewohl, chairman of the Socialist Central Committee in Berlin, were sympathetic. In the prolonged intraparty struggle which ensued, the antimerger Socialists succeeded in winning the overwhelming support (12.4 per cent for merger, 82 per cent against) of party members in West Berlin, and it became evident that even if they forced a party merger in their zone, the Soviets could do so only at the cost of increasing the solidarity and anti-Communist determination of the bulk of the Socialists in West Berlin and the Western zones. After some hesitation, it was nevertheless decided to go ahead, and in April, 1946, the pro-merger Socialists under Grotewohl merged with the Communists to form the new *Sozialistische Einheitspartei Deutschlands* (SED), under the joint party chairmanship of Grotewohl and the chairman of the KDP, Wilhelm Pieck.[6]

This step had many far-reaching consequences besides the one intended of providing a Communist-led party with mass backing and eliminating competition with another working-class party. It was the first important step toward the political division of Germany, for after the spring of 1946 the SPD could no longer operate as a recognized party in the Soviet zone, while the SED could not operate as such in the Western zones since the Western occupying powers refused to license it there. (There the Communists continued to operate independently under their KPD label until they were declared illegal in 1956.) Thus began the tendency toward a development of separate party systems for East and West.

The SED soon went all-out to woo the voters. During the 1946 election campaign, it competed with the CDU for the votes of Christians by calling for political partnership between

[6] Carola Stern, *Portraet einer Bolschewistischen Partei* (Cologne, 1957), Chap. 1.

Marxists and Christians, appealed to nationalist sentiment by asserting that it did not regard the Oder-Neisse border as final, and even welcomed the support of former nominal Nazis and fellow travellers by promising to assure them equal, unprejudiced treatment.[7] But although competing with only two much weaker and less well organized middle-class parties, the SED managed to win only 47.5 per cent of the votes against a combined total of 49.1 per cent for the CDU and LDP. Instead of achieving at least the appearance of an overwhelming democratic legitimation, the SED found itself tied to a parliamentary setting where the resistance of other parties could be broken only by means of pressure.

Starting in 1948 the SED quickly transformed itself, as well as the political structure of the Soviet zone, along lines which now closely resembled Communist practice elsewhere. It de-emphasized its attempt to become a mass party, and sought instead to transform itself into a highly disciplined, efficient mechanism, responding easily to direction from above and capable of controlling both state and economy. Many party members who had joined out of opportunism but lacked the qualities of "good Communists" were purged. New members were accepted only after undergoing prolonged periods of candidacy. The need to transform the SED into a "cadre party" was underscored by the adoption, starting with the 1949–1950 Two-Year Plan, of the principle of the fully planned economy. The consolidation and development of a vast economic bureaucracy that would coordinate and administer the planning mechanism called for large numbers of reliable, trained administrators, which only the SED could produce. Emphasis on ideological purity was accentuated. Those Communists who had earlier advocated a distinctly German road to socialism were forced to recant their heretical views, while Ulbricht and other Soviet-trained leaders emphasized the need for unhesitating acceptance of orthodox Leninist-Stalinist doctrine. The Soviet military administration also displayed its fear of "Western" ideas by decreeing in 1949 that all Germans (even long-time Communists) who had spent wartime exile in any Western country were to be removed from positions of responsibility in the party and the administration.[8]

At the same time, the SED established its position as the fountainhead of all political truth. In 1950, in discussing the resolutions of the SED party conference for the benefit of civil servants, Ulbricht dealt with the suggestion that these were after

[7] Ulbricht, *op. cit.*, p. 74
[8] Stern, *op. cit.*, pp. 118, 127.

all *only* the resolutions of a party. "That is true. But it happens to be the conference of a party which is the spearhead of the German people, the only party which follows a progressive scientific doctrine. . . . Its resolutions constitute a document of the highest significance . . . with which all democratic forces must concern themselves."[9] And well they might, for no leaders of parties, trade unions, or women's organizations could afford to find themselves taking positions differing from those of the SED. All such groups were now united in a cover organization called the "National Front," where the policy of the SED was imposed on the rest. In 1949 free competitive elections ceased to be held, and instead the National Front set up unified lists which were submitted to the voters without an alternative choice. All the parties, as well as other kinds of organizations, were allotted specific quotas within the single list, with the SED's own candidates and SED members running on trade union and other "mass organization" tickets maintaining numerical preponderance. The two middle-class parties, the CDU and LDP, though no longer able to run independent candidates and deprived of most of their original leaders, were distrusted by the regime as channels through which dissatisfaction might express itself. Their role was neutralized by the licensing of two additional middle-class parties, the National Democratic party (NDPD) and the German Peasants' party (DBD), whose functionaries were tested pro-Communists, and which proceeded to rival the two older parties in their efforts to "guide" the nonworking-class, non-Socialist part of the electorate. In addition, the liquidation of organizations perpetuating loyalties no longer convenient to the regime was brought about. Thus the Victims of Nazi Injustice was ordered disbanded because the fraternization of its Communist and non-Communist members was no longer considered desirable. Similarly, neutralist groups which the SED had previously encouraged in the hope of using them to win sympathy in the Western zones were now denounced as vehicles of dangerous, disguised, "pro-imperialist" doctrines.[10]

THE 1953 UPRISING AND DESTALINIZATION

The most difficult testing period for the SED regime came during the transition from the Stalin to the post-Stalin eras. Throughout 1951 and 1952 the SED had to withstand very great

[9] Ulbricht, *op. cit.*, p. 212.
[10] *Ibid.*, pp. 213–15.

internal and external pressures. Internally, it was subject to factional struggles in the top leadership and affected by the various waves of purges which in other East European states were decimating the old line Communist leadership. However Walter Ulbricht's strong hand prevailed and the East German Communists did not tear themselves apart as badly as their equivalents in Poland and Hungary. At the same time, the SED was feeling the tremendous resistance of the bulk of the population to the intensive controls through which the regime sought to increase production, to contain living standards at their low level, and to punish politically unreliable middle-class elements. A consequence of this tough policy was the enormous increase in the number of East Germans fleeing to the West during the first part of 1953. In response to the uncertainty caused by Stalin's death, the regime attempted to demonstrate its control of the situation by depriving certain population groups of ration cards while demanding a 10 per cent increase in the work norms of industrial workers. These measures caused great bitterness among wide sections of the population, and after several weeks the leadership recognized that it had gone too far. In early June SED spokesmen, including the minister-president, Otto Grotewohl, declared that the government had made errors, and promised remedial action.

However the anger, particularly of the workers, broke into the open before the regime could make the necessary concessions. On June 16 construction workers in East Berlin launched spontaneous strikes against the norm increases, and the movement spread like wildfire throughout the rest of the city. Banners calling for a general strike and the release of political prisoners were raised among the demonstrators. On the following day, news of the demonstrations having been spread by radio stations in West Berlin, demonstrations began in most of the other East German cities. Events quickly got beyond the control of local police authorities as the crowds attacked and destroyed SED offices, set fire to official buildings, and stormed the jails and released political prisoners. The SED leadership, finding that its appeals for calm brought no response, was forced to call in Soviet tanks and troops to quell the riots. A state of emergency was declared in most areas and armed troops and police fired on the crowds, causing numerous deaths and casualties before it was possible to disperse them. Giving proof, as they did, of the desperate hostility of large sections of the East German population, while also setting the first example of a large-scale uprising in a Communist-controlled country, the events of June 17, 1953, won world-wide attention.[11] However, as in the subsequent Hungarian uprising, the West could give little effective aid, and order was restored.

Since 1953 the policy of the SED has been marked by short-term fluctuations in which periods of "liberalization" have alternated with stages of "toughness." Shortly after the uprising, the SED, in line with policies then being implemented in the Soviet Union, initiated reform programs which included the promise of an increased emphasis on consumer goods and a greater amount of freedom of expression to trade unions and other groups. Promises to increase the significance of the various legislative organs were among the many not implemented before a new change of course, in 1954, caused the regime to retract or modify many of the concessions it had earlier offered. In 1955, after Khrushchev's denunciation of Stalinist excesses before the Twentieth Soviet Party Congress, the SED once again adjusted to the more relaxed and liberal policies which quickly became the vogue throughout the Eastern bloc. During the Khrushchev era, the SED leadership under Ulbricht followed many of the precedents set in the Soviet Union. One of the reforms in party reorganization taken over involved a shifting of organizational bases from territorial to production of economic units. In the early 1960's this reform was carried through even more thoroughly than in the Soviet Union, reflecting the very high priority the SED leadership had to place on utilizing the party apparatus to maximize production. Ulbricht was himself frequently under attack because of the continued personal build-up he demanded from the party, and there were many who accused him of adhering to "the cult of personality." After Khrushchev's ouster, the SED Politburo in December, 1964, had to explicitly reject these charges aganst him.

Although the DDR entered the post-Khrushchev era as still the least liberalized of the Communist-bloc countries, some minor concessions were gradually introduced. Thus in the communal elections of 1965 voters were offered some limited choice. Although presented with only one list, they were able to vote for and against specific candidates on the list. This merely reproduced a pattern which had been introduced earlier in Poland and elsewhere, but it provided more of an opportunity for electoral choice than had been possible since the very first postwar elections. Most of the intervening elections had followed the usual voting patterns, as in the People's Chamber elections of October, 1963, where a 99.25 per cent participation rate and a 99.95 per cent "Yes" vote for the National Front ticket were chalked up.

[11] Stephan Brandt, *The East German Uprising* (New York, 1955).

SED ORGANIZATIONAL STRUCTURE

Since becoming a "new type" cadre party in 1949, the SED has faithfully followed the organizational pattern of the Soviet Communist party. Party statutes notwithstanding, power and policy control is highly centralized in the Political Bureau, whose ten to fifteen members include the leaders of the party apparatus, the top-level figures in the government, the heads of the most important economic and security agencies, and heads of the mass organizations. As in the Soviet Union, the make-up of the Politburo frequently undergoes changes which reflect the changing power status of differing party cliques. During the period from 1947 to 1960, only five men consistently, or almost consistently, retained membership.[12] Two of these were ex-Social Democrats who held important "show" positions: Otto Grotewohl, the minister-president of the DDR, and Friedrich Ebert, the son of the first president of the Weimar Republic, who is mayor of East Berlin. The three others were all tried Communists who spent their wartime exile in the Soviet Union. Wilhelm Pieck, a cofounder of the KPD in 1918 and later Secretary of the Comintern, was a tried Stalinist who served in top-level prestige positions as cochairman of the SED and, until his death in 1960, president of the DDR. The other two were Walter Ulbricht, the most powerful man in party and regime, and one of his loyal adjutants, Herman Matern, who had in the past helped to destroy Ulbricht's intraparty rivals. Of the other Politburo members in recent years, only one was a premerger member of the SPD, and all were ardent Ulbricht supporters. Men like Fred Oelssner, Heinrich Rau, Karl Schirdewan, and Willi Stoph backed Ulbricht through all his twists and turns and were rewarded for their loyalty as well as their toughness with positions of power.

In theory, the dozen or so powerful members of the Politburo, augmented by a small number of colleagues in the party Secretariat and other key positions, implement policy on behalf of the approximately one and a half million members of the SED. But in practice, the ability of rank-and-file members to call their leaders to account is virtually nil. Organized in some fifty thousand local party organizations, the SED membership is limited by an institutional setting which encourages the carrying out of instructions from top-level party organs but makes effective criticism from the bottom up almost impossible. Though the SED

[12] For a full list of members up to 1957, see Stern, *op. cit.*, p. 326.

strives to assert its popular legitimation by placing top constitutional importance on the decisions of the party convention, this body assembles only for show purposes every four years. The delegates are usually selected so that the convention resembles a cross section of the working masses, which the SED likes to think it represents. Workers and farm hands who have built up good production records are rewarded with delegate positions so that they can listen to the longwinded reports and exhortations of the party leaders. In contrast, for instance, to the pre-1933 Communist congresses where important issues of doctrine were often bitterly fought out, the SED party conventions are very mild affairs. Resolutions and policy statements submitted by the Politburo and the Secretariat are never criticized and always accepted unanimously.

Since the convention cannot even attempt to determine policy, it elects a smaller group of members to do so. This is the Central Committee, normally made up of some 100 to 150 members, and it is in its name that the policy-making apparatus of the SED actually functions. In theory it does this with the assistance of two important advisory bodies; on the one hand, the Politburo, which is authorized to conduct the work of the Central Committee between plenary sessions, and on the other hand, the Secretariat of the Central Committee, which maintains the bureaucratic apparatus through which the party exercises its manifold controls over all aspects of the party structure, the public administration, and society at large. In practice, however, these two organs do not advise the Central Committee, but prepare decisions which the Central Committee normally accepts and publicizes as official policy. In contrast with the party conference, Central Committee meetings are often the scene of fairly lively discussion, but usually over the means of implementing policy rather than over its merits. It also frequently happens that policies are quietly implemented by party functionaries months, and even years, before they are publicly announced as official by the Central Committee. Thus, in effect, the decisions of the Central Committee formalize acceptance of policies which members of the Politburo believe to be desirable and which party functionaries seem to think workable.

However, the real core of SED power lies only in part in its decision-making organs; equally crucial are the organs that supervise policy execution. It is here that the Secretariat under the party's First Secretary, Walter Ulbricht, plays a key role. The Secretariat is the hub of the party's vast control mechanism, the instrument through which it supervises its own organization, the functioning of governmental organs, and the work of satellite groups. Its work is carried out under the direction of Ulbricht and six other secretaries, several of whom are simultaneously members of the Politburo. Each secretary supervises a number of Secretariat sections, which are in turn composed of anywhere from a dozen to several hundred indoctrinated and trained specialists. About half of the Secretariat sections parallel the formal governmental organs. Thus the Transport and Communications Section has the task of providing suggestions for, and control over, the Transportation and Post ministries. Similarly, the Agriculture Section watches the various state and mass organizations which execute policy in the agriculture sector. Other sections concern themselves with intraparty organization and the channelling of party resources. Thus the Top-Level Organs Section coordinates the work of lower-level party committees, gathers information about the important mass organizations, and acts as a kind of personnel office in selecting and assigning top-level party cadre to their proper jobs. Finally there are sections dealing with the problems of propaganda, agitation, science and culture. The Press-Radio-Agitation Section guides the work of official party organs like *Neues Deutschland*, keeps a close eye on the rest of the East German press, and, in general, seeks to manipulate all mass communication media in line with party policy. The sections dealing with cultural, communications, and education problems are particularly important, in that here much of the work is done directly by the party, rather than indirectly through the state mechanism. Altogether the Secretariat comprises some twenty-five such sections with a total staff of about one thousand experts. On the lower echelons, however, recruitment into party membership has lagged. Between 1958 and 1963, the SED increased its membership by 140,000 to 1,610,679 members, but this constituted an annual rate of membership increase of only 1.9 per cent, the lowest figure in the Soviet bloc. Comparable figures were 9.6 per cent for Poland and 12 per cent for Rumania.[13]

CONTROL AND PENETRATION: THE TRANSMISSION BELT

Since the SED, as a genuinely totalitarian party, seeks not merely unchallenged political control but also the transformation of all East German society into its own ideological image, it requires a

[13] U.S. Department of State, *World Strength of Communist Party Organizations* (Washington, 1965).

vast net of auxiliary organizations with which to penetrate all population groups. While the bulk of its own leaders man the crucial control towers, it relies largely on auxiliary organizations to function as transmission belts through which its slogans and exhortations are hammered mercilessly into the consciousness of East Germans. These are the various mass organizations, some led directly by SED functionaries, others by reliable fellow travellers. They include the organizational remnants of the old non-Socialist parties, the huge trade-union federation, the Democratic Federation of German Women, the Free German Youth, the German-Soviet Friendship Society, and sundry other groups. The vast majority of the East German population has been cajoled into membership of at least one of these organizations, and thus receives official propaganda specially filtered for its consumption. The leading mass organizations are united in the National Front which coordinates their activities. Each group, as well as the SED, sends four delegates to the National Front executive council, where decisions are made without dissent. "This means . . . that all questions put up for discussion and decision-making are considered until such time as a unanimous decision can be made,"[14] that is to say, until the SED line is accepted without reservation.

One of the more public functions of the National Front consists in the setting up of the single candidate list for the People's Chamber and other "legislative" bodies (see below, p. 204). But primarily it is a propaganda organ, as when the National Council of the National Front meets to dedicate the people to such things as the speeding-up of the economic plan schedule, the campaign against West German nuclear armament, or "great patriotic efforts on behalf of German unification." Unlike the SED, the National Front is a very loosely organized structure, without direct membership or statutes. Below the national level, the National Front offices maintain informal but tight liaison with the respective SED offices. The leading officers of local National Front councils are in almost all cases SED members, and effective control lies with the local SED first secretary. But the National Front's most important function lies at the lowest level, that of the apartment house or block. There the NF claims to have some 350,000 voluntary part-time workers who fulfill important communal functions such as the distribution of ration cards (until 1958), the gathering of complaints about the functioning of administrative organs, and the collection of pledges of one sort or

[14] Deutsches Institut fuer Zeitgeschichte, *Jahrbuch der Deutschen Demokratischen Republik*, 1959 (Berlin, 1959), p. 59.

another. The volunteers thus serve not only as the local distribution point for the "transmission belt," but also as a safety valve through which the authorities hear of routine complaints. Some observers regard the National Front block-warden system as a vast network of neighborhood spies, but others disagree. "It displays aspects of real Republicanism, in the original sense of the word—and on a level where the individual doesn't even regard his task as 'political.' Observations lead to the conclusion that in allowing people to carry out some sort of honorary community tasks, however unimportant, the state in a certain sense wins them over to its side."[15]

Individually, the mass organizations unified in the National front fulfill more specialized functions. The most important of these, the Free German Trade Union Federation with its more than five million members, has been dominated by the Communists since its founding in 1945, and its leader is usually a member of the SED Politburo. According to *Neues Deutschland*, the trade unions and the works councils which are elected in the various factories are the "links" in the chain which the party must activate in order to raise the workers' class consciousness, work morale and militancy to the highest possible pitch."[16] The local union elections are not as rigged as the general elections, and the SED Communists must make great efforts in order to get trusted functionaries elected to the key works council offices. The second largest mass organization, the Free German Youth, with some three million members, has vast responsibilities in indoctrinating and activating youth, particularly teen-agers, on behalf of the party program, while the women's organization carries out a similar task with its membership. The function of the mass organizations is seen most clearly in the case of the middle-class parties. Originally (at least in the case of the CDU and LDP) set up to articulate middle-class demands on the state, they now function solely to soften up the remaining middle-class elements to conform to the demands of the state. Thus during the year 1958, the parties were set the task of persuading artisans and peasants to join collectives and small businessmen to accept state partnership voluntarily. The DDR's 1959 *Yearbook* credits the CDU and LDP with having brought, respectively, 411 and 658 artisans to join collectives, and 397 and 433 entrepreneurs to accept state partnership. The NDPD was praised for similar achievements, while the DBD, the farmer's party, was recognized for persuading

15 Richert, *op. cit.*, p. 120.
16 Stern, *op. cit.*, p. 258.

13,000 of its members to join agricultural collectives in the course of 1958 (some two years before the final drive in this sector was undertaken). Thus there is competition among political groups in East Germany, but only in the sense that there is competition among different Community Fund solicitation teams.

Insofar as large sections of the population have in the course of the 1960's become reconciled to the regime and integrated into the society, it has been less through the instrumentality of explicitly political organizations like the parties than through the medium of the work-place. By granting not only fringe benefits but better working conditions and higher pay rates, the regime has developed in most workers a loyalty at least to the plant or work group within which they utilize their skills. "The Pressure that led to the provision of fairer working conditions has had a deideologizing effect. One likes to perform a good day's work, both for its own sake and because of the bonus involved, rather than 'in honor of Ulbricht's birthday' or because of 'Friendship toward the Soviet Union.' "[17] Those who now feel "apolitical" are, according to Richert, the very ones who had high hopes for help from the West in 1953–56, and then felt themselves left in the lurch. They see no acceptable solution to the problem of unification, or, especially since August, 1961, any personal opportunity to opt for another alternative. "Since then a new tendency has developed, for which one finds support both in Universities like those of East Berlin, Jena and Dresden as well as in the large factories in Magdeburg and Leipzig. This tendency expresses itself in a striving toward a pragmatic kind of 'people's democracy' of the Polish, Hungarian or possibly even Yugoslav type."[18] The reorientation of potential opponents into pragmatic reformers of the regime has permitted the latter to reduce its reliance on force and on frenetic mobilization drives. Inevitably, therefore, the question of whether the East German regime ought still to be classified as totalitarian posed itself to Western researchers. A series of detailed studies of segments of East German society by sociologists attached to the West Berlin Institute of Political Science addressed themselves especially to this question in a volume published in 1964. Its editor concluded that the regime was in the process of transmuting itself from a totalitarian into an authoritarian type.[19]

[17] Ernest Richert, *Das Zweite Deutschland* (Guetersloh, 1964), p. 238.
[18] *Ibid.*
[19] Peter C. Ludz, ed., *Studien und Materialien zur Soziologie der DDR* (Opladen, 1964).

THE ORGANS OF SECURITY AND LEGALITY

Just as it would be wrong to conceive of the DDR as a state based merely on repression, so it would be inadequate to describe it as a police state. The various police components, of course, play an indispensable role in buttressing the regime's stability, but their role is different from what it typically is in an unpopular Western dictatorship. This is especially true in regard to many aspects of social and political behavior where the line between conduct which is undesirable and that which is criminal constantly shifts, as legal decisions adapt to changing ideological lines and tactical situations. The complex security apparatus is thus as much charged with detecting situations which might culminate in actions that the state apparatus considers undesirable, as it is with apprehending Western agents or East German citizens who are about to make illegal crossings of the zonal borders.

The most apparent component of the East German police apparatus is the People's Police, a uniformed, well armed, centrally directed force which exercises the more obvious control functions, such as the protection of strategic factories, the guarding of the zonal borders, and the dispersing of unruly crowds. It is the instrument of repression best known to the population, but although it too tries to maintain a network of informants, the bulk of the People's Police is made of relatively apolitical youths serving in areas where they are not very familiar with the local population. A more important political police organ, particularly as regards the ferreting out of economic "criminals" and "saboteurs," comprises the civilian members of the Central Commission for State Control. They were in charge of gathering materials for the frequent "show" trials through which the regime sought to reduce resistance to its various socialization and collectivization measures. But most important of all is the police apparatus of the Ministry for State Security. It is this force, with some 7,000 full-time agents and a network of an estimated 150,000 informants, which forms the core of East German political police and counter-intelligence activities. It carries the responsibility for obstructing the development of groups that are hostile to the state, and of detecting and frustrating the infiltration attempts of Western agents. As the Russians have gradually pulled out, it is this body which has taken over many of the functions of the Soviet secret police, and has in the process copied many of the repressive and terror practices through which suspects are "softened up." However, unlike its Soviet equivalent, the Security police has never become a powerful force unto itself, but has remained subject to over-all party direction and closely linked to the official judicial administration.

In determining what kinds of action should be made liable to criminal prosecution, the police work closely with the public prosecutors, 99 per cent of whom are members of the SED. The more the regime seeks to mold opinion, the more chance there is that seemingly private acts, such as divorce, libel, and assault cases, might carry political overtones. As Kirchheimer has written, "in the eyes of the rulers, even the least significant and most ludicrous or banal run-in necessarily assumes a more sinister complexion. In every aimless individual reaction the exponents of governmental power are bound to look for traces of a repetitive, rebellious design."[20] In cases where it decides to intervene the prosecution can operate with such vague, general concepts as diversion, sabotage, and boycott. The regime is especially suspicious, of course, of any contact with persons in West Germany. Its legal commentators have made clear that persons establishing unauthorized contact with people in the West, even if they are of a purely private nature and are unrelated to any political activity, may be punished by prison terms of as much as three years. The catch-all boycott provisions may be applied against anybody who has had any contact with an illegal border-crosser. They have been applied against a lady fortune-teller whose readings were said to have inspired her customers to leave the DDR.[21]

Assurance that the courts actually will hand down decisions which the police authorities desire requires close contact between prosecutors and judges and virtual negation of the concept of judicial independence. The latter is implicit in the Leninist view of law as merely an instrument of class rule, while judicial acquiescence is assured by the character of the judiciary and the ground rules of the judicial system. East German judges are predominantly men installed since 1945, and already in 1953, 85 per cent of them were SED members. Judicial behavior is tightly supervised by the Ministry of Justice, and on the local level each court has a party unit. Frequently the court's clerks and administrative officers enjoy higher rank than the judges themselves, so

[20] Otto Kirchheimer, "The Administration of Justice and the Concept of Legality in East Germany," *Yale Law Journal*, LXVIII (1959), 719.

[21] *Ibid.*, p. 740.

that their influence within the party cell may be correspondingly greater when weak points in individual judges' decisions are discussed by the group.

The capstone of the East German court system is the High Court, which, staffed by the staunchest Communist jurists, transmits to the lower courts the directives of the Ministry of Justice, the attorney general, and other administrative agencies in the judicial area. The High Court sits as a court of original jurisdiction on whichever cases the attorney general thinks of sufficient political significance to submit to it. Decisions in such cases are clear signals to the lower judges. The Court also acts as an appellate tribunal for decisions in the district courts, but in addition the DDR, building on Soviet and Nazi practice, has introduced the institution of the extraordinary appeal. This opens a special route for reversing final court opinions, but one open only to the state. Under it, the attorney general may within one year bring any final judgment by a lower court or by a three-judge division of the High Court itself for review in a High Court plenary session. Invariably the High Court then follows the prosecutor's policy directives.

BIBLIOGRAPHY

BRANDT, STEPHAN, *The East German Uprising* (New York, 1955).

CROAN, MELVIN, and FRIEDRICH, CARL J., "The East German Regime and Soviet Policy in Germany," *JP*, XX (1958), 44–63.

DOERNBERG, STEPHAN, "Die Gruendung der Sozialistischen Einheitspartei Deutschlands und Ihre Geschichtliche Bedeutung," *Zeitschrift fuer Geschichtswissenschaft*," IV (1956), 213–29.

KIRCHHEIMER, OTTO, "The Administration of Justice and the Concept of Legality in East Germany," *Yale Law Journal*, LXVIII (1959), 705–59.

LEONHARD, WOLFGANG, *Child of the Revolution* (Chicago, 1958).

LUDZ, P. C., "Zur Neuordnung des Staats-, Partei- und Wirtschaftsapparats der DDR: Die Stellung der SED im neuen System der Wirtschaftsplanung," *Europa-Archiv*, XVIII (1963), 810.

——, ed., *Studien und Materialien zur Soziologie der DDR* (Opladen, 1964).

NETTL, JOHN P. *The Eastern Zone and Soviet Policy in Germany, 1945–50* (New York, 1951).

RICHERT, ERNST, *Das Zweite Deutschland* (Gutersloh, 1964).

SCHULTZ, JOACHIM, *Der Funktionaer in der Einheitspartei* (Cologne, 1957).

SHERMAN, GEORGE, "The Russian and the East German Party," *St. Antony's Papers*, No. 1 (1956), pp. 85–124.

STERN, CAROLA, *Portraet einer Bolschewistischen Partei* (Cologne, 1957).

——, *Ulbricht: A Political Biography* (New York, 1965).

ULBRICHT, WALTER, *Die Entwicklung des deutschen volksdemokratischen Staates, 1945–1958* (Berlin, 1959).

The Institutions for Implementing Policy

THE CONSTITUTION

From what has been said in the foregoing chapter it is evident that the German Democratic Republic does not have a constitution in the Western sense, that is, one whose provisions regulate relations among the various power-holders in the political system. The SED cannot and does not recognize any power in the state other than itself, and its Leninist ideology would in any case prevent it from acknowledging the sanctity of any legalist framework. Nevertheless, like other Communist states, the DDR does have a quite elaborate Constitution, which among other things guarantees a variety of civil rights, delineates the responsibilities of the various governmental organs and establishes the privileges of the churches. Moreover the Constitution goes further than other East European constitutions in providing, for instance, for a system of proportional representation, which clearly could only make sense in a plural party system with alternative choices open to the voter. In fact, the entire document is basically cut to the model of a parliamentary, multiparty system, and its most influential model is not the Soviet Constitution of 1936, but the Weimar Constitution of 1919, to which in many parts it bears a much closer resemblance than does the West German Basic Law.

The explanation for the curious character of the Constitution is that it was drafted not for the Democratic Republic as it has developed during the 1950's, but during a period (1946 to 1947) when the SED was still proceeding on the assumption that it could come to power within the framework of an all-German parliamentary system. At that time the Soviets were still taking pains to keep the formal governmental structure in their zone much like that in other parts of Germany. In addition to relatively free parties, there were Laender (five) and Land governments. While accepting many pre-Hitler institutions, the SED Constitution-drafters did make some important changes. They refused to accept the principle of separation of powers and instead concentrated power in the legislative organ. They also provided for the gradual reshaping of the traditional German civil service and judiciary, and they gave the state extra powers to socialize property. But private property was definitely protected, could only be "abridged . . . on the basis of laws . . . and against adequate compensation"

(Art 23), small and medium-sized farmers were guaranteed the right to own land privately (Art. 24), and the state was even enjoined "to support farmers, artisans and business men in the development of private initiative" (Art. 20). Other civil rights were guaranteed with still greater forthrightness. Thus all citizens were guaranteed the right to the free and public expression of their opinions (Art. 9), were assured an equal and undiscriminatory claim to education (Art. 35), and the trade unions' right to strike was specifically sanctioned (Art. 14). Indeed some of the guarantees given voluntary groups, such as the assurance that the churches had the right to give religious instruction in public schools through teachers of their own choosing, exceeds similar guarantees in many liberal democratic constitutions in the West (for example, the American).

The Constitution containing these guarantees was adopted in October, 1949, a month after the creation of the Federal Republic. At that time the Communists were still saying that they were ready to combine with the West Germans in a parliamentary regime, and the nature of the Constitution served to buttress this propaganda line. In actual practice, however the Constitution was outdated before it was ever adopted. For in May, 1949, at the time of the elections to the People's Council which adopted the Constitution, the principle of a multiparty system had already been abandoned, and the uniform list system introduced. Many of the other principles of the Constitution, pertaining both to civil and political rights and the structure of the governmental organs, were also soon abandoned. The regime flouted its Constitution by openly refusing higher education to most children of middle-class parents, and pressuring farmers to give up their property without even bothering to pass a coercive law, while the privileges of the churches were increasingly disregarded.

Many inconvenient governmental institutions were done away with even though they were provided for in the Constitution. Thus the Laender together with Land diets were abolished by ordinary law in 1952, and for six years no Laender existed even though the Constitution provided for them. Finally in 1958, when it was decided also to abolish the upper chamber of the national legislature, the long overdue amendments were enacted. However, constitutional amendments (which technically are enacted by the legislature in much the same way as simple laws are) have been enacted with regard to only a few of the provisions where practice has clearly deviated from what the Constitution requires. Up to the end of 1960 only three amendments had been passed in over eleven years. The first, in 1955, provided the constitutional basis for the formal establishment of the East German armed forces; the second, in 1958, abolished the Laender and the upper house of the national legislature; the third, in 1960, replaced the president of the Republic by the State Council. Only in the last instance did the timing of the actual institutional change coincide with the constitutional change, and here both the person of Ulbricht and a position relevant to international relations were directly involved. In hosts of other instances the government has passed laws and decrees clearly in conflict with constitutional provisions, without the question of reconcilability ever being raised.

LEGISLATIVE ORGANS

If the members of the East German assembly, the People's Chamber (*Volkskammer*), actually possessed the powers assigned to them by the Constitution, they would be among the most powerful parliamentarians in the world. They would possess great importance as members of the highest organ of the Republic and great confidence, because the Constitution says that they are "subject only to their conscience and may not be bound by instructions" (Art. 51). Their power would be evident from the fact that all the highest officers of both the executive and judiciary agencies would owe their office to election by the People's Chamber. The president of the Republic and the second chamber (since abolished) would be elected by it, while it would have sole voice in the election of members of the Supreme Court, as well as in the selection of the attorney general. The minister-president and his cabinet colleagues would only hold office subject to its approval and would have to follow policy outlines as laid down by the Chamber. All in all, judging from the Constitution, the DDR would be an extreme example of "assembly government," the type of parliamentary government in which the legislature holds the lion's share of power.

Needless to say, practice could hardly be more remote from legal letter. The People's Chamber is in fact an institution that operates mainly for ritualistic purposes, fulfilling its assigned duties with apparent enthusiasm but without conflicting discussion. It usually meets about eight times annually in order to ratify the nominations and to pass the bills which Communist leaders present to it. However, the Chamber and its members are by no means simple figureheads. They do fulfill fairly important functions.

within the political system as a whole, even if these are not the functions described in the Constitution. The Chamber does have a representative character, not for the purpose of real decision-making, but for the purpose of constituting itself as a reasonably accurate microcosm of a Communist society. This microcosm plays a symbolic role in the manner of certain institutions in constitutional regimes (for example, the British monarchy), and its assent to measures proposed by the executive is understood within such a framework. Individually, the members of this microcosm are expected to do their part to see that the portions of the macrocosm (society) which they represent follow the pattern of their "representatives." In this capacity, members of legislative bodies on the national, regional, and local level play an important role as auxiliary organs to the governmental and party executive in helping to gain popular acceptance of policies and programs.[1]

The emphasis on creating a People's Chamber which is widely representative can be seen in the nomination and electoral procedure. The chief role in the nomination process lies with the secretariats of the SED, the other "parties," and the mass organizations, which nominate candidates for the single joint list which is then run under the name of the National Front. The SED Secretariat selects the candidates for the SED part of the list, but indirectly it also has veto power over the nominations of the other organizations. In 1958 the quotas for the People's Chamber list called for one hundred SED representatives, forty-five each for the four non-Socialist "parties" and the Free Trade Union Federation, twenty-five each for the youth and women's organizations, fifteen for a farmers' organization, and ten for a group representing cultural and intellectual workers.[2] When the National Front has approved the nominations, the candidates are forced to undertake the rigorous task of making themselves known to their constituents. They must attend a myriad of meetings in factories, neighborhoods, and clubs. It is claimed that in 1954 candidates for elective office on the local as well as national level held almost a half million such meetings, attended by about fifteen million citizens. At one of these meetings the National Front candidate is then officially endorsed. Subsequently the entire list is approved in the elections, in which, characteristically, there is an overwhelming turnout (1958: 98.9 per cent of those eligible) and a

[1] Ernest Richert, *Macht ohne Mandat* (Cologne, 1958), p. 106.
[2] Deutsches Institut fuer Zeitgeschichte, *Jahrbuch der Deutschen Demokratischen Republik, 1959* (Berlin, 1959), p. 31.

virtually unanimous endorsement of the list candidates (1958: 99.87 per cent "yes" vote).[3]

This careful selection process results in the desired profile of the legislative body. It is almost a photographic image of the social structure of the East German population as seen through Communist lenses. According to official statements, the social structure is characterized by a working-class predominance, with workers and employees (the categories are defined very broadly) making up 78 per cent of the population. In the People's Chamber delegates of working-class or employee background made up 74 per cent after the 1958 elections; smaller social groups were represented proportionately. The make-up of the legislature also changed as a result of the increasing socialization of the means of production. Whereas private farmers and artisans had played a significant role earlier, by 1958 seventy members of agricultural and artisan collectives predominated over only five remaining representatives of private farmers and artisans.[4]

The data presented in the table on page 206, based on an analysis of the personal backgrounds of members of the West and East German legislatures in the period 1958–63, bear out that the East German legislators more closely resemble the demographic and social composition of their constituencies. While there was a tendency toward a disproportionate representation of middle-aged and older men in both legislatures, women constituted a larger proportion of the East German legislators (24 per cent against 9 per cent), and the legislators below the age of about forty-five were also more numerous (39 per cent against 25 per cent) in the East. As is to be expected in terms of the recruitment base of the dominant SED, the East German legislators were recruited predominantly from the lower strata having little formal education, which constitute the bulk of the population. Whereas only 16 per cent of the Bundestag members on whom data were available were from families in the two lower strata, 56 per cent of the Volkskammer deputies were in this category. When categorized according to their formal education, 60 per cent of the East German deputies had not gone beyond elementary school and only 15 per cent had attended university, whereas the West German proportions were more nearly the reverse.

In its capacity as legislator, the People's Chamber's role has been limited mainly to giving passive approval to bills brought in

[3] *Ibid.*, p. 29.
[4] *Ibid.*, p. 30.

from the outside, although frequently it is not even called upon to do that. When choosing between introducing new rules as laws via the legislative route, or simply introducing them as administrative ordinances, the East German executive much prefers the latter. Despite the enormous changes brought about in all aspects of East German life, the People's Chamber has in some years passed as few as ten new laws, and the over-all average is not much higher. During the six months of June through Decem-

RECRUITMENT PATTERNS IN THE BUNDESTAG AND THE EAST GERMAN VOLKSKAMMER, 1958–63

Age (Year of Birth)	Bundestag %	Volkskammer %
1876–1895	8	7
1896–1915	66	53
1916–1925	20	25
1926–	5	14
No Data	1	—
	100	100
Education		
Elementary School	22	60
High School	25	24
University	50	15
No Data	3	1
	100	100
Sex		
Male	91	76
Female	9	24
	100	100
Father's Social Stratum		
Upper Middle	15	8
Lower Middle	20	34
Upper Lower	4	11
Lower Lower	3	45
No Data		
	100	100

NOTE: This analysis was based on the biographical information of the 544 deputies who were members of the Bundestag in 1961–63 and of the 474 deputies who belonged to the Volkskammer in 1958–60.

SOURCE: Wolf Mersch, "Volksvertreter in West und Ost," in Wolfgang Zapf, ed., *Beitraege zur Analyse der deutschen Oberschicht* (Munich, 1965), pp. 33–35.

ber, 1953, when radical changes in policy caused extensive changes in highly important rules, the People's Chamber passed only two laws, and these concerned themselves with hunting regulations and the protection of rare and useful plants.[5] In important areas like taxation there have been hundreds of administrative rule changes for every change officially imbedded in legislation. Since 1958 the decree-issuing power of the Council of Ministers and the Council of State has become so enlarged that rule changes via the People's Chamber have become even rarer.

Of the bills that are considered in the legislature, almost all originate with the executive, since neither the People's Chamber nor any of its parties—not even the SED—utilize their constitutional power to introduce bills. In the People's Chamber about half the bills considered are passed without any discussion at all, and all are accepted by unanimous vote.[6] The most important function of the members of the legislature consists not in representing the people to the state, but in representing the state to the people. As one German writer put it: "In the deputy, the people have right at their front door a 'hunk of state' with whom they can talk . . . and who has official authority to extend help in case of need."[7]

The regime's anxiety to maintain contact with the people, both for ideological reasons and in order to forestall possible trouble, can be seen from the very large number of persons holding some sort of elected position on the national, district, and local levels. It has been estimated that there are no less than 100,000 elected representatives, or about one for every hundred adult citizens. The local legislative organs have little opportunity to make policy, but they and the local councils have an important function as auxiliary organs for the executive, helping to plan and coordinate the manifold state activities on the local level. They play a particularly important role in helping to realize the objectives of the economic plans, especially since, starting in the late fifties, there has been an increasing attempt to avoid overcentralization of the administration. The regional and local councils maintain auxiliary commissions, and these in turn have at their side teams of local citizens who serve as advisers on the solution of limited local problems. Thus the rigid bureaucracy of full-time state and party functionaries is supplemented and to an extent checked by a large army of part-time volunteers.

[5] Richert, *op. cit.*, p. 31.
[6] *Loc. cit.*
[7] *Ibid.*, p. 103.

THE EXECUTIVE

One of the peculiarities of most Communist regimes is that they generally seek to create the appearance of diversified decision-making, not only by bestowing great constitutional powers on the legislature but also by providing for a plural executive and head of state. In this, they differ both from totalitarian regimes of the right, and also from most constitutional political systems. Thus in West Germany, both the functions of the head of state and those of the head of the political executive are centered primarily in individuals. In East Germany, however, both of the major executive organs, the Council of State, which functions as the nominal head of state, and the Council of Ministers, which is in charge of the actual political and administrative work, strongly emphasize the collegial principle, at least in outward appearance.

Paradoxically, this tendency to emphasize collegial structure has increased in fairly direct proportion to the centralization of power in the hands of one man. Originally there was an individual head of state, the president of the Republic. In 1949 this position was given to Wilhelm Pieck, the "ex-Communist" cochairman of the SED, while the position of minister-president and chairman of the Council of Ministers went to Otto Grotewohl, his "ex-Socialist" colleague. Ulbricht at that time was only a vice-chairman of the Council of Ministers. But increasingly he used his control over the SED party organization to win power at the expense of the other leaders. It soon became evident that the vice-chairman of the Council of Ministers had much more influence on its decisions than the chairman himself. Then, when Wilhelm Pieck died in 1960, the position of the presidency was constitutionally abolished in favor of a twenty-four man Council of State, similar to the U.S.S.R.'s Presidium of the Supreme Soviet. However, the State Council has even greater rule-making powers than the Soviet body, and unlike the latter it is not an organ of the assembly. By having himself elected president of this body, Ulbricht succeeded in outdoing even Stalin by combining in his person the positions of head of state, vice-chairman of the Council of Ministers, and General Secretary of the SED.

The make-up of the East German equivalent of the cabinet has also changed frequently since 1949. The original cabinet was a very large and unwieldy body because the Constitution provided, firstly, that all parties with at least forty deputies in the People's Chamber be represented in the executive; secondly, that all ministers be automatically members; and thirdly, that many leading civil servants be included. In time, this large body came to be known as the Council of Ministers, meeting regularly under the chairmanship of the minister-president. Already in 1952 the Council of Ministers had been given legal authority "to change its own structure by independent decision whenever necessary to conform to the demands of economic planning."[8] This power was frequently taken advantage of, both to reorganize the ministries and to change the make-up of the Council of Ministers itself. One consequence was the creation of a kind of supercabinet, called the Presidium of the Council of Ministers, which in fact became the crucial executive decision-making body. Its size has varied from ten to sixteen, including the chairman, the vice-chairman, and the most important ministers. Two-thirds of its members have always come from the SED, but the "all-party" formula has been superficially adhered to by allotting each of the other parties one of the deputy chairmanships. The Presidium normally meets once a week and in general fulfills the important policy-making functions that in the Soviet Union are exercised by the body after which it is modelled. Attached to it is a secretariat to which are linked the State Planning Commission and the Central Commission for State Control. These top-level coordinating organs fulfill for the state apparatus roughly the same functions that the Central Secretariat fulfills for the party.

Within the Council of Ministers, according to the Constitution, the position of the minister-president is much less powerful than that of the West German Chancellor. Until his death in September, 1964, this position was long held by Otto Grotewohl, whose influence had always been limited. His successor in that position, Willi Stoph, who had served in many top party and government offices and was regarded by many as Ulbricht's potential heir, may be able to transform the position into a much more powerful one. Potentially the powers of the Council of Ministers, as spelled out in an act which went into force in April, 1963, are very broad. It provides that "The Council of Ministers shall work out the main political, economic, scientific, technical and cultural-educational policies which the comprehensive building of socialism requires, on the basis of the program of the SED, the resolutions of the SED Central Committee, the ordinances and resolutions of the People's Chamber, as well as those of the Council of State."

Because centralized economic planning is so dominant a preoccupation of the East German government, the administrative

[8] Ibid., p. 36.

apparatus of the central government is divided fairly clearly between the "economic" ministries and the "political" ones. The latter include the ministries for Foreign Affairs, Interior, State Security, and Justice. As regards structure the political ministries have remained fairly stable, although reorganization took place as the result, for instance, of the official creation of the Ministry of National Defense in 1956. The political ministries have either no "line agencies" at all, or only those which function as its local branch offices. The "economic" ministries, on the other hand, such as the (former) Ministry of Machine Construction or the (former) Ministry of Raw Materials, are responsible for vast industrial enterprises which are mostly directly state owned and all state controlled. The attempt to find an administrative structure which would allow the ministries to exercise central coordination while avoiding excessive bureaucratic duplication has caused this area of the administration to be subject to frequent and radical reorganization. Following the administrative reforms introduced in the USSR in 1962, the East Germans have also sought to further integrate the organizations of party and state. But whereas in the Soviet Union most of the major planning bodies were placed under the jurisdiction of a Supreme Economic Council, in East Germany supervision over the relevant agencies has been maintained by the Council of Ministers itself. After a reorganization in December, 1965, no less than twenty-six of the DDR's forty-six ministries concerned themselves exclusively with administering the economy.

PLANNING AND ADMINISTRATION

Even before this occurred, the State Planning Commission had been the crucial coordinating center for the work of the various ministries, allocating raw materials and setting top-level production quotas. Headed by a chairman who has always been an ex-officio deputy chairman of the Council of Ministers, the Commission relies on the work of about a thousand experts organized in divisions which parallel those of the various ministries or, since 1958, the relevant administrative sections of the Commission. The planning process is a laborious one and begins about a half year before a specific plan goes into effect. Originally the Planning Commission worked out tentative plans and production quotas; these were submitted to the ministries for suggestions, then reexamined by the Commission and transformed into all-inclusive production, investment, labor, and finance plans, which were in turn submitted for approval to the Central Committee of the SED and the Council of Ministers.

Many difficulties beset the regime in its attempts to transform the plans into actual achievements. A bureaucracy which after all consisted primarily of Prussians tended to follow instructions to the letter, resulting in wasteful duplication and excessive formalization of working routines. In an attempt to remedy the situation, ministries were forever being abolished or reconstructed. The area of machine construction was at some periods divided among as many as three ministries, at others combined as a subdivision of one ministry. Since 1958, the former heads of the production ministries have become section heads in the State Planning Commission and form part of a large collegial body which charts the Commission's course. In an attempt to experiment with decentralization, part of the ministries' former functions have been transferred to local authorities and to so-called Unions of Public Enterprise. As a result factory managers have been less bound by explicit directions from East Berlin, but their initiative is still kept under control through the system of "double subordination."[9] This provides for local production units to be subject to the control of both the overall economic planning agency on the local level and to the more specialized technical section of the Planning Commission.

Apart from the low morale and lack of Socialist enthusiasm of the population, the problem of administering the vast planned economy has been perhaps the single most pressing internal problem of the East German regime. A perusal of the speeches Walter Ulbricht has given before East German administration academies over the years shows frequent changes of policy. In 1949 he was calling on county and communal governments "not to let themselves be carried away by talk of self-administration which would disturb the fulfillment of the Plan."[10] The resultant accumulation of tasks for the central ministries led to administrative methods which he described some years later by charting the route of a directive for state-run enterprises from one ministry's Labor Division:

The directive will go from the Labor Division to that deputy minister who is responsible for this division, from him to the Minister, from the Minister to the deputy Minister who is responsible for the Production division, from him to the administrative head of this division, then on

[9] *Ibid.*, pp. 83 ff.
[10] Walter Ulbricht, *Die Entwicklung des deutschen Volksdemokratischen Staates, 1954–1958* (Berlin, 1959), p. 175.

212-COMMUNIST EAST GERMANY

to the deputy administrator until it finally reaches the head of the Labor section of the relevant central administrative agency. . . . Cooperation between the many administrative desks at the central level and the production enterprises is very inadequate and very complicated. The result is that much paper is used up and that scientific-technical work is not pushed forward as quickly as might otherwise be possible.[11]

By 1958 he was praising measures adopted once more to give local government a more significant role in the economic planning process, in the hope that "the simpler the forms and methods through which direction to political, economic and cultural activity, the better can the workers themselves participate in the leadership of the state and the economy."[12]

The tradition of the German civil service as a tightly knit, exclusive professional group, predominantly recruited from middle-class strata, was of course entirely unacceptable to the Communists. They did not bother with halfway measures, but virtually abolished the civil service in its traditional form. A major bulwark of the system, the civil servant's claim to lifetime tenure, was done away with, and under East German law a government employee may be dismissed at any time after being given two weeks' notice. Great effort has been put into replacing the old line, politically unreliable, professional administrators with Communist functionaries. Various sectors of the government compete in seeking to demonstrate the working-class "purity" of their employees. Thus in 1957 two-thirds of the judges were said to be of working-class background, and only two out of 906 were listed as coming from the upper-middle class.[13] About the same time, the army announced that 85 per cent of its officers had working-class origins.[14] Claims for the administration were not quite as high, but in 1955, 60 per cent of government employees were said to come from the working class.[15]

Class background and party membership have been less crucial prerequisites for professional advancement among top-level scientists and other elite specialist groups. Such individuals with the right combination of skills, whom the regime wanted to keep from fleeing to the West, were subjected to fewer pressures to conform. In a study of the membership of the (East) German Aca-

---

11 *Ibid.*, p. 489.
12 *Ibid.*, p. 543.
13 *Ibid.*, p. 533.
14 Deutsches Institut fuer Zeitgeschichte, *op. cit.*, p. 87.
15 Richert, *op. cit.*, p. 158.

demy of Sciences between 1945 and 1961, Hanhardt found that only 16 per cent were members of the SED. Indeed, over 10 per cent were members even though they had been members of the NSDAP during the Nazi period. Among the higher ranking officers of the academy, members without party affiliation seemed to be about as well represented as those who held party membership. The politically conformist members were given more public recognition through official awards, but otherwise their more apolitical colleagues did not appear at a disadvantage.[16]

BIBLIOGRAPHY

ALBRECHT, GUENTER, ed., *Dokumente zur Staatsordnung der DDR* (Berlin, 1959).

Bundesministerium fuer Gesamtdeutsche Fragen, *SBZ von A-Z*, 5th ed. (Bonn, 1959).

——, *Die Wahlen in der Sowjetzone* (Bonn, 1956).

Deutsche Demokratische Republik, *Handbuch der Volkskammer der DDR*, 2d ed. (Berlin, 1957).

DRATH, MARTIN, *Verfassungsrecht und Verfassungswirklichkeit in der sowjetischen Besatzungszone* (Bonn, 1954).

GLASER, KURT, "Governments of Soviet Germany" in E. H. Litchfield, ed., *Governing Postwar Germany* (Ithaca, 1953), pp. 152–83.

MAUNZ, THEODOR, *Deutsches Staatsrecht*, 9th ed. (Munich, 1959), Part II.

POLAK, KARL, *Die Demokratie der Arbeiter und Bauernmacht* (Berlin, 1957).

RICHERT, ERNST, *Macht ohne Mandat* (Cologne, 1958).

ULBRICHT, WALTER, *Die Entwicklung des deutschen Volksdemokratischen Staates, 1945–1958* (Berlin, 1959).

U.S. High Commission for Germany, *Soviet Zone Constitution and Electoral Law* (Washington, 1951).

[16] Arthur M. Hanhardt, Jr., "Die Ordentlichen Mitglieder der Deutschen Akademie der Wissenschaften," *Koelner Zeitschrift fuer Soziologie und Sozialpsychologie*, XVI (1964), 241–62.

PART FOUR

THE GERMANS AND THEIR ENVIRONMENT

11: Divided Germany and World Politics

BERLIN—A HOUSE DIVIDED

Let us imagine the Grimm brothers, the famous German fairy tale authors, writing about Germany in the 1960's:

Once upon a time there was a rich and powerful farmer, who died after committing many dastardly acts and getting deeply into debt. Some of his land was seized by creditors, and the rest was contested by two sons, Konrad and Walter, each of whom claimed to be the right-ful heir and was backed in his claim by different groups of neighbors. Lawyers were hired by the dozen, but the contest could not be effectively settled without launching the whole countryside into civil war. So each of the hostile brothers farmed those pieces of the family land which he had been tilling at the time of the father's death. Most of the farmers thought that Konrad's legal claims were superior, that he was a better sort of man besides being a better farmer, and indeed several of Walter's children cut their way through the barbed wire fences which had been put up across the middle of the farm to settle on their uncle's land. But in addition to having powerful friends of his own, Walter had one great advantage: the old family farmstead was located right in the middle of his land. At the time of the father's death an agreement allowed both the sons and the neighbors to share the house, and a temporary division of the farmstead's facilities were arranged on that basis, with Konrad and the neighbors guaranteed free access across Walter's land. As feeling grew more bitter, the parts of the house were all but barricaded from each other. In time Walter and his friends began to claim that the earlier agreement had lapsed and that the farmstead area formed an integral part of his land. He offered to let some of Konrad's children continue to live in "their" part of the house, but only on condition that they renounce the ties that joined them to their siblings as one family. This settlement was indignantly refused by Konrad and his friends, who insisted that the farmstead belonged to the legal heir to the farm, namely Konrad, and that awaiting a final settlement the old agreements regarding its use should remain in force.

The old farmstead is of course the prewar German capital, Berlin, which has literally remained a house divided for twenty years. It has remained the center of conflict not only because of its symbolic significance for Germans, but because Germany is a miniature of a world divided between East and West. Berlin is both Germany in miniature and also the only large city in the world where the democratic and Communist forces meet head-on. (Vienna, once in a similar situation, escaped that fate with the signing of the Austrian peace treaty in 1955.) Although the two large power blocs also border each other in many other places, and have come into conflict in a number of them, including Korea, Indochina, Laos, and Quemoy and Matsu, Berlin has remained the Communists' favorite place for applying pressure not intended to lead to armed conflict. Its dubious distinction is explained by West Berlin's being completely surrounded by Communist-controlled territory, and by the fact that the instruments for such pressure, the East German Communists, are quite well disciplined and controlled, allowing a fairly fine check on the extent of particular provocations. In addition, the status of West Berlin, directly involving as it does West Germany as well as the major NATO powers, allows the Communists to subtly play on and seek to aggravate latent differences among the Western allies. Finally, Berlin, whatever its political status, is one of the major news centers of the world. If the East Germans block an access road to West Berlin or arrest an American journalist in East Berlin, the news will be halfway around the world in hours, if not minutes. Whenever the cold war settles down into a phase of psychological warfare, Berlin becomes the sensitized area for recording changes in tension.

The story of how Berlin developed this role begins with the wartime agreements of 1944 and 1945, when the victorious Allies agreed not only to divide Germany into four Occupation zones, but to run Berlin jointly, allocating to each of the four major powers a city sector for administration. Then in June, 1948, the Soviets imposed a blockade on all land traffic into West Berlin in retaliation against the introduction there of the new West German currency. In November the city council and administration split into separate parts. During the airlift the West Berliners displayed great courage and endurance, and it was their toughness which finally forced the Soviets to back down and to cancel the blockade after eleven months[1] After that the new Democratic Republic officially declared East Berlin to be its capital, while West Berlin concentrated on economic revival. Eventually the abnormality of relationships was accepted as normal, and throughout most of the 1950's life in the divided city continued with many minor, but few major, upsets. A series of strong Social Democratic leaders, Ernst Reuter, Otto Suhr, and Willy Brandt, provided excellent leadership in the position of Governing Mayor of West Berlin. There was little official contact between the two administrations, but those who cared to could usually travel freely throughout Berlin. While many streets led to dead ends at the sector border, the main thoroughfares were kept open, and the subway and elevated trains were kept running.

The Berlin situation was changed radically on the night of August 13, 1961, when the Communists erected a physical wall to seal off hermetically the two parts of the city. Until that date, Berlin, though divided, had been something of a "clamp that held the parts of Germany together." Relatives from East and West could meet there with comparative ease, and West Berlin was a showcase where in one year visitors from East Berlin and East Germany had bought nine million theatre, movie, and concert admissions. All that was ended when the Communists stopped virtually all German crossings at the handful of check points where traffic could still move across the sector borders. Along the twenty-six mile wall of prefabricated cement slabs topped by barbed wire and frequently reinforced by secondary obstacles, East German soldiers and police patrol ceaselessly. Many of their countrymen have still found means of escape, but many others have died in unsuccessful attempts.

The Berlin wall was primarily Ulbricht's answer to the mass exodus of the DDR's population. As such it has been interpreted as the desperate act of bravado of a regime reeling from manifold setbacks. But the perpetuation of the wall and its designation as the "state boundary" of the DDR have demoralized anti-Communist Germans who had believed that hope of unification remained as long as Berlin was under at least formal four-power control. The Soviets have sought to capitalize on this feeling by developing pressures for direct West German-Soviet negotiations in which they might entice Bonn to weaken its ties to the West. Meanwhile the status of West Berlin, which the Federal Republic

[1] W. P. Davison, *The Berlin Blockade: A Study in Cold-War Politics* (Princeton, 1958).

subsidizes heavily[2] and which it would like to consider one of its constituent Laender, remains a subject of acute controversy.

Throughout this time the endless series of proposals and counterproposals about a German peace treaty got nowhere. The Federal Republic refused to enter into official dealings with the Democratic Republic and the Western powers refused to enter into any negotiations which would entail recognition of the latter regime. Instead they called on the Soviets to arrange for free elections through which citizens of both East and West Germany could choose their representatives for future negotiations. Although they had established diplomatic relations with the Federal Republic in 1955, the Soviets in their turn refused to make any concessions which might endanger the East German SED government, and continued to insist that the two German governments should negotiate together on a basis of equality. When the West refused to proceed on these terms, the Soviets began to talk of arranging a separate peace treaty between themselves and East Germany. Since November, 1958, the Soviets have sought to force the West into a complete renegotiation of the Berlin situation; they themselves proposed turning West Berlin into a neutralized "free city" inside the DDR which would earn its keep by selling its manufactures to both West and East.[3]

Although Khruschev's threat to sign a separate peace treaty with East Germany was not implemented, the Soviets have continued to seek to undercut the prosperous stability the West Berliners have managed to establish. Threats to their supply lines to the West occur frequently, but the city has stockpiles plentiful enough to meet such crises for months. Another form of pressure is applied through the Communist "Three-State Theory," under which the Soviets regard West Berlin as a third German state distinct from both the DDR and the Federal Republic. They like to set up situations that drive the point home. Thus when the State Secretary in the West German Foreign Office visited Moscow in 1965, the highest ranking West German official to do so since Adenauer's visit in 1955, he was made very much aware that he was regarded as speaking for only a part of Germany. For Walter Ulbricht was making a tour of the Soviet Union at the same time, while the West Berlin exhibitors at the Moscow Trade Fair were assigned their own national pavilion. The

[2] Charles Robson, ed., *Berlin: Pivot of German Destiny* (Chapel Hill, 1960), pp. 134-55.
[3] Bruce L. R. Smith, "The Governance of Berlin," *International Conciliation* No. 525 (1959), pp. 189-90.

West Berliners, however, have come to take in their stride all attempts to isolate them, for they have a deep faith that the West will not permit this to happen. Though protected militarily only by tiny American, British, and French garrisons, West Berlin has decided that the best defense lies in being a cultural magnet to the world. To its international congresses, fairs, exhibitions, and cultural offerings come a vast and steady stream of German and foreign visitors, who help to constitute a kind of psychological defense in depth.

THE REVIVAL OF GERMAN MILITARY FORCES

Of those countries that lead the world in economic potential and political influence, most have impressive military establishments that help sustain their claim to recognition as first- or second-rate powers. A few, like Japan, have deliberately avoided the postwar rebuilding of their military establishment for fear of political consequences. Germany has followed a different policy, and this has raised a series of questions on which West German politicians have often been in disagreement. Was it really in the German interest, some have asked, for West Germany to raise strong military forces that might only serve to stiffen Soviet and East European resistance to the primary national goal of reunification? As opinion on this question gradually crystallized in a positive sense, the problem of how a dynamic military establishment could be kept under civilian control and prevented from exerting an antidemocratic influence caused serious concern to those familiar with the past political record of the German officer corps. Finally, with the dispersion of nuclear potential that occurred particularly in the 1960's, another question posed itself as some politicians argued that the Federal Republic should attempt to revise the treaty commitments under which it had agreed to manufacture and utilize only conventional weapons.

In 1945 the victorious Allies seemed determined that a revival of German military power should never recur, and they acted to wipe out all military organizations and to impress on the German people the close connection between German militarism and the disaster of 1945. But a demilitarized Germany was not in the cards. Within five years after Germany's unconditional surrender the very powers who had defeated and dissolved her armies were themselves seeking to encourage the re-establishment of German military contingents. The constitutions of both the Federal Republic and the Democratic Republic contained provisions forbidding large-scale rearmament; both soon had to be amended.

After the near success of the Communist attempt to take over South Korea by force raised further doubts as to the ability of the democratic countries to meet localized Communist aggression, American and British spokesmen in 1950 began to call for the formation of West German contingents. To allay traditional and well-founded skepticism regarding the political effects of the re-establishment of a German army, it was proposed that the German troops be placed under a European army, with other countries doing likewise. The West German government strongly supported these plans, and after some discussion the French cabinet overcame its initial hesitation and agreed to the principles of the European Defense Community (EDC). However, successive French governments proved unable or unwilling to make the plan acceptable to large enough sections of French opinion, and in August, 1954, the treaty was defeated in the French National Assembly.[4] As an alternative it was agreed that Germany be made a member of NATO, and that German armed forces, though organized on a national basis, be placed under the supreme command of NATO. This formula was finally accepted by the French, the Germans, and all the other nations involved.

There were as yet no West German soldiers in uniform when five days after the Federal Republic's admission to NATO the states of the Communist bloc met in Warsaw and formed a counterpart pact, with reciprocal defense guarantees and a joint command for their combined military forces. In this way the effective control exercised through the top-level Communist leaders was augmented by a supranational military organization similar to NATO, whose existence underlined the polarization of the two hostile blocs. A Soviet general was named to command the forces of the Warsaw Pact countries, and a staff organization was established in Moscow. The DDR had not as yet given its "police" formations explicit military status, so although it became a member of the pact, no provision was made regarding its forces. This situation was rectified in January, 1956, with the official formation of the East German People's Army, and a few days later the Warsaw Pact countries announced the admission of East German contingents into the unified command. By 1959 an official East German source described the function of the armed services as "successfully fulfilling, at the side of the glorious Soviet army and of the other fraternal socialist armies, the duties assigned

[4] Daniel Lerner, ed., *France Defeats EDC* (New York, 1957).

to us within the framework of the Warsaw Pact."[5] To tie the People's Army to German traditions, the new army uniforms closely resembled those of the Wehrmacht, despite the fact that the Communists had spent so much time in denouncing the latter as an ally of fascism.

In the Federal Republic, the problem of the reconcilability of old traditions and new roles also caused difficulty. Up to 1945 the ranks of the top-level German military men and those of genuine democrats had, for the most part, been mutually exclusive. "The German democrats had no military heroes in their tradition . . . and the German military had no democrats among their ancestry."[6] The character of West German society and the rapid build-up which was necessary after the long delays over EDC did not allow the training of a completely new military leadership and required the use of officers who had grown up in the antidemocratic Reichswehr and in the service of the Nazi state. In an attempt to prevent the re-emergence of a reactionary officers' corps and a tyrannical military tradition, the West Germans took extraordinary precautions to sift out politically unreliable candidates and to keep a democratic check on the armed forces. When recruitment for the higher offices began, all candidates for positions with the rank of colonel or above were subjected to close individual scrutiny by a special committee set up by the Bundestag. Many candidates were weeded out on political grounds. Then, building on a Swedish model, the Parliament provided for the creation of a parliamentary "Commissioner" whose job it would be to look into complaints from individual soldiers and to report to it periodically on the internal affairs of the military forces.

On the surface the care taken to restrict the West German military to a specific and subordinate role within the political system has paid off. Policy control has remained securely in the hands of the Defense Minister and the Defense Committee of the Bundestag. Generals don't make political decisions in Bonn any more than they do in East Berlin. Their names are barely known to the general public, and there are only brief notices about them in the press when they are shifted from assignments in Bonn to new ones at NATO headquarters in Paris or in Washington. Far from becoming flamboyant national heroes, the military

[5] Deutsches Institut fuer Zeitgeschichte, *Jahrbuch der Deutschen Demokratischen Republik, 1959* (Berlin, 1959), p. 86.

[6] Emil Obermann, "Kraeftespiel um die Bundeswehr," *Neue Gesellschaft*, VI (1959), 96.

leaders have joined the faceless group of supranational civil servants who hardly project themselves as factors shaping political attitudes and enthusiasms. There is little evidence that the military romance has again cast a spell over the German imagination, and indeed the official public relations efforts to make military careers seem more attractive have had only limited effect. Although resistance to draft calls has not been a great problem, recruitment for the permanent officers' and noncommissioned positions has been difficult. In fact a majority of the West German officer corps is composed of natives of East Germany, which is in part a reflection of the fact that well-settled natives have preferred civilian careers. Nor has the magic of Bundeswehr uniforms impressed the general population. When asked in 1965 whether they thought a man looked better in civilian dress or in uniform, 72 per cent of a West German sample opted for civilian dress and only 13 per cent for the uniform. At the same time only 7 per cent of the male members of the sample said they actually liked performing their military duty, while 43 per cent did it against their will and 42 per cent were ambivalent.

Observers of the German political scene have nevertheless developed a certain unease because of the apparent gradual decline of the reform group inside the Bundeswehr which had stood for giving top priority to the development of democratic leadership and disciplinary traditions around the principle of "Innere Fuehrung." Some writers believe that "the new spirit has struck roots in the Bundeswehr," and that "the old traditionalists who speak about the 'Innere Fuehrung' with contempt and ridicule are a shrinking group."[7] But there has been much though inconclusive evidence suggesting quite another kind of trend. Thus the reform group of generals have largely been transferred from positions in the Ministry, while the program at the Bundeswehr "Internal Leadership" school has been watered down and its civilian teachers forced out. A civilian-military power struggle also developed over the question of whether the civilian head of the Defense Ministry's Personnel section should be replaced by a general, as he eventually was in 1965 after much debate in the cabinet. Perhaps these conflicts were taking place because the officer corps was claiming the powers which would be theirs in most armies. But at times their hostility to outside suggestions and criticisms has provoked even those who could hardly be accused of anti-military prejudice. Thus in 1964 the Parliamentary

[7] Eric Waldmann, *The Goose Step Is Verboten* (New York, 1964), p. 151.

Defense Commissioner, who was not only a former CDU deputy but also an ex-admiral, issued a passionate indictment of the Bundeswehr for not really accepting the concept of civilian control, and for reviving a "state within a state" mentality.[8] He became the second Commissioner to resign from this office, primarily because the army's lack of cooperation made his job impossible. His successor also got into a scrap with the Defense Ministry when it appeared that his civil servants were, at the behest of the Ministry, undercutting the control and investigation functions which his Office was supposed to perform.

In a sense the impact that the German military establishment can have on the domestic political system is somewhat limited by the fact that all German military forces are formally under NATO control. But, under the vocal leadership of Franz Josef Strauss, many Germans have come to argue that if NATO should survive, the ground-rules for German participation in it should be different in the late 1960's than they were in the mid-1950's. With German troops constituting the largest contingent under NATO command, and German economic potential the second largest within the Western Alliance, the Federal Republic has been insisting with increasing determination that it should also have a share in the ultimate political-military decisions—those involving nuclear weapons. They do not want to own their own stockpile of nuclear weapons, which would be in violation of the Paris Treaties, but neither do they want to remain militarily inferior to much smaller countries who may be in the process of developing superior weapons.

THE TWO GERMAN STATES IN WORLD POLITICS

A key to the understanding of the German problem lies in the fact that in the course of the 1950's both German states threw off the remnants of Occupation status, and, while they became sovereign in the legal sense, they became more closely tied than ever to the world power blocs led by their respective ex-occupiers. Although all countries in both the Western and Eastern camps have had to yield up considerable amounts of national control over their foreign policies, this has held especially true for the two German rump states on either side of the Iron Curtain. A study of the two states' foreign relations is basically the story

[8] H. P. Secher, "Controlling the New German Military Elite," *Proceedings of the American Philosophical Society*, CIX (April, 1965), 63–84.

of their gradual rise and acceptance within their respective camps. For the DDR, the formalizing of pre-existent ties to the Communist states is, aside from the ardent wooing of neutral nations in Africa and Asia, the sum total of postwar dipolmacy. West German diplomats have had a somewhat greater variety of experience, but the great bulk of the Federal Republic's foreign policy efforts have also been concentrated on forging a strong network of alliances, treaties, and other ties to the Atlantic powers, particularly to the United States. A second area within which the West Germans have been able to develop considerable independent initiative has been in the attempt to create regional political and economic institutions in Western Europe. Here the Federal Republic has, together with France, taken the lead in founding many supranational European institutions. The great bulk of West German foreign policy effort has thus gone into strengthening ties to two major countries, the United States and France. Questions involving relations to other countries have had a far lower priority, although considerable effort has also gone into strengthening relations with other West European countries and laying the political groundwork for the development of West German economic relations with countries in South America, Asia, and Africa.

However, it is within the Atlantic alliance that the West Germans have regained political status and prestige. Under Konrad Adenauer's leadership the guidelines of policy have been to honor treaty commitments and to give diplomatic support to the leaders of the alliance in the expectation that they, in turn, would support West Germany in her efforts to bring about reunification on favorable terms.[9] Critics of the Adenauer policy have from the beginning argued that the Federal Republic's policy of alliance with the West was in fact making German unification impossible, but this position has always been rejected by the Chancellor, who believed that a Western policy of strength would induce the Soviets to ultimately yield up the DDR. This calculation proved to be mistaken, for the Communist willingness to bargain on German unification in fact decreased as the German military build-up and its integration into NATO were stepped up. Thus at the time of Adenauer's retirement as Chancellor in October, 1963, Bundestag President Gersteinmaier could not carry his eulogistic comparison to Bismarck all the way. Unlike Bismarck, Adenauer on leaving office could not, he said, "look back on the

[9] Konrad Adenauer, "Germany: The New Partner," *Foreign Affairs*, XXXIII (1955), 177–83.

implementation of the unification of Germany, an achievement which has up to now been denied to you and ourselves."

As the receivers of a bankrupt nation which had driven nationalism to its furthest extreme, the postwar German leaders were acutely aware of the need to forge a wider, supranational European political framework. Not only did such an aim provide a favorable framework for German political reconstruction, but for many West Germans the postwar opportunity was unique in that it favored turning Germany from a country whose political imagination had always roamed to the East into one which was bound by cultural and economic ties to its Western neighbors.

Building on the functional approach to European unification, the impetus of the six-nation Common Market, and the promise of closer political integration encompassed in the Rome Treaties, Germany, France, Italy, and the Benelux countries built up an infrastructure of increasing economic and political significance. However, crucial differences developed over the speed with which national political institutions were to be replaced by supranational ones, the power relationships to be aimed at, and the admission of new members. De Gaulle developed plans to ensure that French influence would remain decisive. To this end he built on Adenauer's well-known interest in solidifying German-French friendship. This "Bonn-Paris axis," symbolized in melodramatic tours and meetings of the two patrician leaders, alarmed their smaller neighbors, who welcomed all the more Britain's decision to seek Common Market membership. However, Britain's application was dramatically blocked in January, 1963, by a veto of De Gaulle, marking his defiance of the Anglo-Saxon powers and of most prevailing European opinion. The almost simultaneous signing of a French-German friendship treaty suggested a deliberate attempt to wean the West Germans away from their support of American leadership. This posed German leaders with alternatives of the most far-reaching consequences. While ex-Chancellor Adenauer and politicians such as Franz Josef Strauss agitated for accommodation to De Gaulle's plans, Erhard and his foreign minister, Gerhard Schroeder, resisted this pressure and stood by their primary commitment to the American alliance. The struggle over the formation of Erhard's second cabinet in 1965, which resulted in diminishing Adenauer's influence, was seen as a victory for the pro-Atlantic orientation of Bonn's foreign policy.

The German refusal to join De Gaulle in the formation of a French-led European bloc, however, touched off a long-standing crisis affecting the future of both NATO and the European

Economic Community. As De Gaulle found he could not have his way with the Common Market, he initiated a step-by-step policy of undermining the still incomplete structure. A first step consisted of blocking progress toward political unification among "The Six" by demanding national veto powers which would have made a mockery of the planned Political Union. In subsequent negotiations France exerted unremitting pressure to get the other members to agree to its demands, particularly as they related to De Gaulle's vendetta against the Common Market High Commission in Brussels. Why were the French in so strong a minority position within an organization in which they were treaty-bound to implement full economic integration by the late 1960's? One German observer in 1965 thought an important reason was that the French didn't care how selfish or unidealistic they were considered to be by their partners.

Unlike the Germans or even the Dutch, the French government does not run the risk of facing a pro-European protest at home if it acts too obviously in a narrowly selfish way. French public opinion is quite immune to European idealism. . . . They don't care if they are widely regarded as the member state which cares least for the ideals of the Community. . . . This gives them a further advantage. For the other members are never quite sure that in the last instance the French might not be ready to leave the Community and to destroy it. It is because they have these gnawing doubts that the more idealistic and "European"-minded member states are exposed to the constant blackmail of France.[10]

After having earlier pressed his demands by withdrawing French representatives from all Community committees, De Gaulle in his press conference of September 9, 1965, went even further by demanding a revision of the Rome Treaties which had established the Community. Since this threat was combined with the hint that France might well also leave NATO when the treaty forming that organization expires in 1969, there were clear signs that both the Common Market and the Atlantic Alliance would face a period of continuing crisis.

From the mid-1960's on, therefore, the ties that had firmly allied West Germany with the West were placed under strains

[10] "Das Hintergruendige Spiel in Bruessel," *Die Welt*, July 10, 1965. The writer's evaluation of French public opinion might have been different had the article been written after the French presidential elections of November, 1965, in which the strong protest vote against De Gaulle appeared at least in part attributable to "European" commitments of some voters.

affecting all partners. The crisis inside the Common Market had both direct economic and indirect political implications, of which the latter were more important for Germany. Were De Gaulle to carry through his threat to nullify the achievements in the area of economic integration, France would run greater risks than Germany. In 1964, for instance, France bought 11.5 per cent of German exports, but Germany bought 17.4 per cent of what France exported, although both were each other's best customers (while the United States was only the fourth-best customer of Germany and the sixth-best customer of France). But politically and psychologically the Germans had the most to lose if the "European" identification were to become completely undermined. Having foresworn nationalism to a much greater degree than Gaullist France, they were dependent on keeping European institutions viable so that the course of their post-1945 foreign policy might remain meaningful. If the French example were to force them to give greater priority to their national aspirations, the consequences might in turn place severe strains on the Western Alliance and lessen the chances of achieving a viable accommodation between the West and Soviet Russia.

In regard to their position in the Western Alliance, the Germans are exposed because they often give the impression of being unenthusiastic about efforts to reduce Western-Soviet tensions. This is partly because they are the primary inheritors of the rigid policies developed during the Dulles period, and partly because they have the constant fear that accommodation between the major powers will be bought at their expense. They fear that not only Berlin's status but the prospects of achieving unification may be threatened even further in any East-West bargaining process. American officials have in this context frequently been impatient about the constant need for reassurance and "pledging sessions" which German leaders seem to demand. Henry Kissinger has sought to explain this tendency by stressing the underlying insecurity of West Germans: "A divided country which has frontiers that correspond to no historical experience, a society that has lived through two disastrous defeats and four domestic upheavals in forty years cannot know inward security. The need to belong to something, to rescue some predictability out of chaos, is overwhelming. To subject such a country to constant changes in policy—as we have done—is to undermine its stability."[11]

For the DDR, foreign relations are also predominantly con-

[11] Henry A. Kissinger, *The Troubled Partnership* (New York, 1965), p. 25.

ducted outside regularly established diplomatic channels, the major decisions being made at the frequent meetings of Communist leaders of the Eastern bloc. The East German Foreign Ministry, which has traditionally been headed by a representative of one of the satellite parties, is not very significant, especially since it has few diplomatic representatives in countries outside the Soviet bloc, except for Yugoslavia. What contacts the East Germans maintain with neutral countries is largely through trade delegations without diplomatic status. Both states are also handicapped by the fact that they are not members of the United Nations, although here too the Federal Republic is ahead of its rival by virtue of its Observer's Mission at UN headquarters and its membership in organizations like UNESCO. Its isolation and virtually complete dependence on Soviet policy allows the DDR little room for making even secondary foreign policy decisions. In contrast with other Soviet bloc countries like Poland, it has not been able to pursue diplomatic objectives which differ even in minor respects from those of the Soviet Union. Whereas the Federal Republic has been quite free to shift its course between, for instance, support of British or French policies within the European framework, the DDR has not been able to play a corresponding role within the Communist bloc.

WEST GERMAN–EAST GERMAN RELATIONS

The ideological and diplomatic wall which the two German governments have built up between themselves is imposing. Physically it finds its counterpart in the barricaded and tightly guarded frontier which runs through the center of Germany. Road blocks are thrown across highways and villages, farms are cut in two, and there is even a place where the frontier barricades run right through a house. On the East German side police patrol constantly, and since late 1961 the thirty-foot frontier patch of ploughed ground has been developed into a regular line of fortifications, with mine-fields interspersed. Until the sealing off of the Berlin contact point, the 40 per cent of the West German population with relatives in the East could get together with them at least occasionally. In addition, religious, artistic, and other nonpolitical groups met on numerous occasions, and West and East German authorities had extensive technical contacts. However, by the time a thousand West Berlin Christmas trees cast their lonely beacons across the wall in December, 1961, virtually all these contacts had been interrupted. Even bishops and high church leaders were prevented from crossing. In East Germany severe punishment was meted out to those tuned in to West German television, while in West Germany many theaters cancelled performances of plays by East German authors. Yet there are still ways for determined people to move in both directions. Among their number are large numbers of political agents sent across the frontier by various organizations to engage in agitation, spying, and other activities calculated to undermine the political structure of the rival regime.

The job of apprehending agents is difficult for the police authorities in both East and West, especially for the latter, due to the protection of Western legal safeguards. In 1960 the West German attorney general announced that only about 10 per cent of indictments for treason actually resulted in convictions. At that time 130 persons were serving time in West German prisons on this charge, while thousands were in East German prisons. Desertions of trusted functionaries pose yet other problems. In the period from 1959 to 1960 some 9,000 SED members fled from the DDR to the Federal Republic, while many thousands of administrators and policemen have done likewise. In general this sort of movement favors the Federal Republic, although it does work both ways. Thus between 1956 and 1960, according to West German sources, some 5,000 members of the East German army fled to the West, while 161 members of the Bundeswehr went in the other direction. In both states there are sizable groups with pronounced political sympathies with the other side. Not all the 70,000 West Germans who were members of the Communist party up to the time of its official dissolution in 1956 could be placed in jail or kept under constant surveillance. It is estimated that about half continue to be active in underground agitational activities, particularly in the trade unions. In arguing for causes like German unification and world-wide disarmament, the Communists have also been able to sponsor large numbers of "front organizations" which attract non-Communist support. The question of how to contend with these groups without, on the one hand, infringing on the constitutional right of freedom of expression and, on the other, causing retaliatory moves in the DDR, poses a constant problem for West German authorities. Their consolation lies partly in the knowledge that their opposite numbers in East Germany must work equally hard for their salaries, for ardent anti-Communist groups have continued to maintain well organized underground organizations in the DDR.

Aside from attempted subversion, the two German governments engage in a costly and unceasing campaign of propaganda against each other. This propaganda is aimed both at the German population in the two states and at publics in foreign countries. A favorite medium for reaching the former are the air waves, for all parts of both states are of course easily within range of powerful transmitters located across the frontier. The East German radio carries programs featuring speakers whose regional accents correspond to those of their West German listeners, and vice-versa. The circulation of printed propaganda is more difficult since newspapers are not allowed to cross the frontier, and other periodicals are severely restricted. However masses of propaganda are printed and smuggled in both directions in manifold ways. Communist underground groups in West Germany distribute leaflets and publications in the factories; soldiers in the Bundeswehr receive brochures in the mail which combine barracks-type cartoons with bitter attacks on their officers and political leaders; special material is put out for West German pacifists and other critics of the government's policy. In 1960, an estimated twelve million pieces of illegal Communist literature were distributed each month.

Especially since 1961, there has occurred a further sundering of ties and contacts between all kinds of groups and organizations in East and West Germany. Where official organs and organizations led the way in ignoring each other, private and nongovernmental groups were increasingly forced to follow suit. Thus religious organizations such as those of the Protestant church, which had held joint West-East meetings in the 1950's, were unable to continue these. Scholars and academicians even in quite nonpolitical fields like linguistics found it increasingly more difficult to attend scholarly congresses in the other part of Germany than to attend international meetings abroad. When one of the two governments favored a particular encounter for tactical reasons the other was likely to undermine it. Among the few groups able to maintain at least the appearance of an all-German organization were the sport organizations affiliated with the German Olympic Committee which did enter a joint German team in the 1964 Olympic games in Tokyo. But this was done only because the International Olympic Committee had consistently refused the East German demand for a seperate team. In 1965 the East Germans renewed their demands, strongly re-enforced by the other Communist countries, and in a tumultuous meeting in October, 1965, the International Olympic Committee gave way and admitted the East German Olympic Committee as a full member. This paved the way for separate "German" and "East German" teams to enter the 1968 Olympic games in Grenoble and Mexico City, although they are scheduled to enter the stadium together singing the hymn from Beethoven's Ninth Symphony which eulogizes the impending brotherhood of all mankind. This compromise was sweetened somewhat for the West Germans because their team would continue to be recognized as the "German" one without qualifying adjective, while others took comfort from the fact that twice as many German athletes could now be entered. Ironically, the city where this decision was hammered out was Madrid, where thirty years earlier German "teams" had fought against each other in the Spanish Civil War.

However, particularly since the end of the Adenauer period, there has also been a cautious countertrend in West German policy toward opening up new channels of contact with the Communist countries in general and even directly with the East German regime. The contacts with the East German regime have had to be most circumspect since Bonn could hardly afford to seem to recognize the DDR when it was trying to prevent other countries from doing just that. There have been, however, numerous official contacts on lower levels, particularly with regard to developing procedures that would ease the lot of the Berlin population. Thus arrangements were worked out to permit West Berliners to visit relatives in East Berlin during special holiday periods, which received extensive favorable publicity. There have also been administrative contacts in other areas, particularly in regard to questions of transport and West-East German trade, which is not inconsiderable. Other West German attempts to "open a window to the East" by normalizing relations with East European countries have been less surreptitious. Under Foreign Minister Schroeder, Bonn has moved ahead with a firm policy of establishing contacts with countries like Poland, Czechoslovakia, and Hungary, which it had scorned to do in the Adenauer period. This has led in the first instance to the exchange of trade missions, but not to full diplomatic contacts. Part of the price countries like Poland appear to ask for the latter is West German recognition of the Oder-Neisse line, and other de facto boundaries. Especially because powerful expellee pressure groups oppose such recognition, West German politicians are loath to think of forcing acceptance through anything short of an over-all settlement in the peace treaty.

The German problem, encompassing as it does the question of uniting the two presently hostile German states, as well as related problems of boundaries and balance of power in Central Europe, has proved the most untractable of the numerous difficult legacies of World War II. Proposals to solve it have been far less successful than, for instance, plans to control the testing and use of nuclear weapons. "Yet it is probable," wrote Henry Kissinger in 1965, "that over the next decade the cohesiveness of the Western alliance will be tested more severely by the problem of Germany unity than by who presses the button for nuclear war." In an attempt to make a contribution to the gradual solution of the problem, he has proposed a plan and timetable whose major components are as follows:

1. The Western allies would "declare their willingness to acquiesce" in the existence of an East German state which would be independent, neutral and demilitarized, and linked to the Federal Republic in a loose confederation.

2. Under a treaty the East German government would guarantee free elections, and these together with the demilitarization provisions would be monitored by a commission of neutrals.

3. After fifteen years the same commission would supervise a plesbiscite to determine whether East Germany would remain a separate state in a loose German confederation, or whether it preferred unification.

4. Both states would recognize existing frontiers, including the Oder-Neisse line.

5. Soviet troops would be withdrawn from East Germany after the establishment of a freely-elected government, and in the Federal Republic foreign troops would withdraw a distance equal to that between the Oder and the Elbe rivers.

6. The Federal Republic would renounce access to the ownership of nuclear weapons.[12]

It is a shape something like this that a peaceful and successful reunification plan may eventually take, although the balance of power between the blocs will determine the relative weights of the concessions made by each side.

---

[12] Kissinger, *op. cit.*, p. 221.

BIBLIOGRAPHY

ADENAUER, KONRAD, "Germany: The New Partner," *Foreign Affairs*, XXXIII (1955), 177–83.

BLUHM, GEORG, *Die Oder-Neisse Linie in der deutschen Aussenpolitik* (Freiburg, 1963).

CURTIS, MICHAEL, *Western European Integration* (New York, 1965).

DAVISON, W. P., *The Berlin Blockade: A Study in Cold-War Politics* (Princeton, 1958).

DEUTSCH, KARL, and EDINGER, LEWIS, *Germany Rejoins the Powers* (Stanford, 1959).

——, *et al.*, *France, Germany and the Western Alliance* (New York, 1966).

ERLER, FRITZ, "The Struggle for German Unification," *Foreign Affairs*, XXXIV (1956), 380–93.

FREUND, GERALD, *Germany between Two Worlds* (New York, 1961).

GREWE, WILHELM G., *Deutsche Aussenpolitik der Nachkriegszeit* (Stuttgart, 1960).

HAAS, ERNST B., *The Uniting of Europe: Political, Social and Economic Forces, 1950–1957* (Stanford, 1958).

HARTMANN, FREDERICK H., *Germany between East and West: The Reunification Problem* (Englewood Cliffs, N.J., 1965).

KISSINGER, HENRY A., *The Troubled Partnership* (New York, 1965).

McINNIS, EDGAR, *et al.*, *The Shaping of Postwar Germany* (New York, 1960).

OBERMANN, EMIL, *Soldaten, Bürger, Militaristen: Militaer und Demokratie in Deutschland* (Stuttgart, 1958).

PLISCHKE, ELMER, "Integrating Berlin and the Federal Republic of Germany," *JP*, XXVII (1965), 35–65.

PRITTIE, TERENCE, *Germany Divided: The Legacy of the Nazi Era* (Boston, 1960).

ROBSON, CHARLES, ed., *Berlin: Pivot of German Destiny* (Chapel Hill, 1960).

SECHER, H. P., "Controlling the New German Military Elite," *Proceedings of the American Philosophical Society*, CIX (April, 1965), 63–84.

SHELL, KURT L., *Bedrohung und Bewaehrung: Fuehrung und Bevoelkerung in der Berlin-Krise* (Cologne, 1965).

SIEGLER, HEINRICH, *Dokumentation zur Deutschlandfrage* (Bonn, 1959).

SMITH, BRUCE L. R., "The Governance of Berlin," *International Conciliation* (1959), pp. 171–230.

SPEIER, HANS, *German Rearmament and Atomic War* (Evanston, 1957).

——, and DAVISON, W. P., *West German Leadership and Foreign Policy* (Evanston, 1957).

WALDMANN, ERIC, *The Goose Step Is Verboten* (New York, 1964).

WHITE, JOHN, "West German Aid to Developing Countries," *International Affairs*, XVI (1965), 74–88.

WISKEMANN, ELIZABETH, *Germany's Eastern Neighbors* (London, 1956).

Political Germany,
Viewed Comparatively

The student of comparative politics and government, as we have suggested in the preceding chapters, is offered many challenging opportunities to compare forms of German political behavior and institutions with those in other countries. He can compare the distribution and regularity of German voting behavior with that in France. He can investigate differences in the financing of political parties, or, for that matter, of the churches. By examining changes in the number of contending political parties and seeking to explain why their number has decreased more than it has in other countries, he will be led to discussions of the role of ideology, and of the differential effect of electoral systems. Similarly, term papers can be devoted to comparing the functioning of the upper and lower houses of the German parliament with their equivalents elsewhere, or to differences in attitudes toward elections as borne out by the comparison of German attitude surveys with those made in other countries. Such are the very worthwhile exercises through which the student of comparative politics can develop his skill.

But what other approaches might he also employ to enhance his understanding by posing questions or hypotheses in a comparative frame of reference? Some social scientists, especially historians, formulate their questions and hypotheses with particular reference to past patterns of behavior of nations or national elites. Although dubious about cross-national comparisons, they are willing to compare contemporary political structures and practices with their predecessors in the same country. In the case of Germany, they have concentrated their attention on whether Germans might revert to policies and practices that in the past alienated them from the Western democracies. A few have adhered to the implicit assumption that it would be only a matter of time before Germans dropped the "democratic masks" of the postwar period and returned to their "natural" forms of behavior shaped by inherited nationalist and authoritarian values. Others, employing concepts more economic in nature, have suggested that West German democracy has not really been tested since it has not been forced to survive a severe economic depression. They have tended to argue that German political and social practices have not really changed enough to prevent a reversion to instability of the Weimar type if domestic pressures became sufficiently great.

Another mode of analysis, one with a cross-national comparative emphasis, might develop hypotheses on the basis of certain structural similarities between the German and certain other political systems. Thus, specific German political processes might be compared with those in other highly industrialized countries like the United States, Great Britain, and Canada. Since these countries tend to have many of the same kinds of socio-economic interest groups, it is possible to ask how particular cultural and institutional factors affect the manner in which demands are articulated. How have centralized or decentralized interest groups, ideological or pragmatic party systems, operated in different ways to bridge regional antagonisms within federal and unitary governmental systems? What were the similarities in the origins and growth of "breakaway" regional parties in industrially underdeveloped regions like Bavaria, Quebec, and the American South? How do different recruitment patterns of legislators relate to different styles of aggregation within parties and parliaments? Are the feedbacks to policy decisions affected by whether certain communication media are linked nationally or decentralized, are publicly or privately owned?

TRANSCENDING THE NATION-STATE

A quite different kind of research approach might compare Germany with other divided countries, for example, Korea. Such a comparison might consider the place nationalist appeals play in the programs of political parties, or the extent to which the recruitment of political elites is affected by large-scale internal migration. The kinds of processes and the national or subnational systems selected for comparison will be determined largely by one's implicit or (preferably) explicit model. This should relate the variables one is most interested in investigating. Suppose that one were interested in the interaction between national politics and pressures generated within the surrounding international environment. With this frame of reference, he might see the behavior of Germans affected less by the instability under Weimar or the domestic tyranny under Hitler than by the experience of having lost two bloodletting wars within a single generation. The model of Germany he might thus develop is that of a polity which sought to master its international environment, but which itself became the victim of its miscalculated attempts. In past centuries, an aggressive Sweden was defeated in its attempts at aggrandizement, and subsequently receded more into the role of an inner-directed armed neutral, a stance strongly affecting the nature of its domestic politics. Is Germany likely to undergo a similar long-term development?

Another model of Germany, also consonant with an assumption of great environmental influence on its political system, might conceive of that country's citizens as striving for membership and acceptance in a larger supranational community. While recent progress toward European political unification has been halting, the supranational integration of the Common Market countries will no doubt continue. The question is at what rate, and whether the Germans' dedication to European unification is genuine and lasting. Many attempts at supranational federal systems have failed in recent decades, as in the West Indies, Central Africa, and Malaysia. Will the past experiences and the present political skills and practices of the Germans, as the largest and most powerful unit within the European community, contribute toward a more viable solution in Western Europe? A German president of the EEC High Commission, Walter Hallstein, has strongly defended supranationalism against De Gaulle's onslaughts. Is this an omen for the future? Or will the Germans misuse their power within the federation, just as Prussia misused its influence within the earlier federation of the German Empire?

It may well remain difficult for Germans to define their roles in the international system, but their ability to cope with this problem will be a good indicator of their total learning experience in politics. In the past, educated Germans have tended too often to reduce the complexities of political competition to simple formulas. One widely prevalent German doctrine has posited that politics is really concerned with a very simple set of relationships—the cultivation of one's friends, and the frustration of one's enemies. This *freund-feind* doctrine, which was particularly elaborated by the legal philosopher Karl Schmitt (who became an apologist for the Nazis), has continued to shape the thinking of many contemporary Germans; hence, they have tended to divide the world and its political publics into two simple categories—one composed of West Germany's friends, another of West Germany's enemies. No politician played on this tendency more skillfully than Konrad Adenauer, who for twenty years deliberately fueled the Germans' hate and fear of the Russians while nurturing his alliance to the West. That is why his sensational about-face at the age of ninety left his followers dazed and aghast. They could not believe their ears as, at the 1966 CDU convention, they listened to their departing chairman suddenly refer to the Soviet Union as a nation which had joined the rank of peace-loving peoples. The deafening silence that greeted this apocalyptic declaration was a sign not of skepticism, but of shock on the part of those whose black-and-white picture of the world was suddenly undermined by their own prophet. It had taken considerable effort to dismantle the "friend-enemy" doctrine in the arena of domestic politics; now they were being challenged to accept more complex pluralistic concepts in the area of world politics also.

NEW GERMANY OR LITTLE AMERICA?

In political science, one's selection of a basic unit of analysis is important. This is borne out when one approaches the inter-relationship between wealth and political behavior. If one concentrates on the individual, it would probably be difficult to show that persons who are most wealthy by comparison with their neighbors are also more democratically inclined, but when one selects the nation as the unit of analysis, a positive correlation emerges more clearly. National wealth correlates highly with national tendencies toward stable democracy. Moreover, since industrialization correlates highly with wealth, a country like Germany ought to be among the most safely democratic in the world. Assuming continued West German economic growth, one might develop a strong argument about the inevitability of further and continued German democratization—possibly in East as well as in West Germany. But the historically-minded student of German politics shrinks from pushing this argument too strongly. He remembers that Eduard Bernstein followed just such an hypothesis in predicting an inevitable trend toward liberalism in Germany just after 1900. The reasons Bernstein's prognosis proved a bad one were connected not only to the trauma of World War I, but to peculiar resistances in the German social system and in the values it had molded.

The values some say were so important in frustrating the attempt to implant democratic practices during the Weimar period were by no means unique to Germany. Particular components of this value system, which is sometimes described by the umbrella term "traditional," contributed to the persistence of authoritarian family structures, the resistance to change in social mores and customs, and the persistent attachment to fairly rigid and narrowly-based ideologies. Strong traces of just such tendencies can, however, be identified in a large number of cultures, some of which developed very strong, and others quite weak, traditions of self-government and shared decision-making. Among European societies, for example, the family structure and class divisions among the Dutch have been not too dissimilar historically from those prevailing in Germany. Why, then, did authoritarianism prevail in Germany and not in Holland?

It is the dominant tendency among contemporary sociologists to perceive West Germany as becoming increasingly remolded into a replica of the "American-type," egalitarian, achievement-oriented, unideological consumer society. But to a certain extent such changes are taking place throughout prosperous Western Europe. Is West Germany going to become more of a "Little America" than the other countries? At the present time, class and religious subcultures appear more exclusive and politically relevant in Holland than in Germany. If deideologization continues to proceed rapidly in Germany, will this permit us to project that in twenty years' time Germany may well have the most genuinely "modern" as well as the most thoroughly democratic political culture in Western Europe?

Depending on how one defines modernization and which leading indicators of the process he selects, he might also compare contemporary changes in German society with those taking place in certain developing countries, particularly those in Asia. Like many Asian societies, German society in the recent past wavered between adherence to "Eastern," or collective, and "Western," or individualist, values and modes of social organization. Because this dilemma was articulated in the early writings of men as diverse as Thomas Mann and Mahatma Gandhi, an analysis of their work might usefully lead into a comparative analysis of the impact of liberal, individualist values on societies as different as those of Germany and India. Such studies might assess the degree of congruence between the social values expressed in the everyday life of the population and the political values implicitly embedded in the political institutions imported from abroad. Particularly apt comparisons might be made between Germany and Japan; although possessing quite different cultures, the two countries do have in common similar patterns of reaction against periods of authoritarian rule as well as rather similar patterns of entry into the era of high mass consumption.

INSTITUTIONALIZING STABILITY

To the political scientist, "Bonn Democracy" has over the past two decades almost become synonymous with "political stability." Why and how did this occur? From a very early point, at times before the Allies were ready to let them, West German political leaders assumed responsibility for protecting the frail democratic institutions against potential wreckers. In time, psychological controls have come to be more important than legal and physical controls. West Germans were told by their own leaders and opinion-shapers that their rehabilitation in the eyes of the world required voluntary abstinence from certain kinds of political behavior. But a much more effective functioning of external and domestic control mechanisms is only one factor that has made Bonn different from Weimar, for the Federal Republic has possessed prerequisites for the establishment of a stable political system which its democratic predecessor did not have. Its founders were not discredited by charges of having accepted a dishonorable peace treaty, but rather were credited with cleverly speeding up the timetable toward the return of German sovereignty. The cold war also paved the way for the acceptance of Germany into the Western camp on a level of formal equality. Because it is based on the ego-restoring and profitable tie to the Western alliance, Bonn's foreign policy, again in sharp contrast to the experience of the Weimar regime, has had an over-all stabilizing effect on domestic politics. An even more direct prerequisite for the maintenance of democratic institutions has been the fact that the political system could stabilize itself during a period of sustained economic growth, during which social tensions lessened and economic expectations could to a large extent be fulfilled. Finally, although democracy is still understood in varying ways among different West German political groups, there is no doubt that their leaders and chief instruments are sincere and single-minded in their commitment to the values of the Constitution. This, too, marks a vital difference with the Weimar "Republic Without Republicans."

The cold war, the far-reaching German reaction against a planned economy, and the restoration of the traditional social structure have created a climate hostile to proposals calling for experiments in either the political or economic area. Even new or partially new institutions have become instruments for established forces or traditions. Thus the Bundesrat has become essentially an instrument allowing the bureaucracy greater scope for influence, while the Constitutional Court has served the purpose of adapting German legalism and the doctrine of the "rule of law" to democratic constitutionalism. Above all, however, it has been the office of the Chancellor and the personality of its first incumbent — both with strong Bismarckian traits — which have contributed the essential element of the stable pole around which the political game has revolved.

For many apolitical Germans these institutions have helped to transform the game of democratic politics from an unruly, dangerous amateur rodeo into a professional match supervised by a management which virtually guarantees spectators against injury, if not also against disappointment. With a professional captain drawn from an old family, with a coaching staff molded by centuries of experience, with teams made up of licensed experts, and with rules enforced by legally trained referees, the German public has gradually come around to the view that this game can after all be observed with safety, and perhaps someday even participated in with all-around healthy enjoyment.

Can one then venture to predict that West Germany's political system will become more and more like Britain's? Only with reservations. A German tendency to look to British government as a model has existed for well over a century, but the Westminster-style parliamentary system has not been fully replicated even today. There remain important differences in regard to the relationship between parliament and cabinet, the relation of government to the opposition, and to the role of the bureaucracy. Moreover, on the national level, German voters have yet to implement the first postwar instance of that alternation between competing leadership teams which the parliamentary system is supposed to facilitate.

In the recent past, during the Adenauer era, the main impediment to the evolution of Bonn parliamentarianism was the position of the Chancellery. Because of his strong constitutional and party position, Adenauer was able to impose upon the entire government a pattern of decision-making that was incompatible, in manifold ways, with the model of responsible party government. It was not inappropriate to describe the West German politics of that period as "Chancellor Democracy." Many politicians and ordinary Germans disliked the paternalist authoritarian style of the first Chancellor, but not to the extent of doing anything very radical about it. Many of Adenauer's followers, on the other hand, thought that the German system required a tough leader in the Chancellorship lest the entire system disintegrate. This accounts for their strong opposition to the succession of Ludwig Erhard, and their continued use of every opportunity to undercut his position.

Erhard's different conception of the Chancellor's political role has radically reshaped the nature of West German politics. Where previously all policy controversies revolved around the position taken by the Chancellor, suddenly there was a great vacuum. For some time after 1963, the governmental machinery seemed to reel and waver as its components sought to adjust themselves to the wholly different style of operations. Ministries conducted independent warfare against each other, and parliament threatened to become dominated by factional politics. Even Erhard's personal victory in the September, 1965, elections brought no dramatic turning point.

The post-Adenauer experiences might cause the West German political executive to develop according to any one of three quite different patterns. One pattern the Erhard period might lead to is that of a closer approximation of the British system, with the Chancellor reduced to the position of a "first among equals" in the cabinet. By fighting to succeed Adenauer as CDU chairman, Erhard sought to continue the identity of government and party leader roles which the British pattern presupposes. Should Erhard continue not to establish a very great authority but still operate the executive effectively, it is possible that he might lead the German system to resemble more closely that of some of the smaller European countries, with their patterns of uncharismatic collegial leadership. If that tendency prevails, the future inheritors of Bismarck's title might be bland and inconspicuous uncle figures, as the recent prime ministers of the Scandinavian countries have been. But such a tendency might very well evoke a reaction, particularly if it is associated with frequent cabinet instability due to factional revolts. In that case, there might well develop pressure to fill the Chancellery with another Adenauer or perhaps a De Gaulle, who would become a personal guarantor of stability.

PARTICIPATION OR DELEGATION

German political processes, whether under authoritarian or democratic regimes, have always differed radically from American processes in the emphasis they have assigned to the leader's function of responsibility and the follower's, or citizen's, function of participation. As a consequence of the manner in which Germans were roused from medieval particularism, all segments of German society, not just the governmental machinery, have been strongly infused with bureaucratic traits. The individual as such was less often called upon to make direct political and other choices than he was in the more voluntarist, and originally less highly organized, American society. When he possessed residual decision-making power, he tended much more to delegate such powers to elected or appointed office-holders of organized groups with which he strongly identified. Usually these leaders were invested with clearly delineated powers and responsibilities, which they were frequently able to utilize more efficiently precisely because they were less subject to the changing whims of their followers.

To what extent can this system of roles and attitudes, which is truly distinctive of German political culture, be held responsible for the traditional weakness of German liberalism? American political scientists have led the way in suggesting that the lack of direct participation in political processes by enough Germans might indeed be identified as the most fatal flaw. Thus, in Almond and Verba's *Civic Culture*, the German system is still categorized as one tending toward a "subject" political culture. The implication is that Germans have usually been poor democrats because they have always been too ready to delegate authority upward, whether for purposes of more efficient municipal services or of mystic national revival.

Perhaps German techniques of centralizing authority are even now becoming antiquated in terms of efficiency. It is argued that the challenges to advanced industrial societies posed by technological change can no longer be met through the kinds of organizational techniques the Germans perfected in an earlier era. Organizations composed of highly educated specialists do not have to be, and perhaps cannot be, subjugated to the uniform rules that may have been rational when applied to personnel with lesser skills who performed more routine tasks. These conclusions seem obvious, but German firms pay large fees to American management specialists to drive the message home to their own executive personnel.

Many educated Germans of the postwar generation have come to chafe at the overly bureaucratic and hierarchical elements in German social and political organizations. The German scientists who enjoyed the greater informality of American universities have been hesitant to return to German universities with their more hierarchical and less adaptable authority structures. In East Germany, traditional German techniques for effecting decisions and rationalizing organizations have also been partially replaced by patterns molded by Soviet-style collectivism. At the present time, it is difficult to foresee how much further the tendency to adulterate "German" techniques of problem-solving in favor of American and Soviet models will go.

Is it inevitable, therefore, that Germans, in both East and West, will remain essentially buyers and borrowers in the international market of social and political patterns and techniques? In the immediate past, judging by the very limited number of translations of works of contemporary German social scientists, interest in their products has been rather low. Hopefully this will change. Certainly German political scientists have potentially an immense amount of German experience to investigate for the benefit of a worldwide audience. In regard to the willingness of the Germans to delegate authority, perhaps they can demonstrate that this quality has more beneficial aspects than Anglo-American commentators have conceded. The fact that most Germans abstained from participating directly in demonstrations on behalf of genuinely-felt issues like reunification and the Berlin wall, delegating instead authority to the Allies and the diplomats, probably helped reduce world tensions. More generally, it may be possible to demonstrate that in certain kinds of situations the Germans faced, such as the rebuilding of their society, delegation was a more preferable device then participation. The broth produced by the kitchen masters in Bonn may not have been to everyone's taste, but there was plenty of it; more chefs in the kitchen might have led to soup lines.

Highly advanced industrial societies are also highly urbanized societies, and the current problems of American cities are vivid proof that extensive political participation does not necessarily lead to efficient municipal government. A good case can probably be made that American cities became such ill-ordered conglomerations in good part precisely because participation in political processes was too extensive and delegation of power to responsible experts too limited. Similarly, the planning and architecture characteristic of Soviet cities suggests that better decisions might have been made if the arm of the party had been less powerful and delegation of authority more extensive. Developing countries that follow either pattern may well have to cope with problems comparable to Chicago's traffic or Moscow's plumbing in fifty years' time. Should they balk at this prospect, they might well try to contain their own "explosions of participation" and examine more closely some beneficial by-products of the German experience.

INDEX

INDEX